MAKING MORAL DECISIONS

A textbook for Intermediate 1 and 2
Scottish Qualifications Authority
National Qualifications
in
Religious, Moral & Philosophical Studies

Joe Walker

Hodder & Stoughton
A MEMBER OF THE HODDER HEADLINE GROUP

BIBLIOGRAPHY

The publishers would like to thank the following individuals, institutions and companies for permission to reproduce photographs in this book. Every effort has been made to trace ownership of copyright. The publishers would be happy to make arrangements with any copyright holder whom it has not been possible to contact.

Associated Press AP page 71, 73; Frank Capri page 37; Bettinann/Corbis page 13, 101, Jeremy Hornet/Corbis page 10; Frank Lare Picture Agency/Corbis page 144, Paplin/Corbis page 151; Reuters Newmedia Inc./Corbis page 2, 46, 56; Richard Duszczak page 116; Ronald Grant Archive page 89, Lambert/Archive Photos page 125; Metro page 47; PA Photos page 19, 33, 95, 103, 109, 135, 159; Graham Burns/Photofusion page 85, Steve Eason/Photofusion page 94, Equal Opportunities Commission 123, Crispin Hughes/Photofusion page 127, Nicky Johnston/ Photofusion page 55, Warren Powell/Photofusion page 118, Joseph Sohm/ChromoSohm Inc page 117, Helen Stone/Photofusion page 65, Sam Tanner/Photofusion page 24, 40, Mike Wilce/ Photofusion page 80; Popperfoto/Reuters page 110; John Reilly page 8; Alex Bartel/Science Photo Library page 160, Simon Fraser/Science Photo Library page 157, Francis Leroy, Biocosmos/Science Photo Library page 15, Michelle Del Gurcio, Custom Medical Stock Photo/Science Photo Library page 30, Petit Format/Nestle/Science Photo Library page 17, Chris Priest/Science Photo Library page 31; Ed Young/Science Photo Library page 141, Scottish Executive 132, Michael Bond/ Scottish News Agency page 78; SMN Archive page 142; Stuart Conway 139, UN DPI page 93; Graham White page 148

The "Three Faces" poster (p 81) forms part of an ongoing and award-winning CARE programme (Co-ordinated Action on Racism in Edinburgh) which has been developed by the Black & Minority Ethnic Communities Safety Group (BMECSG). The BMECSG is a Working Group of the Edinburgh Community Safety Partnership which is supported by the Community Safety Unit of the City of Edinburgh Council. Tel: 0131 469 3871

The illustration was drawn by Richard Duszczak

Orders: please contact Bookpoint Ltd, 130 Milton Park, Abingdon, Oxon OX14 4SB. Telephone: (44) 01235 827720. Fax: (44) 01235 400454. Lines are open from 9.00 – 6.00, Monday to Saturday, with a 24 hour message answering service. Email address: orders@bookpoint.co.uk

British Library Cataloguing in Publication Data
A catalogue record for this title is available from the British Library

ISBN 0 340 80203 0

First Published 2001
Impression number   10 9 8 7 6 5 4 3 2
Year   2007 2006 2005 2004 2003 2002

Copyright © 2001 Joe Walker

Cover photo from Peter Samuels/Corbis
Typeset by Dorchester Typesetting Group Limited
Printed in Great Britain for Hodder & Stoughton Educational, a division of Hodder Headline Plc, 338 Euston Road, London NW1 3BH by J. W. Arrowsmith Ltd, Bristol.

ACKNOWLEDGEMENTS

The author would like to thank the following: Lorna and David, as ever, for their patience and understanding while he was yet again shut away at the ink well and occasionally therefore unavailable to cook the dinner.

Thanks to Mike Kincaid, formerly RE Adviser for Fife, Brenda Hamilton, Principal Teacher of RMPS at Bathgate Academy, and Stuart Holden, RMPS Field Officer at the Higher Still Development Unit, for reading and commenting upon the first proposal. Thanks also to Brenda and pupils at Bathgate Academy for trying the materials out in draft form.

Others have also looked over the materials as they have been developed: John Stevenson, Head of Education at the Church of Scotland; Patricia Stevenson, SQA Principal Assessor for Intermediate 1 and 2; Chris Foxon, Lecturer in RE at Strathclyde University; and Aman de Sondy, Student RE Teacher.

Thanks also to pupils at Liberton High School who have had the materials tried out on them in various forms. In particular to Nikki Summers, Claire Niven, Ross Brain and Hannah Baker.

Thanks also to those at Hodder & Stoughton who have been very patient and supportive during my various projects. In particular, Mel Thompson, Rachel O'Connor and Elisabeth Tribe, as well as many unsung desk editors and others who beaver away as a book makes its way from idea to production.

ABOUT THE AUTHOR

Joe Walker is Head of Religious, Moral and Philosophical Studies at Liberton High School in Edinburgh. He was Secretary of ATRES for four years. He was part of the original Central Support Group during the development of Standard Grade Religious Studies and has marked Standard Grade since its inception. He was, for four years, a member of the Scottish Examination Board and then Scottish Qualifications Authority, Religious Studies Panel. As part of this work, he has been responsible for vetting, setting, moderating and many other tasks for the SQA. He is the writer of a range of support materials and NAB items for the HSDU, then SQA, at all levels, including Advanced Higher Bioethics. He was Development Officer for RME for the City of Edinburgh Council. His other books with Hodder & Stoughton are: *Our World: Religion and Environment* (0340 605499); *Their World: Religion and Animal Issues* (0340 721162); *World Issues: Religion and Morality* [with Jim Green] (0340 781815); *Environmental Ethics* (0340 757701).

This textbook supports the delivery of SQA National Qualifications at Intermediate 1 and 2 in Religious Moral and Philosophical Studies. The aim is to support teaching that may be bi-level in nature, although not exclusively. The material may be used with certificate classes but is also suitable for use with non-certificate S3 and S4 pupils – or with those who will follow the Making Moral Decisions Unit as a stand-alone unit. Teachers should satisfy themselves that they are working from the most recent SQA arrangements documents and that they understand the methods of assessment employed in the Higher Still Programme. The text is not designed as a distance learning programme. The text aims to be as contemporary as possible but, inevitably with issues such as these, the circumstances can change rapidly. The focus is on an approach that draws out the religious, moral and philosophical themes which lie 'behind' the actual moral issues themselves. The aim has been to present this as objectively as possible so as to allow for discussion and reasoned debate, as well as provide a range of relevant information with which to illustrate the topics. It has also been the aim to use Scottish examples where possible, although not hopefully to the point of parochialism. It is considered that pupils will be more engaged in the issues where the context is one with which they are familiar. There has also been the use of anecdote and story wherever possible, as a way of drawing pupils into the issues under consideration. Christianity and Islam have been used as exemplars of moral responses based on religious authority. It is hoped that this best reflects the religious make-up of contemporary Scotland. However, candidates are free to base this moral stance on any religious tradition. Activities are split into Intermediate 1 level *i1* and Intermediate 2 *i2*

The author would welcome comments, advice or suggestions for any subsequent publications or revisions to this one, as well as any comments that arise from the use of this book. Feel free to allow your pupils to contact him with their views. There's nothing like direct interaction with your 'audience' to keep you on your toes!

Contact: mobyjoe1uk@yahoo.co.uk

CONTENTS

1 MAKING MORAL DECISIONS

A word from the author

Some cold, dark, miserable mornings I wake up and wonder whether or not I should go to work that day. Unless I'm ill I always go. Why?

◆ Not going has **consequences**. Other teachers will have to look after my classes – not much fun if you thought you had some time to get on with your own work. The pupils won't get their own teacher and so they might fall behind in their work. If it happened too often I'd have to explain myself to the Headteacher who might begin to wonder whether I was up to the job or not. Besides, think of the mess I'd have to clear up in my classroom on my return. Also, if I did stay off for any reason for too long, I might end up losing my job – and I need the money!

◆ My **conscience** wouldn't allow me to 'skive'. I'd spend the entire day feeling guilty, because I enjoyed a rest while my colleagues were working hard. My parents always taught me to tell the truth and do my best. If I pretended to be ill I wouldn't be doing either.

◆ There are **rules** that say you should only be off work if you're ill. These rules are for everyone's benefit. I should try to follow them if I expect to benefit from them.

◆ I want to set a good **example** to other teachers in my school, as well as to my pupils. If I stay off without good reason then this might encourage others to do the same. This would affect everyone.

◆ Most of the time I **enjoy** my job – it gives me personal satisfaction. To avoid it therefore doesn't make much sense – because by being off, I deny myself the benefits that my job brings.

◆ Something tells me that to stay off without good reason is therefore **wrong**.

◆ Even more than this, like all teachers, I have gone into work many times when I shouldn't have – like when I've had a cold – because I think it's right to try as hard as you can to be reliable. I take my responsibilities as a member of the school seriously.

HOW MORAL DECISIONS ARE MADE

GOOD REASONS

What other reasons might there be for me always doing my best to get to work?

Your teacher asks you to dance naked on your desk. Without really thinking about it you'd (hopefully!) come to the conclusion (almost instantly) that this is wrong. Or at least, it's wrong if it's done for no reason(!). When deciding what is right and wrong, we usually want to think about the reasons behind actions. Most issues of right and wrong aren't straightforward, they are not in 'black and white'. Whether something is right or wrong is usually quite complicated. Take, for example, killing. Most people would agree that if you walked up to someone in the street and stuck a knife in their stomach for no apparent reason, then that would be wrong. What if you were at war, however, and you did exactly that to an enemy soldier? Also, imagine chopping off a friend's leg for a laugh. That would be quite different to a surgeon cutting off someone's leg to save their life. In each case, the reason behind the action gives you some idea about whether the action is wrong or not. But is that enough? Someone who kills someone else may think they have a perfectly good reason for their actions – even if we disagree. For example, someone may decide to kill someone to 'put them out of their misery' when suffering from some serious illness – is that 'right'? How we decide what is and isn't a 'good reason' is difficult, and so makes the whole idea of right and wrong quite slippery.

CONSCIENCE

What about your conscience? One person's conscience might be quite different to another's. Besides, should we accept that something is right just because it 'feels good'? Is your conscience enough of a reason to decide that one thing is right while another is wrong? Where does your conscience come from? Does it depend too heavily on the kind of upbringing you have had? Some people argue that the motivation behind an action is what makes it right or wrong, not what the consequences are. However, if that is so, then there are many examples of people throughout history who did things which were 'wrong' for what they probably thought were the 'right' reasons.

FIGURE 1.1 *A courtroom scene. Society makes rules which we have to live by. The courts are there to punish those who break the rules*

RULES

Who makes rules in society? What are these rules based on? What should we do when these rules themselves seem to be wrong? Should we follow rules strictly or be flexible about them? How should we respond when the rules are broken? How can we match rule-breaking with an appropriate punishment?

All societies have rules and laws. These are usually agreed by the people who live in a particular place and exist to benefit everyone, even if they sometimes restrict our freedom. We agree to follow the rules individually so that we all get the benefits collectively. Rules and laws can change as times change. The trouble with most rules and laws is that they try to be 'tight' so that they cover every possibility. Of course, life is so complex that this isn't always possible, and this is why we have people who interpret the rules for us, like lawyers and judges. They themselves have to take advice when the rule or law covers something they are not specialists in.

TRADITIONS

Many of our ideas about right and wrong come from the traditions that we follow. Where we live, and also when we are living, play their part. In some countries, certain things are acceptable, quite different things in others. Some things were once considered right and now aren't and vice versa. Some people think that traditions are worth holding on to, others that traditions should only be kept up where they actually produce positive results. For example, some people argue that women should have certain roles in society because that is traditional – but are all traditions equally valuable?

BORN BAD?

Some people believe that humans are born with instinctive ideas about what's right and wrong. Some believe we are born more likely to do bad things than good things, others believe that it's the other way around.

Most people argue that we gradually learn what is right or wrong as we grow up. We learn by our own experience as well as from the example of others, including significant people like our parents. We also learn that certain actions bring punishment and others reward. The ones that bring reward we come to think of as right and the ones that bring punishment as wrong. We may not actually believe that this is the case, but it's most practical to live as if it is.

Because of this, some people argue that we are born 'neutral'. Our only aim is to survive until adulthood and so we behave in a way that makes this possible. What is therefore right or wrong depends on what we think might bring us the greatest advantage individually or collectively.

ABSOLUTE AND RELATIVE MORALITY

- Absolute morality is the principle that there are some things which are always wrong. These may be summed up in laws, religious codes, traditions or just by agreement within societies. It can also mean that there are absolute codes of behaviour, which make certain things always much more likely to be wrong than right. For example, applying absolute morality to killing could mean **either** *killing is wrong in any situation for any reason* **or** *killing is generally wrong, except in very special circumstances.*
- Relative morality means that what is right and wrong is decided in every situation according to what the situation is. The idea here is that no two situations are the same so it is difficult to have any hard and fast rules – even ones that you can 'bend'. So, for example, *whether killing is wrong or right depends on the circumstances of the events surrounding the killing.* This is often known as **situation ethics**.

DISCUSSION POINT

Are there some things which are 'always wrong'?

ARE 'THINGS GETTING WORSE'?

Some people argue that today's world is much less concerned with right and wrong than it once was. They might say that people are more selfish than they were and less likely to have any 'solid' ground on which to build up their own ideas of right and wrong. They would probably argue that people don't help each other out so much nowadays and that we're all more likely just to 'look after number one'. Whether or not this is true is a matter for discussion. There is also an argument about whether the possibilities of life today are so complicated that our ideas about what's right and wrong haven't caught up yet. For example, scientific developments give us possibilities unheard of even a few years ago – have we been able to make sure that our moral thinking about some of these issues is keeping up with developments?

DISCUSSION POINT

Are people less concerned about right and wrong now than they were in the past?

WHAT'S THE POINT?

Some of the issues in this book you might never face in real life, so what's the point in studying them?
- Thinking about certain specific issues helps you clarify your own views generally.
- You get the chance to study the views of others.
- It's part of growing up to become a responsible member of society.
- It develops your critical and analytical skills.
- It opens your eyes to the complicated world you live in.
- It helps you find your place in society.

As an example, use the following case study and ask yourself:

◆ What punishment should the boys have received?
◆ What would you have done if you'd been the killers' parents or Mark's parents?
◆ Whose fault was this, the boys' themselves, or society's as a whole?
◆ Why was what they did 'wrong'?
◆ What 'caused' this tragic event?

CASE STUDY

Mark Ayton, 19, was killed after a drunken scuffle between teenagers in Balerno, Edinburgh in November 1997. His head was repeatedly kicked, leaving the imprints of his attackers' bootlaces on his face. Mark was Scottish, but had lived in England and so had an English accent. His father believed this was the 'reason' behind the attack. The killers, Iain Wheldon, Graham Purves and Ross Gravestock, were all 16 at the time of the attack. They came from supportive, financially comfortable families. They were the sons of a police chief inspector, a managing director and a senior civil servant. Newspapers at the time reported that Mark's death was the result of 'a few moments of senseless, inexplicable violence'.

MORAL STANCES

MIX AND MATCH

When you make any moral decision, your decision is probably based on a number of things. Some of these will be quite obvious, like what the law says, or what your parents will 'approve' of. However, lying 'underneath' your decisions may be a particular viewpoint, of which you may or may not be aware. This **viewpoint**, or **approach** or **stance**, will affect your decisions – tending to push them one way rather than another. It may be a very strong stance, which almost 'makes your decisions for you', or a weak influence, which simply 'nudges' you in a particular direction. You may be able to identify this stance, because it is part of something which is a complete way of life for you, affecting every decision you take. On the other hand, it might just be something that is called into action when you have to make a moral decision – or maybe even only when that moral decision is a difficult one.

This moral stance may be something you share with others or may be yours individually. It might be predominantly one thing or a loose collection of things, which you mix and match to produce a response to a particular moral issue. It may have a name and a history or it may not.

In your studies in RMPS, you are expected to be aware of two moral stances at Intermediate 1 level and three at Intermediate 2 level. You should be able to apply these moral stances to the issues you'll study. Perhaps one of these is your own moral stance anyway – or you may discover that it is, even though you weren't aware of it!

DISCUSSION POINT

Are you aware of having a particular moral stance? What varieties of moral stances are there in your class?

RELIGIOUS AUTHORITY: CHRISTIANITY

Christianity was 'founded' by Jesus of Nazareth, known as 'The Christ'. His followers were not sure what to make of him. After his death and resurrection they were convinced that he was the Messiah. This means that he was sent by God to re-establish the link between God and his creation, mankind. Christians believe that Jesus is the Son of God, and also God himself (God in human form). Jesus died, and according to Christians, rose from death and was followed in the form of the Holy Spirit. Jesus based his teachings on the Jewish scriptures, but interpreted them in his own way, adding his own 'slant' or entirely new teachings. The first Christians tried to make sense of his teachings as they encountered new situations. As they moved outside the Jewish world, they had to explain his teachings to people who had no background in the Jewish scriptures. People like the Apostle Paul wrote letters to the young Churches to explain how they should live their new lives as Christians. As Christianity became more powerful, its own scriptures were agreed and written down, forming the New Testament (many of the Jewish scriptures becoming the Old Testament). These Biblical teachings would be the subject of explanations and commentaries throughout the years, and Christians today still try to fit the teachings of the Bible to situations that could never have been imagined at the time they were written. For Christians therefore, the sources of guidance about what is right and wrong are:

♦ **Biblical materials:** Many Christians understand the Bible as literally true and try to live by it in practice. They believe that it is the 'inspired word of God' and so cannot be wrong. They use the Bible as a reference book in their own lives, picking out passages and directly applying them to modern situations. They argue that although Bible times were different from today, people were just the same and the situations were just the same, except set in a different context. Other Christians understand the Bible more flexibly. This means that they think it was written in a particular time and place and so the teachings don't easily transfer to the modern situation. This means that you have to 'read between the lines' to try to apply Bible teaching to current moral problems. To do this you have to work out what the Bible teaching meant in its day for those who heard it then, and whether it can be just as easily applied today. Some Christians go even further and argue that the Bible is a starting point, with general trends in it, which are useful. However, it can't be used simplistically, by just applying the teaching from then to now without any adaptation. These Christians argue that as times change, Christian teaching must change too. Each Christian viewpoint must be applied freshly to each new situation in the modern world.

♦ **Tradition:** Many Christians follow also the traditional teachings of their own Church. As Christianity developed, the Churches began to understand key Christian Bible teachings in their own ways. These became traditions that the followers of each Church started to keep as well as the teachings of the Bible. In many cases, these traditions were devised by important figures in the Church like Augustine, Thomas Aquinas and Martin Luther. In many Christian Churches today, these traditions are just one 'step' below the teaching of the Bible. In some Churches, these traditions are explanations of Bible texts. In others, they are believed to be the direct handing down of teachings from the first followers of Jesus.

◆ **Authority:** In many Christian traditions, guidance on moral decisions is given by important leaders of the faith. For example, in the Orthodox Churches, the teachings of the Patriarchs are important. In Roman Catholicism, the teaching of the Holy See takes the form of the teaching of the Pope – who is seen as the direct spiritual 'descendant' of Peter, Christ's principal disciple. In Churches like the Church of Scotland, decisions about morals are made by a yearly Assembly, where representatives of the Church gather to agree on matters of belief and morality. In some Churches, there are very strong leaders who interpret the faith on matters of morality for the 'ordinary' members.

◆ **Prayer and direct revelation:** Many Christians believe that God speaks individually to each person about what is right and wrong. There is no need for someone to act as a 'go-between' because everyone can contact God for themselves. Of course, this could be subject to abuse as someone might say that God told them that a certain action was right. However, most Christians who take this approach use a system of 'cross-checks' to make sure that what they think God is 'telling them' makes sense. For example, they would compare what they felt they should do with what seemed right, or what the Bible said was right. They might also compare what they thought was right with the teachings of other Christians, in particular, people who had spent a lot of time learning the Bible and its languages etc. Groups like the Society of Friends (Quakers) believe that God speaks individually to them and also 'through' them so that others might hear his message. God may give 'spiritual gifts', like prophecy, teaching and speaking in tongues. These can be his ways of directly teaching people about what is right and wrong.

Some Christian moral principles

◆ Christians believe that life should be lived showing concern for others regardless of who or what they are. The Golden Rule is that Christians should 'Love one another'.
◆ Kindness, generosity and fairness in treating others are all therefore important.
◆ Christians should protect the weak and vulnerable.
◆ Generally, the needs of others should be met before your own.
◆ Justice is an important concern for Christians.

- While Christians should seek justice, they should avoid judging others – God will do that.
- Christians should aim to make the world a model for the Kingdom of God. This means putting their beliefs into practice for everyone's benefit.

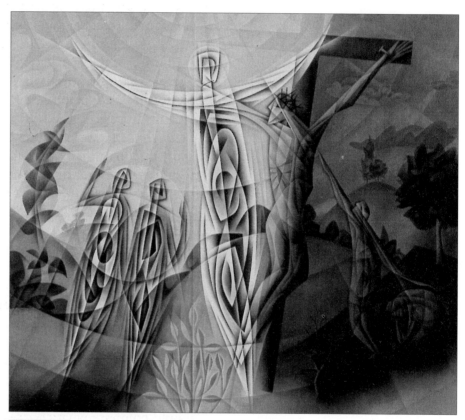

FIGURE 1.2 *A contemporary depiction of Jesus Christ*

RELIGIOUS AUTHORITY: ISLAM

The religion of Islam began with the Prophet Muhammed. Muslims believe that he received the Qur'an from Allah. This holy book was Allah's final words of guidance to humankind. Islam shares many key figures with Judaism and Christianity, like the prophets Ibrahim (Abraham) and Isa (Jesus). Through all these messengers, Allah tried to turn humans away from wrongdoing and back towards him. Muhammed is believed to be the final prophet of Allah, and the Qur'an, Allah's final revelation. This means that how Muslims should live their lives is summed up in the teachings of the Qur'an. This is considered to be the actual words of Allah as given to Muhammed by the angel J'briel on the Night of Power. Pre-Islamic Arabia was made up of a tribal culture where worship of many gods took place. There was also an element of nature worship. Muhammed's message was that there is only one God. This idea, *tawhid*, also involves the belief that Allah is the creator – all-seeing and all-knowing. All actions are judged by Allah (including their intentions). A Muslim will have to account for how he or she has lived his or her life at the final day of judgement. This means that all moral actions and beliefs for a Muslim take place under the ever-present watchful eye of Allah. So, for Muslims, the sources of guidance about what is right and wrong are:

♦ **The Qur'an:** This is the actual word of Allah (provided it is in the original Arabic). It gives guidance on all kinds of moral situations and is the highest authority because it is the actual words of Allah. However, Muslims believe that there are times when the Qur'an does not give clear guidance for all modern situations. In this case, Muslim scholars will try to explain what it is the Qur'an meant at the time and try to apply the same principle to a modern situation that is similar. Commentaries are written about the Qur'an to try to explain what message it has about particular modern-day situations. Of course, there can be disagreements about what the Qur'an means and this can lead to different moral viewpoints within Islam, as well as different beliefs and practices.

♦ **The Sunnah:** This is the example set by Muhammed during his life. This may be in the form of Hadith, what Muhammed himself said, or simply reports about what he did in a certain situation. The Sunnah does not have the same status as the Qur'an because it is the 'teaching' of a human, Muhammed. However, Muslims believe that because Muhammed was the prophet of Allah, he must have the best idea of all about what is acceptable and unacceptable behaviour. So where the Qur'an doesn't give completely clear guidance on an issue, Muslims will try to do what Muhammed would have done in the same (or a similar) situation.

♦ **The Shariah:** Throughout the ages, Muslim teachers have tried to work out what is the best way for Muslims to live their lives. The teachings of the Qur'an and the Sunnah have been turned into laws, which deal with specific situations. These Shariah can be very different depending upon which you follow and which you don't. Different cultures and traditions within the Islamic world have different Shariah laws about the same situations.

♦ **Culture and tradition:** Like other religions, Muslims may have different ideas about what is right and wrong depending on where you live, who your teachers are and what is considered 'normal' in your society. Like many religions, as Islam spread around the world, it mixed with the cultures of other places. Although its central teachings remained unchanged, certain moral situations might have been viewed differently in different settings.

♦ **Authority:** In Islam, the *imam* is the teacher for the Muslim community. In some Muslim traditions, there are also teachers known as *ayatollahs*. These teachers interpret the Qur'an, Sunnah and Shariah for ordinary Muslims. Because of their knowledge and spiritual importance, what they teach often becomes important for ordinary Muslims when making moral decisions.

♦ **Experience:** In some traditions, like Sufism, personal prayer and reflection is a highly valued as a way of working out what is right and wrong in any situation. Sufis believe that Allah speaks to everyone's heart. In this way, by combining this experience with the teaching of the Qur'an you can work out what is right and wrong.

Some Muslim moral principles

The Islamic Propagation Centre International states that:

♦ Whatever leads to the welfare of the individual or society is morally good in Islam and whatever is harmful is morally bad.
♦ Allah sees the individual at all times and cannot be hidden from – If you live a life that aims to please Allah you won't go wrong.
♦ Allah has revealed the right way for humans to follow.
♦ The community (*ummah*) should help each member to live morally.
♦ Humility, modesty, control of passion and desire, truthfulness, integrity, patience, steadfastness and fulfilling one's promises are emphasised in the Qur'an.

FIGURE 1.3 *A Muslim child studying the Qur'an*

EGOISM

Egoism, as a moral stance, is not exactly lived in the same way as a religious faith. Egoism is a moral philosophy. In ancient Greece, the Epicureans stressed the idea of personal satisfaction. Epicurus (341–270 BCE) himself believed that 'the beginning and root of every good thing is the pleasure of the belly'. He thought that pleasure was the absence of pain – 'being neither pained in the body nor troubled in the soul'. The Epicureans, however, didn't think that this meant you should be able to do anything at any time. If you did so, then you might actually cause more pain than pleasure in the end. Your own self-interest was your only goal, but to achieve your best interests, you might have to deny yourself certain things. For example, imagine you like deep-fried Mars bars. As an Egoist, you won't deny yourself the odd one or two, but if you ate twenty of them, then you might actually cause yourself more harm than good. So, you could end up denying yourself something you liked, because by denying it to yourself you actually act in your best interests. More modern philosophers like Nietzsche (1844–1900) argued that the only way to give meaning to life was to take control of it for yourself and act in your own interests. The Egoist philosopher, Max Stirner, added that Egoist philosophy is the realisation by individuals that they are individuals and, as far as they're concerned, the only individual. In 1905, another Egoist philosopher, James L Walker, defined Egoism as 'the principle of self; the doctrine of individuality; self-interest; selfishness'. Thomas Hobbes (1588–1679) argued that human nature was basically selfish. It was in the individual's best interests to 'join together' with others who also want to protect their self-interest. If everyone looks after their own self-interest, then everyone should be happy. For the Egoist, the source of guidance about what is right and wrong is

♦ **The self:** Egoists may read philosophical texts and may even 'follow' the teachings of Egoist philosophers, but the main source of understanding about what is right and wrong is the individual Egoist. Egoist morality is mostly relative morality. Each situation is judged according to that situation's components. There may be some general principles, but these can be abandoned if they come into conflict with what seem to be the Egoist's self-interest in any individual situation. The difficulty for each Egoist is in working out what is in their own self-interest and how best to bring it about. Actions which promote your self-interest in the short-term might be different from those that promote your self-interest in the long term. The real difficulty for the Egoist is in predicting what will be in your self-interest. This is because the outcome of any moral decision could be difficult to predict and might bring you either pain or pleasure depending upon how things 'work out'.

Some Egoist moral principles

♦ Egoists believe that all moral decisions should be based on your own self-interest. Decisions should be made on the basis that they are most likely to contribute to your own pleasure.
♦ Moral decisions are therefore made by taking each situation on its own merits and working out what seems to be the best approach at the time.

◆ However, Egoists might also follow more general principles if that's in their own interest. For example, the Egoist might think that the general rule 'do not kill' is valuable because it protects you even though it limits your freedom too. The Egoist will apply such rules in a flexible way.

◆ There has to be a balance between short-term and long-term benefits. Bringing about one or the other might lead to different decisions.

◆ The Egoist can also make decisions for the good of others, provided that doing so is ultimately in his or her own self-interest.

UTILITARIANISM

This is also a moral philosophy, not a religion. However, Jeremy Bentham first used the term in a letter in 1781. He said, 'A new religion would be an odd sort of thing without a name' and then he suggested that it should be called 'Utilitarianism'. Bentham (1748–1832), whose stuffed body is still wheeled out at meetings of University College, London, argued that morality is only useful if it produces 'happiness'. This happiness has to be shared among the greatest number of individuals. It means that as few people as possible are 'unhappy' (or 'suffering'). This suffering is sometimes called 'pain' – although you have to be careful because for some people, pain is a form of pleasure! He called this system the principle of Utility.

John Stuart Mill (1806–1873) also argued that moral decisions should be made on the basis of maximising pleasure and minimising pain for the greatest number. He thought that individual happiness was important, but that it wasn't the greatest form of happiness: 'The happiness which forms the Utilitarian standard of what is right in conduct is not the [individual's] own happiness, but that of all concerned' He added, 'An action may be said to [conform] to the principle of Utility, when the tendency it has to [improve] the happiness of the community is greater than any which it has to diminish it.'

Utilitarianism can be divided into the following categories:

◆ **Rule Utilitarianism:** Some general rules are more likely to produce greater happiness than others. Utilitarians don't need to judge each situation as completely new because certain things are almost always more likely to lead to pleasure than pain. How closely you stick to these 'rules' depends on how helpful you think they are. This leads to a 'strong' version of rule Utilitarianism, where you try to stick to the general rule as closely and as often as possible. There's also a 'weak' version, where rules can be treated in a more flexible way.

◆ **Act Utilitarianism:** Here, decisions are made, based on what the probable outcome of any action will be. If the action is more likely to cause pleasure than pain then it is thought of as a good act.

The trouble for the Utilitarian is in working out what the likely outcomes of any action are going to be. How can you be sure that your actions now will actually lead to benefit for the greatest number in the future? Also, perhaps your idea of pleasure is not the same as other people's – so you end up causing the majority pain because you think it's pleasure!

Some Utilitarian moral principles

- The individual must act in a way which is likely to produce the greatest happiness for the greatest number of people.
- Judging what will probably produce the greatest happiness is up to individuals, societies or governments to decide.
- Mill argued that the rights of minorities should not be ignored because a society like that would be a cruel (and therefore unhappy) one.
- Utilitarians may act selfishly or selflessly depending upon which one is most likely to produce the greatest benefits for the greatest number.
- Everyone is considered equal – everyone's rights are of equal value.

FIGURE 1.4 *John Stuart Mill*

APPLYING YOUR MORAL STANCE

How flexible you are about using your moral stance to help you make moral decisions is up to you. Some people will stick very closely to the stance, continually checking their decisions against its 'rules'. Others will use it as a starting point to make their own moral decisions. Some people will stick to one stance exclusively, whereas others will mix them up in different situations. For example, a Christian believes in the importance of caring for others. Suppose doing so causes pain for the majority? Should he continue with his actions, or apply a more Utilitarian approach?

Humans are complicated beings, and the specific moral issues you are about to study are complicated too. Making moral decisions isn't easy.

2 MEDICAL ETHICS

THE TREATMENT OF EMBRYOS

CASE STUDY

Alan and Louise Masterton want to use genetic technology to make sure their next child is a girl. Their daughter died in July 1999. They argue that it is a basic human right to choose the sex of their child, saying they don't want a 'designer baby'. The Human Fertilisation and Embryology Authority (HFEA) allows parents to choose the sex of their child when the family has genetic disorders that affect only one gender. It doesn't allow choice for 'cosmetic' reasons – as it says this is. The Mastertons intend to take the HFEA to court.

The couple attend St Aidan's Church of Scotland in Broughty Ferry. Mr Masterton has argued that choosing the gender of their next child is no more 'playing God' than using contraception.

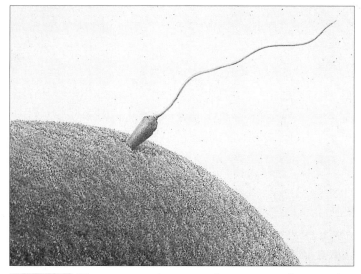

FIGURE 2.1 *The sperm and ovum at the moment of conception*

WHEN DOES LIFE BEGIN?

When sperm and ovum meet, they combine genetic information, in the form of DNA, to make the person they will become – or are becoming. From this moment, the single fertilised ovum (zygote) divides. It is known as a blastocyst or pre-embryo until the 14th day of development. At this point, cells begin to specialise (the 'primitive streak') ready for their role as body parts. This could mean that consciousness or the ability to feel pain are present from this point onwards. As many believe consciousness is an important part of being 'alive', the scientific community has agreed that until the 14th day, the pre-embryo is not strictly a 'person'. Others think that life begins at some other point, eg:

- six days after fertilisation when the pre-embryo attaches itself to the walls of the uterus (implantation); it is now viable or able to survive
- at 54 days when the brain begins properly functioning
- at 26 weeks when the spinal cord, brain stem etc are developed enough to 'experience'
- at some point where the foetus could survive *outside* the mother
- from the actual moment of birth.

Some also argue that life begins *at the moment of conception*. From here, all the information required to complete the pregnancy is present. After this moment, everything else is an unbroken process of *becoming*. This would mean that the ten-day-old pre-embryo is no more or less a person than the 14-day-old one. Many religious people believe this is the moment when we become a person, and the point where we obtain a soul (ensoulment). However, many non-religious people also believe this is when life begins because, from that point, the pre-embryo is a *potential* person.

WHY THIS MATTERS

When life begins has taken on particular importance in the recent past because of developments in science. Embryology involves the use of pre-embryos for scientific research. In the UK, this research can be done only until the 14th day of development. After this, the pre-embryo must be implanted in the uterus or destroyed. Research is usually done on 'spare embryos'. These are embryos 'left over' after IVF treatments. Here, drugs are used to cause super-ovulation, then many oocytes are removed at the same time. These are then fertilised in-vitro (so-called test-tube babies). The most viable – the most likely to survive – are implanted in the uterus to become foetuses. The others can be used for research purposes. There are at least three types of research:

1 **Gene therapy:** The pre-embryo is removed so that 'unwanted messages' in the DNA can be altered (or 'engineered'). Many medical conditions are caused by 'faulty' genes. If we can replace these or correct them, then we can stop the condition ever happening. It is then possible to replace the pre-embryo and allow it to develop in

the normal way. However, some worry that this process could lead to simple cosmetic changes – for example, choosing the features you want in your child ('designer babies') or avoiding 'unwanted' features.

2 **Applied research:** This is usually done in relation to helping people who have fertility problems or in attempting to understand some of the mechanisms behind genetic conditions. The genetic information is studied to understand it better. This could lead to improvements in treatments or procedures.

3 **Pure research:** This is where there is no clear goal in mind except study. It might lead to applications that weren't thought of in the first place.

All of this work is carefully regulated by the HFEA. This licenses such research and checks that it stays within strict guidelines. It states: *Our aim is to support the best clinical and scientific practice while guarding against the undoubted risk of exploitation of people at a time when they may be particularly vulnerable.*

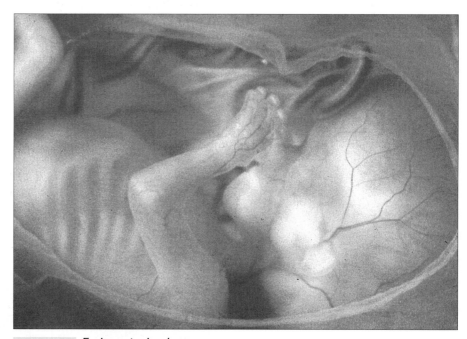

FIGURE 2.2 *Embryonic development*

RESEARCH OR NOT – THE DEBATE

Many objections to embryo research are based on the principle that, however you look at it, the use of actual or potential humans for research purposes is wrong:

◆ The pre-embryo can't agree to being used for research so it is wrong to exploit it in this way.

◆ Using pre-embryos where they will be destroyed afterwards can't be right.

◆ Altering the embryonic structure is 'playing God'. It could also have harmful consequences, which might be unpredictable.

◆ It could lead to a 'slippery slope'. If we decide that one thing isn't desirable, what next – people who might not turn out to be very bright? Also, who decides that certain characteristics in a developing person are 'desirable' and others 'undesirable'? What right does anyone have to make those kinds of decisions? This means that by genetic engineering we could create the world we want. Besides, gene therapy isn't *treatment* it is destroying what 'isn't desirable'.

◆ This could lead to the 'problem of eugenics'. If we can change anything at the genetic level, what's to stop us creating only 'intelligent' people or 'beautiful' people? This would also mean that anything 'less than perfect' might be discarded. What kind of a world would that be?

On the other hand, scientists argue that *not* to use such a powerful process for good purposes is equally wrong:

◆ Research on embryos is the only way to study certain genetic conditions.

◆ If we can put certain genetic conditions right, then we should. This doesn't devalue people, but no-one would surely want to give birth to a child whose life would be one of constant pain or disadvantage if that could be avoided. Some things in life *are* less desirable than others.

◆ We already 'play God' with nature every time we take a pill or accept medical treatment.

◆ Ruling out someone having a terrible genetic condition does not automatically lead to the creation of 'designer babies'.

◆ Embryo research is strictly regulated. This means that abuses of the technology won't happen. To end it all because someone might go too far doesn't make sense.

◆ The pre-embryo is *not* a person as we understand it. There is a difference between the use of a potential person and an actual one. A sperm or ovum is a potential person, but we don't regulate their treatment.

DISCUSSION POINT

Is the use of embryos for research wrong?

THE VALUE OF LIFE

Apart from the argument about when life begins, there is also the question of what value life should have. There are two clear positions on this:

1 **The sanctity of life argument:** This is often based on religious beliefs but not always. The idea is that life is somehow special or sacred. This may be because it is thought of as a gift from God or

FIGURE 2.3 *Pro-life protestors*

because it represents a person who has the right to exist for their own sake. Where life is seen as sacred we have to treat it carefully. This means treating it with respect from the moment it begins – and we're back to the start of the argument now – right till its natural end. If life is sacred, then no-one should have the right to 'interfere' with its natural development or to destroy it, without some exceptionally good cause. Some who accept this viewpoint think that all embryo research is wrong because there's never a good enough cause to destroy an innocent life. Also, if life is special in this way, we have to accept it for what it is and not try to make it the way we want it to be. Instead of trying to alter undesirable qualities in a person, we should accept them and learn to live with them.

However, some would argue that although life is sacred, there may be occasions where a society 'sacrifices' some lives for the benefits of others. This happens in war, for example. With embryos, where research can provide benefits for many at the expense of a few, then – reluctantly – we might have to accept this. Besides, many who accept that life is sacred, do not accept that the pre-embryo is a life.

2 **The quality of life argument:** Others argue that life only has value when it has 'quality'. Consciousness and self-awareness are often thought of as necessary for life to be regarded as having quality. The pre-embryo does not have consciousness (not fully anyway), therefore it is not 'alive'. So using something that is not fully alive, which could benefit those who are (or will be), is not wrong. Where genetic engineering of the embryo can improve the quality of the person's future life it should be carried out. It would be wrong to hold back medical technology that could make life 'better' just because there is disagreement about what 'better' means. Even pure research is of value, because the benefits might not be known while the research is carried out, but could be great when all that's been learned is put together.

MORAL RESPONSES

Christians generally argue that life is sacred and should only be taken by God (Job 1:21). If embryo research involves the acceptance of destroying 'spare' embryos then it is wrong. Life is a gift from God and so should be cared for at all costs. In the Psalms, it is stated that God knows you from the time you are in the womb. This is taken to mean that you are a person before birth. If this is so, then you deserve the rights that any person should expect. Also, Jesus is traditionally thought of as being fully a person from the moment of conception (Luke 1:15).

Many Christians will also argue that God chooses the person you should become. Altering the genetic structure of the embryo means that you are 'playing God' in deciding which kinds of people are valued and which aren't. It is up to society to accept variety – not to make people the way it wants. The Roman Catholic Church opposes the use of embryos for research purposes, because from the moment of conception there follows a process of becoming a person. It does accept gene therapy where it is of medical benefit to the developing embryo. The Church of Scotland argues that life should be protected from the moment of conception, but it also accepts research on pre-embryos up to the 14th day. Both reject the use of genetic engineering for cosmetic purposes.

> You created every part of me; you put me together in my mother's womb …. When my bones were being formed … when I was growing there in secret, you knew that I was there.
>
> Psalm 139:13–16

For the **Muslim**, life is also thought of as sacred and a gift from Allah. How we treat living things throughout their lives will be part of the final judgement of mankind by Allah. The embryo has its soul 'breathed in' by Allah during its development and from this moment on it is a person. There are disagreements about when this is – some say 42 days, others 120 days. This means that some Muslims will accept research on embryos up to one point in its development, others to another point. For Muslims, life may be taken where there is good cause. Some argue that this means you can use a pre-embryo, or embryo, for research purposes if the possible benefits of doing so are great enough. Also, many Muslims argue that if you can use gene therapy to 'treat' a possibly serious genetic disorder then you should do so. Allah has given humans the wisdom to know when things are done for the right reasons, and we should put that wisdom into practice. Again, Allah knows you in the womb, so in some sense you must be a person. This means that you should be treated with care. Many Muslims say that the Qur'an shows an understanding of the process of the developing embryo long before science 'discovered' the process:

> We created man from an extract of clay. Then we made him as a drop in a place of settlement, firmly fixed. Then we made the drop into an alaqah (blood-clot), then we made the alaqah into a mudghah (chewed-like substance).
>
> Surah 23:12–14

Egoists would have few problems with the use of embryos for research purposes at any stage of their development. Provided that there were benefits to be had for the Egoist, whether or not the embryo is a person does not really matter. Such an Egoist might also not be too concerned about what kinds of research were done on embryos or that they were created only for use in research. Most other moral responses would probably think differently about this. An Egoist might even be prepared to accept the buying and selling of embryos and embryonic materials provided that he benefited. In particular, if the Egoist was going to benefit directly (for example, if he had an illness that embryo research could help cure), then he or she might support embryo research whatever the drawbacks.

However, an Egoist could take a broader view of the whole issue. Many people argue that using embryos for research purposes makes the world a less caring place – because we are able to treat 'the innocent' so uncaringly. If this is true, then unregulated embryo research might make the world a more unpleasant place to live – not to the Egoist's liking. For example, if we can routinely accept the creation and destruction of embryos for our own ends, what's next? Perhaps the Egoist! Perhaps we could force people to become pregnant and then surgically remove their embryos. If this were to happen to an Egoist, she probably wouldn't consider it in her self-interest.

The **Utilitarian** position is that the use of embryos is acceptable provided that it can bring benefits that outweigh the drawbacks. Many Utilitarians will argue that the 'spare' embryos from IVF treatments will go to waste anyway – so their use for beneficial purposes can't be wrong. Some might go as far as to say that embryos could be sold or created for the purpose of research if such research would be useful. Many Utilitarians base their arguments on the quality of life. Some will claim that an embryo, and especially a pre-embryo, isn't alive in the same way that a person is. This means that it doesn't need to be given the same rights as a person. They will argue that even those who believe in the sanctity of life sometimes seem to ignore this belief when convenient. For example, during war we accept the need to kill 'the enemy' to bring about a situation that we think is 'desirable'. We can even accept the killing of 'innocent life' if that can have good consequences overall (eg the dropping of the atomic bomb on Hiroshima). Why then, if embryo research could lead to cures for all kinds of terrible illnesses, should we let an idea like the sanctity of life get in our way?

The ethical philosopher Peter Singer (in *Rethinking Life and Death*) argues that we should recognise that the quality of human life varies. He also claims that just as we accept 'brain death' as the end of life, we should accept the start of full brain function as the beginning of life. Finally, he argues that when life begins is not really the issue. Society accepts the need to take life on purpose where this will have a beneficial outcome for the majority. For the Utilitarian, the taking of embryo 'life' is just the same.

ACTIVITIES

Knowledge & Understanding

1 What do the Mastertons want to do? Are they right?
2 What happens to the embryo on the 14th day? Why is this important?
3 When do some others believe 'life' begins.
4 What is meant by 'gene therapy'?
5 Which organisation regulates the use of embryos?
6 In your own words, state one argument in favour of embryo research and one opposing embryo research.

7 What is meant by the 'sanctity of life'?
8 State two different opinions a Christian might have on embryo research.
9 What do some Muslims believe happens to the embryo at 42 or 120 days of its development?
10 How might an Egoist argue that using embryos for research is wrong?

Analysis

1 You have been asked by the government to draw up a list of reasons when it is acceptable to choose the gender of your child by using techniques to 'alter' or 'select' the embryo. Discuss in groups and draw up your list. Give reasons for your choices.

2 Design and make your own information sheet entitled 'When does life begin?'

3 Use your imagination. It is the year 3001, anyone can 'design' their own baby. What kind of baby would you want to have? What problems could there be with a world where this was possible?

4 Your local hospital has advertised for people to sell their embryos for research purposes. You disagree with this. Write a letter explaining your views.

5 Write out two lists for display in your classroom:
Why a religious person would oppose embryo research.
Why a religious person would support embryo research.

6 Two Egoists are having a discussion. One supports embryo research, the other opposes it. Based on their Egoist beliefs, what might each one say? Write a dialogue that they might have.

Evaluation

'Embryos should never be used for research purposes.' State whether you agree or disagree with this and give at least **two** reasons for your answer.

Assessment question

Outcome 2 Imagine the Prime Minister wants to change the law so that embryos can be used for research without any kind of regulations on what is done and when. There is a discussion about this during a cabinet meeting. One of the MPs in the cabinet is a religious person and another is an Egoist. What might each one say to the Prime Minister?

Homework

Write a letter to the Mastertons, expressing your views about what they want to do.

ACTIVITIES

Knowledge & Understanding

1 In your opinion, should the Mastertons be allowed to choose the gender of their child? Explain your answer.

2 Based on what you have learned, when do you think life can be said to have begun? Explain your answer.

3 Explain what is meant by a 'potential person'.

4 Why might people respond differently to the use of embryos for different kinds of research?

5 What is meant by the 'slippery slope' argument?

6 In what circumstances might a scientist argue that we already 'play God'?

7 What might someone mean when talking about the 'quality of life'?

8 What is the Church of Scotland's position on the treatment of embryos?

9 Why might someone think that the Church of Scotland is contradicting itself in its beliefs about embryo research?

10 How might a Utilitarian justify the use of embryos beyond the 14-day limit?

Analysis

1 You are a scientist working on embryo research. You have received a letter calling you a 'heartless murderer'. Write the response you would make.

2 Draw up a list of rules which, in your opinion, the HFEA should apply to embryo research. You could compare it afterwards with the HFEA's own Code of Conduct.

3 Carry out a class debate: 'This house believes that embryo research is wrong because it is an attack on the sanctity of life'.

4 Is the idea of designer babies so awful? Discuss in your class how society might change if this was accepted. Why do some oppose/support it? You could make a display of your findings under the broad title 'What if?'.

5 Imagine embryo research led to the finding that you could cure criminal behaviour by genetic engineering. Would you support this kind of engineering as a standard 'treatment'? Discuss and note down your findings. What other things might 'benefit' from genetic engineering?

6 In your own words, list three views a Utilitarian might have on embryo research. For each one, add your own response to this viewpoint.

Evaluation

To what extent do we have a duty to future generations to carry out embryo research now?

Assessment question

Outcome 3 'Embryo research is a necessary evil' How far do you agree?

Homework

Imagine a world where designer babies were common. What problems could this bring?

LIFE SUPPORT MACHINES

CASE STUDY

My husband was fit, active. Very sporty. He had a good job, three children he loved. I suppose we had the perfect relationship. Then one morning he got in the car to go to work. Just a 15 mile journey. I got a phone call an hour later. All I remember were the words 'road traffic accident' and the awful tone in the nurse's voice ... 'you'd better get here as soon as you can'. It made no sense. The man who'd juggled the boiled eggs a few hours ago to the delight of the children, was now in a hospital bed surrounded by wires, machines, tubes. At any moment I expected someone to appear shouting 'April fool' or something like that. It was all just so unreal. I wasn't emotional, because I didn't really believe it was happening. 'Brain starved of oxygen' ... 'Irreparable damage' ... 'no chance of recovery' ... 'brain dead'. I heard the words being said, as if from far away. But his body was warm, he looked a normal colour. I held his hand and could feel his pulse, a heart still beating. There was breath too ... a normal movement of his chest as he breathed in and out. I was taken to a little room. There was a pinboard with lots of scraps of paper ... and family snaps, one of the doctor's children I suppose. I had to make a decision about whether or not the life-support system should be 'switched off'. Did he have a donor card? The medical staff were wonderful, no pressure ... but they were doing their job. I suppose they couldn't get too close to me, I was another patient's wife ... they had to get on with things. They'd have families to go home to. They didn't want to take my sorrow with them. Juggling boiled eggs just a few hours ago ... .

KEEPING YOU 'ALIVE'

Luckily for most of us, life support machines are the stuff of TV shows like *ER*. When they're real, and we are responsible for them, it's different. Medical science now lets us keep vital bodily functions going – even after what we think of as the person attached to the body has 'gone'. Hearts can still be made to pump blood, lungs to draw in oxygen and other organs helped to do their work. Alternatively, many of these functions can be completely taken over mechanically. Even after 'death', you can be 'brought back' by medical technology and 'kept going'. For anyone visiting you, you will be warm to the touch, have a heartbeat and breathe. You may also make involuntary movements. To describe such a person as dead is difficult for many to accept. Removing life support systems is known as *involuntary euthanasia*. This can mean either 'assisting' the person to die, 'allowing' them to die or 'withholding' treatment which 'maintains' life – depending on your point of view.

DISCUSSION POINT

What do you think is the difference between 'assisting' death and 'allowing' someone to die? Is one more acceptable than the other?

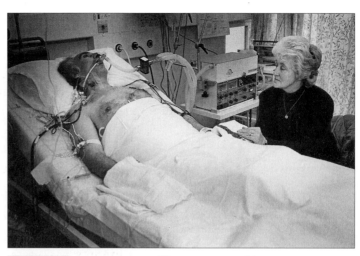

FIGURE 2.4 *Someone on a life support machine*

WHEN DO YOU DIE?

There are differences of opinion but the most widely accepted definition of death – at least by doctors – is the idea of brain-stem death. This means that there is no 'higher order' brain activity, nor any lower order functions, such as breathing or digestion. It means that the person has no consciousness and is not 'thinking'. You might think this is quite straightforward to determine. However, there is a condition known as the persistent vegetative state (PVS). Here, a patient shows no brain function, but their organs may continue to work – sometimes with help. When someone is in a PVS, it is up to the relatives to decide whether that 'person' should continue to receive life support or not. This depends on whether or not they think that what the person in the situation has is 'life'.

The decision to 'switch off' the machine would be made on behalf of the person, because he or she cannot make it.

SANCTITY OF LIFE **V** QUALITY OF LIFE

Decisions about involuntary euthanasia are often made based on one of these ideas. But even if you hold only one of these beliefs, you can still come to different conclusions about whether life support should be switched off or not.

Sanctity of life

◆ Life is sacred and so we should do everything we can to keep it going. If technology helps us do this, then we should use it. 'Switching off' a life support machine is always wrong, because there is always hope. Where life is concerned that hope should be enough.
◆ Life is sacred but there comes a point where there is a difference between taking a life and prolonging unnecessary suffering. Life support should be used but not beyond the point where using it

DISCUSSION POINT

At what point do you think death occurs?

becomes inhumane. Life should *not* be maintained at all costs but death should be allowed to take its natural course. We should not keep a person in some kind of mechanical no-man's land, in between life and death.

◆ Life is sacred but what we count as 'life' has to be clear. There comes a point, if someone is on life support or in a PVS, when we can say that the person is no longer living in the way that we understand it. Switching off life support is just accepting that the person has already 'gone'.

Quality of life

◆ Sometimes a person's quality of life is no longer good enough to justify keeping life support systems going. To enjoy a good quality of life involves many factors – most of which are not possible when you're on life support. Life support maintains body functions but does not keep you alive in the full sense. So there comes a point where it is best to switch it off.

◆ What counts as a good quality life is difficult to decide. Perhaps in some way, which we don't understand yet, the person in the PVS does 'experience' something. We know so little about the workings of the brain in this condition that to judge a person on life support as not having a 'good enough life' to continue supporting it is dangerous. Besides, the needs of surviving relatives have to be taken into account. We exist as members of families and communities and this is part of our value as human beings. Switching off life support should therefore be done after a great deal of thought.

SOME OTHER CONCERNS

There are other issues raised by the question of when – or if – life support machines should be switched off:

◆ There is always the hope that a 'cure' might be just around the corner. Switching off a machine shows a lack of faith.

◆ Even when machines have been switched off some people survive unassisted for a long time. This raises the question of how long we should carry on looking after them.

◆ Where there is a dispute about whether or not life support should be switched off the courts often step in. They have to decide what to do. This is based on what the person would have wanted if they had had all the facts that the court has. Of course, it is very difficult to do this because most of us don't give much thought to this kind of issue – and if we end up on life support, by then we can't think about it. So predicting what a person would have wanted is very difficult.

◆ At difficult times like these, relatives may not be able to make clear-headed decisions. They might feel under pressure to switch a machine off. Sometimes this is because they believe that the resources being used to keep their loved one 'alive' would be better spent on someone else in the hospital with a 'better chance'. It can be very costly to keep someone on life support. Other times, there may be pressure on them to consider organ donation. When someone is on life support, there are often very deep and complex emotional issues. There might even be disagreements among relatives about what to do. All of this can make the decision even more difficult.

♦ The emotions which follow the switching off of life support can take relatives a long time to deal with. Making all the options clear is important so that the relative can make as informed a decision as possible.

♦ Although complete brain death is quite obvious, the status of the brain in a PVS is more difficult. PVS patients, for example, will 'react' to painful stimuli, but we don't know if that means they 'experience' the pain. *With the PVS, there is no broadly accepted, published set of specific medical criteria with as much detail as the brain death criteria.* (RE Cranford, *Ethical Issues in Modern Medicine*, p174)

RIGHTS AND RESPONSIBILITIES

Some argue that this is what the debate is all about. What rights does the person on life support have? Do you have to be 'conscious' to be given rights? Do you stop being a person just because your brain no longer functions? Would this mean that a brain-damaged person shouldn't have the same rights as someone with 'normal' brain functions?

What responsibilities do we have to people on life support? Should we keep them going whatever the cost – even if this means other, 'more hopeful' cases lose out? Is there a duty to die?

The issues are complicated. It seems that, while medical science offers us more choice and greater opportunity, it also gives us even more complex moral decisions to make.

DISCUSSION POINT

Should life be defined by whether or not your brain is functioning?

FACTS AND FIGURES

♦ It is estimated that there are around 1000–1500 people in PVS in British hospitals and nursing homes.

♦ A Gallup poll in 1990 showed that 66% of 1018 people asked favoured involuntary euthanasia where there was no hope of improvement in a person's condition.

♦ The longest period of survival in a PVS is just over 37 years.

CASE STUDY

On 15 April 1989, 17-year-old Tony Bland was crushed by a crowd during the Hillsborough football disaster. His brain was deprived of oxygen and he ended up in a PVS. Tony's parents and his doctor agreed that Tony's artificial feeding should be withdrawn. Because the case was so well known, the hospital went to court to 'lawfully discontinue all life-sustaining treatment including the provision of food and water by artificial means'.

After a lot of legal discussion, the case went to the House of Lords – Britain's highest court. The Lords decided that Tony's treatment brought him 'no therapeutical, medical or other benefit'.

Tony's life support was withdrawn.

MORAL RESPONSES

Christian belief about withdrawing life support is finely balanced. On the one hand, there is the belief that life is sacred and should be maintained whenever possible. Any treatment that prolongs life should be tried. On the other hand, there is a point where treatment is just putting off the inevitable. There comes a point where treatment can be withdrawn so that God's will might be done. This means that instead of using medical knowledge to treat the illness, we use it to make sure that the dying person is pain-free. The question is one of intention. If the aim is to 'kill' the person by withdrawing treatment, then this is not acceptable, but if it is to 'allow them to die' then this can be. Christians believe that God is with them at death, as he was throughout life. So to prolong the process of death, when it is seen to be inevitable, is wrong. In particular, the Hospice movement has taken an 'aggressive' approach to death, where it accepts that patients are in the final stages of life, but doesn't try to cure them, just make this final stage as easy as possible. In this way, the Christian can accept that life is sacred, but also accept that keeping it going isn't always within our power.

> While seeing no virtue in the prolongation of dying ... we disapprove of the deliberate termination of life, and see the alternative as 'good terminal care'.
>
> Church of Scotland, General Assembly Deliverance, 1977

Muslim attitudes are similar. Life is a gift from Allah and should only be taken where there is good cause. Here, the key issue is compassion for the person who is dying. It would not be compassionate to keep 'alive' someone who can no longer function as a full human being. Some Muslims talk about the idea of giving the dead 'relief' from the agony of their dying. If such relief can be given, then it can be seen as an act of compassion to do so. This would not be 'killing' but 'allowing to die'. Islam is entirely based on the idea of submission to the will of Allah. So withdrawing life supporting treatment could be thought of as a way of putting the dying person's life into the hands of Allah and accepting his will. According to the Shariah, or Muslim law, a person is thought to be dead when the heartbeat and breathing have completely stopped and can't be restarted and when the brain has stopped functioning and has begun to 'disintegrate'. At this point, the person should be given into Allah's hands by withdrawing unnecessary 'treatment'.

> It is he who gives life and causes death. And when he decides upon a thing He says to it only: 'Be!' – and it is.
>
> Surah 40:68

Egoists could respond in a variety of ways to the issues surrounding life support machines, depending on whether it is you on life support or someone else:

◆ Life only has value where your own self-interest can be achieved. If not, then there's no real point in keeping your 'life' going any longer. Prolonging your death is therefore pointless.

◆ As long as you can be kept 'alive' you should be. Even if this is time consuming and costly for others, that doesn't matter. There's always hope that you'll improve or that a cure will be found – which would be of no benefit to you if your life support has already been switched off.

◆ If it is another person on life support, someone you care for, then it would depend on what you thought was best for you. Perhaps it is best to keep them 'alive' so that you still 'have them', or perhaps it is best to allow them to die, so they are not a 'burden' to you any longer.

◆ If it is someone you don't know, then you'd probably want life support withdrawn, because it is costly and could mean that the money used for this was not available for treatment that you might need. It also ties up medical staff who wouldn't be there for you if needed.

◆ Alternatively, a society that could turn off life support thoughtlessly, without looking at the individual case, could make for a much more harsh society generally. This could mean that if you were ever in the same situation, little thought would be given to your needs. Such a society wouldn't be in your self-interest.

Utilitarians tend to follow quality of life arguments. There is no point in prolonging life unnecessarily when the quality of that life doesn't amount to much. They would not accept maintaining life at all costs. Also, the Utilitarian would not necessarily have a problem with withdrawing life support, with the intention of 'killing'. This is because killing can be regarded as acceptable where it is of benefit to the greatest number. Keeping people on life support unnecessarily (ie in completely 'hopeless' cases) wastes scarce medical resources. It seems strange to keep 'alive' someone who will inevitably die, if this means withholding treatment from someone who has a better chance of recovery. The time and money spent on the person on life support would be better spent on someone who had a chance of surviving, for example, in treating a cancer patient. The Utilitarian would claim that the value of life comes from the fact that you can carry on normally, have self-awareness and engage in relationship with others – not some idea of the sacredness of life. Maintaining life support is only right where there is some benefit to the person receiving it. For many Utilitarians, the belief is that there comes a point where there is no benefit to the individual and significant drawbacks for society generally, so such life support should be withdrawn.

ACTIVITIES

Knowledge & Understanding

1 What can life support machines 'keep going'?
2 When do doctors believe you 'die'?
3 What is a PVS?
4 State one argument, about life support, used by someone who believes that life is sacred.
5 Why might someone think that when you're on life support you have little quality of life?
6 What do the courts think about when making a decision about the withdrawal of life support?
7 Describe the case of Tony Bland.
8 What did the decision about Tony Bland say about the 'value' of life?
9 What two views might a Christian have about withdrawing life support?
10 In what way is withdrawing life support showing submission to Allah for a Muslim?
11 In your own words, state one attitude an Egoist might have about life support.

Analysis

1 Imagine you have a relative on life support. You have to make the decision about whether or not to switch it off. You take a week to decide. Write a week's diary entries where you think about what you will do.
2 Your local hospital asks you to design an information leaflet about life support machines, entitled 'Switching off life support: Things to think about'. Design the leaflet.

3 Some people draw up 'living wills' – these say what should be done if they ever end up on life support machines. Draw up your own. This should state what you believe about the quality of life as well as if (or when) you believe life support should be withdrawn from you in such a situation.
4 Your relative is on life support. The doctors say that the case is 'hopeless' but you believe that life is sacred. Write out what reasons you would give for refusing to withdraw life support.
5 Your Egoist brother wants you to 'pull the plug' on your relative because he wants to 'get on with his life'. You are a religious person. Write the discussion you might have.

Evaluation

'Life should be kept going at all costs.'
Do you agree? Explain your answer with at least two supporting reasons.

Assessment question

Outcome 1 Two people are on life support in hospital. One is an Egoist and one a religious person. Each has written a 'living will', stating what they'd like done in such a situation. What would be in each one's living will?

Homework

You are a doctor. You are supervising someone on life support. The relatives have asked you if it should be withdrawn. What things would you advise them to think about?

Knowledge & Understanding

1 Why is it difficult to say when a person has actually died?

2 What problems does the PVS present?

3 How might a person who believed that life is sacred still justify switching off life support?

4 How might someone who supports the quality of life argument argue that life support should be maintained?

5 What pressures might relatives of someone on life support be under?

6 Do you think that a person's rights change once they are in a PVS? Explain your answer.

7 Do you think the courts should take into account the results of the Gallup poll when making decisions about life support cases?

8 What does the religious person mean by talking about the 'intention' behind withdrawing life support?

9 What position might a Utilitarian take on the issue of withdrawing life support?

Analysis

1 You are a hospital administrator. You have a limited budget. You must decide whether to buy two more life support systems or to use the money for something else. You gather together a committee of various people, including religious people, Egoists, Utilitarians, as well as doctors and members of the public. In groups, work out your positions and have a meeting to decide what you should do.

2 Following this meeting, you have made your decision (whatever it is). Write a statement from each of the three moral stances stating whether they would agree with the decision or not and why.

3 A patient is on life support. This patient had already drawn up a living will, which stated that if he ever ended up on life support it should be maintained indefinitely. You are the lawyer for the hospital where the patient is. In the opinion of the doctors, the case is 'hopeless'. You go to court for permission to withdraw life support. Act out the court case, and then write up a report of the event afterwards.

Evaluation

To what extent should the decision to withdraw life support be based on the idea of the quality of life?

Assessment question

Outcome 3 'It is never right to withdraw life support'. To what extent do you agree?

Homework

Draw up a list of arguments for and against this statement: 'The decision to withdraw life support should always be left up to medical staff'.

ORGAN TRANSPLANTS

CASE STUDY

Jetmund Engeset is the most senior transplant surgeon in the North of Scotland. He argues that the bodies of accident victims should be 'kept alive so that their organs can be harvested for transplantation'. He says, 'People are incredibly selfish and should think about their fellow human beings. Is it really better to put their organs in a hole in the ground or on the fire?' He proposes 'elective ventilation' of brain-dead corpses so that their organs remain in good condition for transplant. For some, this raises the bizarre possibility that corpses could be 'kept alive' indefinitely, while their organs are removed as needed. At the moment, life support is only legally allowed when it is of benefit to the person on it. Elective ventilation would be illegal as it means keeping people on life support for the benefit of others. Engeset wants the Scottish Parliament to debate the issue. He claims that elective ventilation could solve the problem of lack of organ donors.

DISCUSSION POINT

What do you think of this surgeon's suggestion?

FIGURE 2.5 *An organ ready for transplant*

THE NEED FOR TRANSPLANTS

Organ failure can be caused by many factors: accident, disease, genetic disorders or just wearing out. Organs which can be replaced include the heart, lungs, kidneys and liver, as well as bone marrow and other tissue. These could be replaced when the person in need of them would otherwise have a normal life. Transplants have become regular occurrences in medicine. However, some people argue that just because this is medically 'ordinary' does not mean that it is always morally easy.

THE MORAL STATUS OF THE DEAD

When you are alive you have certain rights. What happens to these once you are a corpse? Some people believe that from this point, you have ceased to exist and so don't have rights in the same sense as you did when alive. Others argue that you have some rights. Others argue that you have all the rights you had – that is, until your body is disposed of. Many people, including those with religious beliefs, talk about the 'integrity' of the body. This means that you are only 'you' when you are whole – if you remove organs then in some ways you have harmed the integrity of the person. On the other hand, many believe that if you can help someone – even after your death – then you should. If, as a dead person, you can still have rights, why shouldn't you still have responsibilities?

Some also argue that human foetal tissue and organs should be used for transplant. This is even more difficult because you could never be sure if the person that the foetus *would have become* would have agreed with this. At least if you have lived fully before you die, then people can be sure about what you would have wanted after death.

There is also an issue about how far people in a Persistent Vegetative State (PVS) should be thought of as potential donors – and how this might affect the treatment they receive.

GIVING

There are particular moral problems linked with getting hold of (or harvesting) organs. At the moment, your organs can only be used if you carry a donor card, which says that in the event of your death any or all of your organs can be used for transplants, **and** if your relatives give their consent to the use of your organs. Taking organs without this consent is illegal. Some people believe this need for 'donation' of organs is wasteful because individuals might never 'get round to getting a donor card' or might be superstitious and see having a donor card as 'tempting fate'; and then some relatives might find the decision too difficult to make at a difficult time. Some people also don't give their organs for reasons of belief. This means that many possible organs are 'lost'.

◆ Some argue that donation should be compulsory. Your organs are no longer any use to you after your death. It should therefore be seen as a *social duty* to give them for the use of others. This duty would also take away the pressure on relatives to make difficult decisions at such a time.

◆ Another approach is to make donation compulsory, unless you have 'opted out'. So, instead of carrying a donor card, you would carry a 'non-donor' card, which would state that your organs are not to be used. Without this opt-out card they would be used automatically (e.g. as in Singapore).

◆ Some people worry about the pressure relatives might be put under to donate your organs when you are considered dead. This might be a particular problem when you are in a PVS, where there might be pressure to switch off life support in order to harvest organs in their best condition. Some also worry that doctors, keen to obtain organs, might make hasty diagnoses of death.

Organs can also be donated by people while they are alive. Bone marrow and various organs that we have 'sets' of (like kidneys) can be donated without harm to the donor. This raises a whole new set of issues. How far do we have the right to give away parts of our body? For example, imagine you had a child who needed a heart transplant. Do you have the right to donate your heart (and therefore sacrifice your life)? Should a doctor agree to such a procedure? Currently, you can only donate organs where that wouldn't seriously harm your own survival chances. Some worry about the pressure on

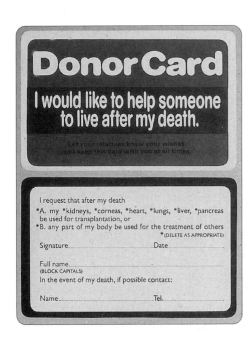

FIGURE 2.6 *A donor card*

relatives again. Perhaps you don't really want to donate your organs while you are alive but feel that the pressure is on you to do so – so you feel you 'should'.

There is also the very difficult issue of whether or not you should be allowed to sell your organs:

◆ You should be able to sell your organs because they are yours to do with as you please. What right does anyone have to deny you this opportunity – especially if you are very poor and have no other way to support your family? It's no different to 'selling' your labour.

◆ The selling of organs should not be allowed because it is a way of the wealthy exploiting the poor. Someone would have to be seriously struggling to do such a drastic thing. Such a person should be helped – not taken advantage of. It could also lead to people using violence to obtain organs.

DISCUSSION POINT

Should you be able to sell your organs?

RECEIVING

There are also issues about who should receive organs. Currently, need is decided by medical factors only. Organs are given to the person who needs them most. But is this fair? Should other things be taken into account? For example, should a young person's needs come before an older person's? What about some kind of 'social' consideration? For example, an organ becomes available; two people need it, both the same age and both with the same medical needs. One is a hardworking father of four children, the other a single man who is serving a life sentence for murder.

Already doctors have to make medical decisions about need – should there be other factors taken into account too? Who would decide these? There are only enough resources to meet a limited amount of need in any health service, transplants are expensive and not always successful. Perhaps the money used on them would be better spent in another area where success was more likely.

What also about the *cause* of your need? For example, should the person who requires a liver transplant because of damage caused by alcohol abuse be given the same chances as someone whose liver damage has been caused by disease?

DISCUSSION POINT

What factors should be taken into account when deciding who should get a transplant?

THE APPLIANCE OF SCIENCE

Perhaps the best way to meet the need for organ transplants is to find some other way of getting them than from the living or the dead – people that is.

Xenotransplantation

Already, animal organs may be transplanted into humans. This involves the need for lots of drugs because the human body does its best to 'reject' such organs. Some scientists have argued that the way to deal with this is through genetic modification. This would mean

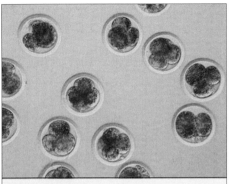

FIGURE 2.7 *Xenotransplantation. This female piglet was cloned by injecting genetic material from fetal pig skin cells into an egg, and transplanting that egg into a surrogate mother*

'altering' genetic information in animals so that they developed 'more human' organs. Research into the genetic modification of pig hearts to match human needs was recently halted. This was because of fears that the processes could develop new and very dangerous diseases, which could cross from animals to humans. There are also issues here about the rights of animals as well as the 'integrity' of a human with animal organs – although some argue that using animals in this way is no different to using them as food sources.

Stem cell growth/cloning

Some think the way forward is simply to grow human organs from human stem cells. These are often obtained from aborted foetuses (which raises it own issues).

In 1999, researchers in Tokyo University successfully grew frog eyes and ears in the lab using the animal's own embryo cells. Human skin can already be grown from a patient's own cells. Perhaps complete organs are the next step. Cloning would have the benefit of compatibility – the organ would be less likely to be rejected because your own cells are used. It would also avoid the need for the use of foetal cells. However, this is probably a long way off yet.

Bionics

Perhaps human organs could be replaced with mechanical organs. Of course, this would raise the question of when a person becomes a machine.

FACTS AND FIGURES

- ◆ There are almost 6000 people waiting for kidney transplants at any one time in the UK.
- ◆ The world's first heart transplant took place in 1967.
- ◆ It is estimated that xenotransplantation could generate five billion dollars in revenue over the next 15 years.

MORAL RESPONSES

Some **Christians** do not donate their organs. This is because they believe that the body should be 'whole' so that it can be physically resurrected. Most Christians, however, do support organ donation because they see this as an act of 'charity'. However, they do not believe that it should be made compulsory because this would then take away your own freedom to choose and so it wouldn't be an act of kindness any more. While alive, you should be able to choose whether or not you donate your organs. The use of the dead as organ donors is acceptable provided that this is what they would have wanted and their relatives are comfortable with it. There should be no pressure on anyone to donate and it should not lead to 'hasty' diagnoses of death nor to families being persuaded to switch off life support machines before they are ready to.

Christians oppose the selling of organs. This is because of the abuses that might go along with it but also because it is seen as exploitation of the weak by the strong. For this reason, too, the use of foetal tissue is completely opposed by the Roman Catholic Church and seen as morally doubtful by the Church of Scotland. Most Christian groups support the use of animal organs for donation, provided there is no unnecessary suffering involved for the animals. As far as the creation of 'spare parts' by genetic modification is concerned, again there is caution. Christians welcome such developments provided that they are safe and that they don't lead to humans 'taking over' the creative role that should belong to God.

The fundamental Christian ethical argument in favour of organ transplantation must be Christ's commandment to love one's neighbour.

Church of Scotland, Report on human transplants, May 1990

The **Muslim** view on organ transplants varies. Some say that they are wrong because the body must remain whole to be raised on the day of judgement. Others disagree, saying that organ donation should be seen as an act of compassion and that if good can come out of your death then it should. Again, there should be no pressure on relatives or the dying because this could lead to abuses. In Singapore, where you must opt out of organ transplants, organs are automatically taken unless you are a Muslim – where it is assumed that you might have religious objections. Even as a Muslim, however, you can state that you want your organs removed.

Muslims would also oppose the selling of organs. Muhammed did not allow humans to eat the 'living flesh' of animals because this was an abuse (in Muhammed's time a living animal might have been used as an ongoing food source on a journey). In the same way, 'plundering' the organs of the living for the benefit of others could be seen as abusive. It is also a way of exploiting the poor. Muslims might also have problems with the use of animals as sources of organs – particularly animals which are *haram* (unclean). Pigs, for example, are *haram* and so the use of pig organs or tissue would not be acceptable (although again, *some* 'progressive' Muslims might argue that in a life or death situation you can suspend this ruling). In general, the 'power' given by the ability to transplant organs should be handled carefully.

Egoists could take a number of positions depending upon how this helped their own interests. Egoists wouldn't be likely to donate organs out of kindness, unless this was to a close relative who really mattered. They might support the selling of organs, which would benefit them if they needed either an organ, or the money. In fact, the Egoist might not be very bothered about where organs come from provided that there is a ready source of them to meet their own needs. For example, the 'early' switching off of life support for someone in a PVS would be acceptable if it meant getting hold of organs as needed. Also, using the brain dead as 'organ factories' would not be unacceptable. Egoists would also support the use of animal organs, however they were 'sourced', provided that this didn't mean an increase in harmful diseases. They would also support scientific development that resulted in the 'growth' of organs from scratch – even if this meant the use of foetal tissue.

The only probable concern an Egoist might have would be if donation were made compulsory. You might therefore fear that your own life could be 'cut short' so that your organs could be harvested. Other than this, the use of organs seems like a good way to further your own self-interest.

The **Utilitarian** position is similar to that of an Egoist in some ways. Organ donation is acceptable provided that its benefits outweigh the drawbacks. With proper controls about when and how it is carried out this should mean that abuses are kept to a minimum. The Utilitarian would want to make sure that people didn't feel under pressure to donate their (or their relative's) organs before they were ready to. Utilitarians could support the selling of organs provided this was tightly controlled and meant that no-one was being taken advantage of. They could argue that as your organs are yours, no-one has the right to deny you the opportunity to benefit from them – especially when otherwise you might be very poor and unable to support your family.

Utilitarians might be likely to support an 'opt-out' approach, where your organs are taken after death unless you had specifically requested that they should not be. This system would help deal with the shortage of organs and so produce a great deal of happiness at 'no real cost'. Some Utilitarians argue that withholding your organs after death is irrational because, after all, they're no use to 'you' then. Utilitarians would also support using organs from any source provided that this didn't involve unnecessary suffering. For example, the use of foetal tissue is not the same as using organs from a complete 'person'. Also, as someone in a PVS can't have much quality of life, switching off life support to harvest organs can't be wrong. Utilitarians might also support keeping the brain dead respirated so that their organs can be systematically harvested for use. Some Utilitarians worry about the suffering of animals used for organ transplants and the possible harm that the spread of disease from animals to humans might cause. Utilitarians would also support the use of artificial organs, as well as the development of organs from stem cells, provided the suffering caused didn't outweigh the eventual benefits.

ACTIVITIES

Knowledge & Understanding

1 What does Jetmund Engeset think should happen? Why?
2 What organs are usually transplanted and why are they needed?
3 Why might someone argue that a corpse has no rights?
4 Why might some people not have an organ donor card? Think of as many reasons as you can.
5 Why might relatives feel 'under pressure' to donate their loved one's organs?
6 Give one argument against the selling of organs.
7 Do some people 'deserve' organs more than others?
8 Explain one way in which science could help cut the shortage of organs.
9 Why might a religious person want to donate his organs?
10 What concerns might religious people have about organ transplants?
11 What might an Egoist feel about the idea of selling organs?

Analysis

1 Write a letter to Jetmund Engeset explaining your view of his proposal.
2 Design your own 'Charter for the newly dead'. List what rights and responsibilities the 'newly dead' should have.

3 Imagine you are someone who wants to donate his heart to his 18-year-old daughter. You secretly meet with the doctor in charge of your daughter's case. Write the discussion that might take place.
4 It has been decided to allow people to sell their organs. Draw up a list of rules that you think are needed to cover such a practice.
5 It has been agreed that animals will be genetically modified to 'grow' human organs. There is a meeting in your town about it. Run the meeting in your class. Include the views of religious people as well as Egoists.

Evaluation

'Religious people should always donate their organs.'
Do you agree? Give at least **two** reasons for your answer.

Assessment question

Outcome 3 'People should be allowed to sell their organs if they want.'
Do you agree? Give at least **two** reasons for your answer

Homework

If you carry a donor card, explain why you do this. If not, explain why you do not. Discuss this with relatives and friends. Write down some of their views to add to your own.

Knowledge & Understanding

1 Why might someone oppose Jetmund Engeset's views?

2 Do you agree that even after death we have responsibilities to others? Explain your view.

3 Why might the need for organs be important for the status of someone in a PVS?

4 What would the advantages and disadvantages of an 'opt-out' approach to organ donation be?

5 What 'pressures' might be linked to organ donation?

6 What do you think should be taken into account when deciding who should receive organs?

7 Should foetal tissue be used for transplant? Explain your answer.

8 Would the Egoist always support the use of the newly dead as organ donors? Explain.

9 Why might a Utilitarian support an 'opt-out' approach?

10 State one major difference between the views of a Utilitarian and a religious person about organ donation.

Analysis

1 You are First Minister of the Scottish Parliament. Your government has decided to support the views of Jetmund Engeset. Issue a press release that explains your position.

2 Carry out a class debate: 'This house believes that it should be compulsory to donate organs after death.'

3 You are responsible for someone in a PVS. The doctors suggest that you switch off the life support so that the organs can be used. You meet with your family to explain. Act this out as a role play. Ideally, one other member of the family should disagree with your decision.

4 The 'hardworking father of four children' has been denied an organ transplant which has gone to a murderer instead. You are the wife of the 'hardworking man'. You take this decision to court. Write what happens in the form of a short play.

5 It has been decided to legalise the selling of organs. Write a speech which might be made by a religious person in response to this.

Evaluation

'Some people deserve organ transplants more than others'. How far do you agree?

Assessment question

Outcome 3 To what extent do you agree that organ donation should be 'opt-out' as opposed to 'opt-in'?

Homework

You are the judge in the case described in Analysis question four above. Write out the decision you make and your reasons for it.

VOLUNTARY EUTHANASIA

CASE STUDY

In 1975, Derek Humphry helped his first wife, who had cancer, to commit suicide. They believed that the right to die was a question of individual freedom. Derek began to set up groups that shared his belief. In 1976, he set up the Hemlock Society to support people's right to euthanasia. By 1990, he was President of the World Federation of Right to Die Societies. At its conference, in 1990, he explained what the Society is about:

> We are definitely not about murder or killing, or getting rid of less fortunate people within our communities; nor are we about unhappy or unbalanced people escaping this world because they cannot cope with it; we are about compassion and love for our fellow man and woman. It is about caring. These feelings alone are not enough; they must be accompanied by thought, advance planning, and perhaps new laws to ensure the individual's control and choice. Let us never lose sight of the main target: helping human beings to suffer less.

In 1980, the Voluntary Euthanasia Society of Scotland published a book. *How to die with dignity.* Written by Dr George Mair, this describes effective ways to carry out euthanasia.

FIGURE 2.8 *Derek Humphry*

WHY DIE?

Euthanasia means deciding when, where and how you die. There could be many reasons for choosing to end your own life:

◆ The pain of illness might mean you would rather die than suffer.
◆ You may feel that the quality of life you live is no longer acceptable – for example, if you suffered from a progressive disease like Alzheimer's or if some ability you valued (like your sight) was lost.
◆ You may want to choose the time, place and method of your own death – to 'die with dignity'.
◆ You may want to die before you become a 'burden' to others.

Euthanasia can be:

◆ **active:** by taking certain fatal drugs, for example
◆ **passive:** by refusing life-saving treatment

Currently, voluntary euthanasia in Britain is not illegal but helping someone to die is. It is often called 'assisted suicide'. In Britain, if you 'assisted' in someone's suicide – whatever your reasons – you could be charged with murder. Many people call it doctor-assisted suicide. They want medical help to carry out euthanasia so they can be sure it's effective. Doctors could face murder/manslaughter charges if they help in any way. Many feel this is wrong because only doctors have the proper medical knowledge to help make death 'painless'. Why should they not be allowed to use this knowledge if asked?

THE RIGHT TO DIE?

Supporters of voluntary euthanasia argue that everyone has the right to choose the time and method of their own death. This is personal autonomy – no-one else's business. Life belongs to the person who lives it, they should choose when it ends, just as they chose how it was lived. Opponents say that life is not entirely 'at our disposal' – and besides, if voluntary euthanasia was too easy then it might lead to all sorts of abuses.

SUPPORTING VOLUNTARY EUTHANASIA

◆ It is about human freedom to choose and control your own life. Everyone has the right to choose when and how they die.
◆ It is an act of compassion. Surely it is better to have a doctor help you to 'die with dignity' than to 'fade away' while suffering pain and indignity. It is also a way for your family to show their love by helping you in your final moments.
◆ It relieves burdens on families who might otherwise have to support a dying relative, which could be time-consuming, expensive and emotionally difficult. This also relieves the burden on society – allowing medical resources to be used for more 'hopeful' cases, not to keep you 'alive' when you don't even want to be.

DISCUSSION POINT

What would be the advantages and disadvantages of making voluntary euthanasia legal?

DISCUSSION POINT

Is your life yours to do with as you please?

◆ It is about the doctor's right to treat the patient. Being a doctor is not just about saving lives, it's about doing what's best for the patient. If sometimes that means helping to end their suffering, then why should this treatment not be possible? We already accept that some treatments are 'ordinary' and others 'extraordinary'. Even opponents of euthanasia sometimes think that we should 'allow people to die' while not actually 'causing them to die'. Voluntary euthanasia takes the responsibility away from the doctors, so they don't have to bear the burden of such a serious decision.

◆ The value of life is related to its quality. Many people feel that there comes a point where life is 'no longer worth living'. Although we might not agree with their conclusion, we should respect their right to make such a decision and then not stop them doing something about it. Besides, there is no real value in suffering – especially unnecessary suffering.

◆ It would be good for society as a whole if we could 'compassionately' help someone to die. This means that you would never have to worry about the effects of something which changed the quality of your life seriously. You know you could safely end your life when you chose to. This would make society generally more caring.

Opposing voluntary euthanasia

◆ Freedom should have limits. No-one is free, for example, to kill someone else for no reason – why should we be allowed to kill ourselves? Also, how can we know that someone's decision to ask for voluntary euthanasia is completely 'free'. There could be all sorts of pressures on them. They may be unable to make such a decision in a calm way at such a difficult time.

◆ Voluntary euthanasia, however it is carried out, is not facing up to the end of life with courage. It is not an act of compassion but an act of hopelessness. If a family assists in voluntary euthanasia, it isn't showing love, it's abandoning the person. Besides, there is value in suffering. People often learn more about themselves in such situations than at any other time. It can also bind families together. Without the natural processes of death and dying, perhaps people would never confront the 'big issues' in life. There can be value in some suffering for the person dying as well as the family.

◆ Families and society should accept the 'burden' of the dying. Resources should be available to treat all. Supporting a person towards the end of their life – without speeding up the process – is true compassion. Why be with them all through their life and not see it through to its 'natural' end?

◆ Voluntary euthanasia is not treatment. Medical science is now so advanced that pain and suffering can be kept to a minimum, even in the most severe cases. This means that choosing death doesn't ever need to be an option. Most people are not afraid of death but dying. Proper palliative care can do away with this fear and so make voluntary euthanasia unnecessary. Besides, having the option of voluntary euthanasia might put a strain on the doctor-patient relationship that needn't be there.

◆ How can you put a 'value' on life? Life is sacred – a gift to be used wisely. What we think of as a poor quality of life is just another kind of living. The trick is to learn to adjust to a different life – not just end it because it's not what we're used to or what we like. Besides, if we agree as a society that certain lives are more 'worth living' than others, then what's next – should we allow people to carry out euthanasia because they lose their jobs or lose their partners?

◆ There are no benefits to society in making voluntary euthanasia more easily available. It would just make life more uncaring – because we would know that at some point in the future, euthanasia might be 'suggested' to us. Many people who 'feel' they are a burden might opt for euthanasia when they don't really want to. It could also lead to people being 'persuaded' to carry out euthanasia when they don't want to so that their families could 'get on with their lives' (or get their hands on their relative's money, for example). There are too many possible pressures which could be exercised to make voluntary euthanasia a good idea. Making voluntary euthanasia easier might also lead to making other kinds of euthanasia 'compulsory'.

FIGURE 2.9 *Caring for the dying*

FACTS AND FIGURES

◆ Derek Humphry's book, *Final Exit*, describes ways of ending your life. Attempts to ban it were unsuccessful.
◆ In the USA, since 1935, 11 doctors have been charged with murder/manslaughter for assisting people to die.
◆ The British Medical Association has repeatedly argued against legalising voluntary euthanasia.

CASE STUDY

Dr Jack Kervorkian was recently charged with manslaughter and imprisoned in the USA. He believes that everyone should have the right to choose when and how to die. He has even designed a machine that administers lethal drugs at the push of a button. The button is pushed by the person who has chosen voluntary euthanasia. He has constantly challenged the US legal system to arrest him as he's quite open about what he does. He was finally arrested after a video he had made of him assisting someone to die was shown on TV. At his trial, the judge said, 'You had the audacity to go on national television and show the world what you did and dare the legal system to stop you. Well, sir, consider yourself stopped.' Dr Kervorkian's case is currently the subject of legal appeal.

A bill allowing doctors to end the life of suffering patients was passed by the Dutch Parliament on 28 December 2000. The patient must face 'constant, unbearable physical suffering' and must be at least 16 years old. They must also have asked over a period of time to be helped to die. Each case will be looked at individually. Opponents argue that this will lead to exactly the kind of abuses that you might expect from easy euthanasia.

SOME 'FINAL' QUESTIONS

◆ Should everyone have the right to carry out voluntary euthanasia?
◆ From what *age* should it be possible to consider it?
◆ When might such a decision be thought of as 'doubtful'? (for example, if someone was severely depressed or on powerful drugs)?
◆ Who should decide whether it is right or not? The courts? The medical world? The individual? Governments?

MORAL RESPONSES

For the **Christian**, voluntary euthanasia is almost always opposed. This is based on the idea that life is God's to give or take away. In 1981, the Church of Scotland made its position clear: 'On the same basis of the Christian belief in God's sovereignty over life, there can be no support for the concept of the permissibility in law to kill a fellow human being even when he requests it.' The Church of Scotland document, *Euthanasia: A Christian Perspective* (1997), summarises its beliefs:
◆ Human life is not our own property – it is 'on loan' from God
◆ As we are in the image of God we have different responsibilities to each other from all other creatures.
◆ Jesus suffered as a human, suggesting that suffering is part of what it means to be human.
◆ We have responsibilities to each other, which we would be ignoring if we allowed euthanasia.
The Church believes that euthanasia is not an issue of personal freedom but of care for each other. If people were sure that while dying, they would be well cared for, then the 'need' for euthanasia would disappear.

Roman Catholic teachings are similar. The Church believes that the terminally ill are a 'call' from God for the Christian community to care for them. Euthanasia is an act of 'hopelessness', whereas Christianity is a religion of 'hope'. In 1991, the Pope called any kind of euthanasia 'a grave violation of the law of God'.

No-one can keep himself from dying or put off the day of his death. That is a battle we cannot escape; we cannot cheat our way out.

Ecclesiastes 8:8

Muslim teaching is similar. Euthanasia is seen as a form of suicide, which is believed to be wrong. Only Allah has the power to take your life away. If you do it yourself, then you are interfering in Allah's will for your life. It is part of your submission to Allah to accept whatever he has in store for you. Muslims believe that there can be value in suffering and that euthanasia is a form of not facing up to your suffering. Muslim life is based on accepting Allah's will for you – including the time and method of your death. Accepting your death is the final and greatest act of submission to the will of Allah.

Endure patiently whatever may afflict you, for that shows determination.

Surah 31:17

Allah suffices for anyone who relies on him.

Surah 65:3

Muslims also believe that it would be wrong to ask a doctor to take your life because this is asking him to commit murder.

Anyone who kills a believer deliberately will receive as his reward a sentence to live in Hell for ever. God will be angry with him and curse him and prepare dreadful torment for him.

Surah 4:93

Like Christians, the process of dying is seen as an opportunity for the community to support and care for a person in the last stages of their life. To 'abandon' the person by allowing – or helping – them to carry out voluntary euthanasia is not the proper way for a community to support its members.

More than any other moral stance, **Egoism** believes that personal freedom is of the greatest importance. If you want to end your own life, however and whenever you want to do it, that is your concern and no-one else's. Egoists would want to have the option of voluntary euthanasia when they had chosen it. They might want to carry out euthanasia for all sorts of reasons – from relieving the pain of serious illness all the way to just wanting to die because they are 'tired of life'. Generally speaking, the Egoist would want euthanasia to be as easy to obtain as possible. Even if he had decided to end his own life, the Egoist would want it to be done in a way which ensured that he didn't suffer. The best way to do this would be to have a doctor help him or her to carry it out. The Egoist would not be concerned about the pressures this might put the doctor under, nor that making euthanasia easy to obtain might lead to 'abuses' (unless those abuses were more likely to lead to pressure being put on him to end his life before he was ready to). The right to take your own life, when you want to and how you want to, is probably the most obvious case of making a moral decision based on self-interest.

Utilitarians generally support the right to choose the option of voluntary euthanasia. For the Utilitarian, whether your life is worth living any longer is a case of weighing up life's benefits against its drawbacks. Particularly where someone was in great pain, the Utilitarian would support voluntary euthanasia as a way of minimising pain and maximising happiness. Provided that the choice was completely free and that there was protection for individuals from unwanted pressure to choose euthanasia, the Utilitarian would think having it freely available would make society 'happier'. This is because you could live your life, certain that when you no longer wanted to live it – for whatever reason – you could end it painlessly and with medical help. Utilitarians would think that such a society was far more caring than one where people were 'kept alive' even when they didn't want that to happen. They might argue that doctors should be able to 'treat' patients in this way if that is what the patient thought was best and the doctor agreed. Besides, Utilitarians might say that making euthanasia more easily obtainable just makes more official what already happens in hospitals anyway. It is surely in the best interests of the majority if it is 'decriminalised'. Why should a doctor be prosecuted for helping a patient make their life more 'comfortable', especially when the patient requests it. Utilitarians would also accept the idea that society should explore other alternatives. There's no real freedom of choice for you if the choice is either death or endless suffering. Utilitarians support the Hospice movement and also the patient's right to be kept alive as long as he or she chooses. A society keen on maximising happiness would explore all the possible options, but not 'ban' options with which people were happy. The only concern the Utilitarian might have would be if making voluntary euthanasia easier to obtain led to more 'abuses'. However, many Utilitarian moral philosophers argue that where voluntary euthanasia is already tolerated such 'abuses' don't seem to happen any more than where it is illegal.

ACTIVITIES

Knowledge & Understanding

1 What does Derek Humphry think the Right to Die Societies are all about?

2 State **one** situation where someone might 'want to die'.

3 In your own words describe **two** arguments supporting voluntary euthanasia.

4 Choose **one** of these arguments and explain whether you agree with it.

5 In what way might voluntary euthanasia make a 'society more caring'?

6 Describe **one** way in which someone might argue that voluntary euthanasia is wrong.

7 Why do you think the book, *Final Exit,* was banned?

8 Describe, in your own words, the Church of Scotland's views on voluntary euthanasia.

9 State **two** reasons why a Muslim might oppose voluntary euthanasia.

10 Why would an Egoist probably support voluntary euthanasia?

Analysis

1 Discuss whether or not you would want to carry out voluntary euthanasia. In what situations do you think you'd be most likely to want it? Draw up a questionnaire and ask people for their views. Write a brief report of your findings.

2 As a class, split into two groups. One should be for voluntary euthanasia and one against. Give yourself a reasonable time-limit and create a display board that explains your side's position. Use artwork, writing, images etc.

3 You are a doctor who has 'helped patients to die'. You have been called before the General Medical Council to explain your illegal actions in the following four cases. In each case, you helped the person to die. As a class, act out the meeting in the form of a role play. You should include representatives of a variety of moral stances in your role play – including religious people. You might find it helpful to add further detail to the 'cases':

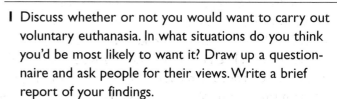

Nadim was 18. A promising football player, he lost the use of his legs in a car accident. The thing he most wanted in life – to be a football player – was now impossible.

Alison was 33, with two children. She had early Alzheimer's and was beginning to suffer its effects. She didn't want her children to see her deteriorate.
Alan was 67. He had terminal cancer. He knew he had only months to live and that these wouldn't be easy months. His wife had died from the same thing a year ago.
Marion was a single woman. She was 48 years old. She was depressed because she'd had a long list of failed relationships. Her life no longer 'had meaning'. She said she wasn't physically ill, but 'mentally terminally ill', and would probably kill herself anyway.

Evaluation

Do you agree that 'helping someone to die' should be made legal? Give **two** reasons for your answer.

Assessment question

Outcome 3 'Voluntary euthanasia is about personal freedom.' Explain whether you agree or not and give at least **two** reasons.

Homework

You are the doctor in Analysis question three. Write your response to ONE of the case studies.

ACTIVITIES

i2

Knowledge & Understanding

1 Are some reasons for wanting to carry out voluntary euthanasia more 'valid' than others? Explain.
2 Do you think there is any difference between active and passive euthanasia? Give reasons for your answer.
3 What is meant by saying that voluntary euthanasia is about 'personal autonomy'? Do you agree?
4 Which of the arguments supporting voluntary euthanasia do you think is the 'strongest'? Explain your answer.
5 Which of the arguments opposing voluntary euthanasia do you think is the 'strongest'? Explain your answer.
6 What happened to Dr Kervorkian? Do you agree with him being imprisoned? Explain your answer.
7 Why do you think the British Medical Association has 'repeatedly argued against legalising voluntary euthanasia'?
8 What reasons do religious people usually give for opposing voluntary euthanasia?
9 In what ways are the Utilitarian and Egoist views about voluntary euthanasia similar?

Analysis

1 You are a committee of the General Medical Council. The government has decided to fully legalise voluntary euthanasia. Draw up a list of guidelines which you think doctors should have to follow. (You could later compare these with the Dutch guidelines which already exist.)
2 Using the case studies in the Intermediate 1 Analysis section, write a response that would be made about each one from each of the three moral stances.

3 Imagine you are a member of the Church of Scotland who is opposed to its stance on voluntary euthanasia. Write a letter to the Board of Social Responsibility explaining why you, as a Christian, support voluntary euthanasia. (You could also do this from a Muslim perspective if you prefer.)
4 Carry out a class debate: 'This house believes that *helping someone to die* should remain illegal.'
5 Write an article for a newspaper entitled: 'Voluntary Euthanasia – What's the big fuss about it?'. Explain what the issues are as well as different opinions about them.

Evaluation

How far do you agree that helping someone to die is 'an act of compassion'?

Assessment question

Outcome 3 In the case of voluntary euthanasia, personal autonomy is not the only issue.'
To what extent do you agree?
Note: remember to consider arguments for and against as well as your own personal conclusion supported by reasons.

Homework

Choose one of the case studies in the Intermediate 1 Analysis section. You are judging the actions of the doctor for the British Medical Association. Explain the decision you reach in this case and give the reasons for your decision.

HUMAN RELATIONSHIPS

SEXUAL BEHAVIOUR

IT'S ONLY NATURAL

From the earliest times there have been restrictions on when, where, how and with whom sexual relationships could take place. In native societies, there were very clear rules about sexual behaviour – the taboos. Punishments for breaking these taboos could (and still can) be serious. In modern society, there are still 'rules'. Some believe these should be strictly followed, others that they should be flexible. Some believe that society is ready for a complete change in attitudes to sexual behaviour. Some also believe that there should be no rules at all because sex is not a moral issue – just natural.

DISCUSSION POINT

Should there be 'rules' about sexual behaviour?

CASE STUDY

Girls are twice as likely as boys to feel pressured into having under-age sex because it is seen as 'cool'. Research carried out in Scotland showed that a desire to impress their friends played a greater role for girls than boys in making decisions about sexual behaviour. A sample of 129 14- and 15-year-olds in Ayrshire were asked their views about sexual behaviour. When asked, 'Why do you think younger people are having sex?' 41% of girls said 'to impress or look cool' compared with 19% of the boys. Girls reported feeling under pressure from their partners to have sex. 21% of girls and 11% of boys felt forced to have sex to keep or please their partners.

Scotland on Sunday, 20 August 2000

CASE STUDY

School nurses are pressing for the right to hand out the morning-after emergency contraceptive pill to pupils on demand in Scottish secondary schools.

Sunday Herald, 20 August 2000

YOU CAN'T AVOID SEX

It is often argued that sexual behaviour today is such a 'problem' because sex is 'everywhere'. Some believe that sex is more obvious nowadays than it was – and for people at a younger age. While some believe that this is a more healthy approach to sexual matters, others believe that the easy availability of sexual materials makes the whole business of sexual behaviour more complicated and pressurised.

Pornography

Previously, this was not easy to obtain in any form and there was little on TV that could be described as pornography. Now, however, the internet provides unrestricted access to all sorts of materials and can be accessed by anyone anywhere. The growth of satellite and cable TV has also meant a growth in the availability of pornography. Some believe that the laws covering pornography have been weakened so that much 'stronger' materials are more easily available.

Sexier Exposure

Some believe that people are exposed to sexual issues more often and at a younger age these days. 'Tweenager' magazines, aimed at pre-teens, cover sexual issues more explicitly (it is claimed) nowadays. Boy bands, pop videos, teen idols, etc are now 'sold' much more on their sex appeal (for example, Buffy, Britney etc). Also, for

FIGURE 3.1 *Britney Spears*

DISCUSSION POINT

Do you think sex is more evident nowadays? If so, is that a problem?

adults, sex is increasingly evident. There has recently been growth in the sale of 'lad mags', like *FHM*, which some people argue are just a mild form of pornography, while more and more TV commercials use sexual imagery.

FIGURE 3.2 *Even companies like Marks and Spencer use sex to sell*

THE AGE OF CONSENT

At the moment, a heterosexual sexual relationship is legal in Scotland from the age of 16. This age has been chosen because it is thought to be the time when physical and emotional development are, on average, about equal. Recent reports show that young people are reaching puberty earlier than they were in the past. On average, girls are reaching physical sexual maturity at around ten years old. Some argue that the age of consent should be lowered because:

◆ If you are 'ready' for sex then why shouldn't you be able to have a sexual relationship?
◆ It would just make lawful what already happens anyway, but take away the guilt and worry.
◆ It would therefore bring sexual relationships 'out into the open'. This would lead to fewer abuses.

Others argue that the age of consent should remain the same (or even be raised) because:

◆ Even if you are physically 'ready' you might not be emotionally ready.

DISCUSSION POINT

At what age do you think a sexual relationship should be legally allowed?

◆ Lowering the age of consent would take away protection from vulnerable young people who may feel even more pressure to have sex.
◆ Just because something's already being done doesn't make it right.
◆ It could result in even more abuses as people take advantage of younger boys and girls.
◆ A sexual relationship involves powerful emotions, as well as commitment and understanding. All of this would be too much for someone under 16 to cope with.
◆ It would result in more casual sex, with all the medical and social problems that come with this.

SAME-SEX RELATIONSHIPS

CASE STUDY

In 1999/2000, a campaign was run in Scotland over the 'Section 2A' issue. The law stated that when teaching about sexual behaviour in schools, teachers should not be allowed to 'promote' homosexuality as an acceptable way of life. Instead, they should stress that heterosexual relationships were the best option. So if your teacher said something like, 'It's OK to be gay' they would have been breaking the law. The Scottish Parliament wanted to remove this law from the statute books. A group led by Brian Souter, owner of the Stagecoach bus company, carried out an independent referendum on the issue. 66% of Scots chose not to vote. 89% of those who did vote wanted to keep the clause. However, the Scottish Parliament did repeal the law, but added mention of the special nature of heterosexual marriage.

Homosexual relationships have always existed. In many societies throughout history they have been tolerated, encouraged or just accepted. Sometimes, however, homosexuals have been persecuted for their lifestyles. Male homosexual acts were illegal in Britain until relatively recently, although lesbianism has never been illegal. Homosexual sexual behaviour raises strong emotions. In schools, to be called 'gay' is often thought of as one of the 'worst insults'. Very few school pupils therefore 'come out' as homosexuals during their school lives. But if the statistics are right, then every school must have a reasonable number of people who are homosexual.
Opponents of homosexuality argue that every teenager goes through a 'phase of confusion' about their sexuality and that the task is to help them through this so that they come through it and end up in a 'normal' relationship.
Others say that we should help young people to work out their sexuality – whatever that ends up being. What are the arguments?
◆ Homosexuality is just a matter of personal choice – no-one else's business. Where two 'consenting adults' are involved, it has no harmful effects for anyone.

- You're born a homosexual. You can't change it. You should just accept it.
- Homosexual relationships are no different to heterosexual ones. They can be loving, caring and long term. The idea that homosexuals are 'more promiscuous' is wrong.
- Homosexuality is 'unnatural'. Society needs relationships to be heterosexual so that it can continue.
- It might be true that you are born a homosexual. But then it should be seen as an 'illness' and we should try to 'cure' it.
- Homosexuals are more promiscuous. This takes away all the special qualities of a sexual relationship.

Homosexual pressure groups argue that anti-homosexual beliefs are based on prejudice and ignorance – old-fashioned ideas of what's right and wrong. Those who oppose homosexual practice say that they want to 'protect' vulnerable people – in particular younger people from this kind of 'unnatural' relationship.

DISCUSSION POINT

Is homosexuality 'wrong'?

FACTS AND FIGURES

- In a recent study, 32% of 15-year-old boys and 37% of 15-year-old girls report having had sex.
- In 1999, gay couple Barrie Drewitt and Tony Barlow used surrogate mothers to produce their own family. They are named as 'parent 1' and 'parent 2' on the childrens' birth certificates.
- Girls who first have sex at 12 are twice as likely to catch a sexually transmitted disease as girls who first have sex at 15.

LOVE OR LUST?

Is sex somehow 'special'? Some think it is just an activity, which doesn't need to have any emotional strings attached. Sex is physically enjoyable and if you choose to do it with as many people as often as you like, that's up to you. The argument is that where two adults agree to have sex for pleasure, with no long-term relationship involved, then that's no different to agreeing to do anything else with anyone.

Others disagree. They say that sex is a very personal and intimate way of showing your love for someone. Sex means giving yourself completely to a person and taking big emotional risks. You can only do this if you're prepared to commit yourself to the relationship – perhaps even in marriage. Most supporters of marriage would argue that you should be sexually faithful to your partner while married. Also, many involved in long-term unmarried relationships would agree you should remain sexually faithful. A relationship involving sex gives both partners responsibilities to each other. The level of commitment that sex involves means that you should be totally committed to the person – not just 'use each other' for pleasure. Some go further and argue that casual sex is wrong because such relationships without commitment 'weaken' society.

DISCUSSION POINT

Should sex involve commitment?

MORAL RESPONSES

Almost all **Christian** teaching states that sex is a gift from God that is special. It should only take place within a long-term, stable relationship. For most, this means marriage. In 1994, the Church of Scotland set out its position:

> Sexuality is a blessing and gift from God to be experienced and enjoyed without shame or guilt; and marriage is appointed as the right and proper setting for the full expression of physical love between man and woman.

Sex is seen as an act of commitment between two people and so should not be 'devalued' by being treated lightly. Casual sex is therefore wrong. The level of commitment required also means that the age of consent should not be too low. Apart from the potential for exploitation of the young by older people, a child should not be expected to cope with the emotions of a sexual relationship too soon.

As far as homosexuality is concerned, most Christian churches see it as wrong. In 1967, the Church of Scotland saw homosexuality as 'a source of uncleanness, deterioration in human character, and weakness'. In its Report on Human Sexuality in 1994, it takes a more balanced approach, but the Assembly of that year stated: 'while we note the presence of differing views, we see no compelling reasons to alter the Church's position that the practice of homosexual acts is contrary to God's will for mankind'. The Roman Catholic Church, while it says that homosexuals should be treated compassionately, still believes that homosexuality is sinful.

Key Christian texts in relation to sexuality are: Leviticus 18:22 and 20:13; Genesis 19:1–11; Judges 19:16–30; Romans:1:24–27; 1 Corinthians 6:9–11; 1 Timothy 1:8–11; Jude 7.

Muslim teaching also states that sex should take place only within marriage. Sex is the way a husband and wife show their love for each other. It is also the source of creating a family – an important part of marriage for the Muslim. Sex is a gift from Allah and so to be enjoyed. Casual sex is wrong, so too is sex with someone else while you are married. In many traditional Muslim societies, polygamy is practised – so sex with more than one partner is permitted, provided that you are married (see marriage section for more details). The Qur'an is quite clear that having sex without being married is wrong – it suggests a punishment of whipping. But sex with someone else while you're married can be punished by being stoned to death (Surahs 4:15–16 & 24:2). Also, in many Muslim societies, people (usually girls) are married at a very young age. However, almost always, such girls remain with their families until it's thought they're old enough to begin their married life involving sexual intercourse. Muslims believe that there can be differences of opinion about the age of consent – but that whatever age that should be – everyone involved should have their own interests looked after and protected by law. In Britain, there has been no support from within the Muslim community to lower the age of consent.

As far as homosexuality is concerned, this is completely prohibited. It is seen as unnatural and something that Allah will not look favourably upon. Sex can only take place within full marriage. As marriage is not possible for same-sex partners, sex between them would be illegal sex and punishable according to Surah 4:15.

As far as sex is concerned, the **Egoist** might say that 'anything goes'. Sex would be seen as a pleasurable activity, which no-one would have any say in other than the people involved. It would not need to be part of a marriage and one-night stands would be perfectly acceptable. Also, even if you are married, there's nothing to stop you having sex with other people – whether your partner knows or agrees or not. For the Egoist, this is a matter of exercising personal freedom – however you choose to do so. The age of consent for the Egoist might be whenever you feel 'ready' to have sex – whether in a relationship or not. Some Egoists might argue that the law in this case can't be equally applied because the age of consent is only an average point at which you are emotionally and physically ready for sex. Some Egoists might go even further and argue that there should be no legal restrictions on when you can have sex. If life is about pursuing your self-interest, then the law shouldn't get in the way of that. As far as homosexuality is concerned, again this is a matter of personal freedom. There's nothing 'wrong' with homosexual sex if that's what you enjoy. No-one has the right to stop you doing what you want. While religious people usually argue that sexual images are too obvious and widespread today, Egoists would claim that there's nothing wrong with this if it produces pleasure. Sex is a natural function of human life – perhaps the most natural. To surround it with 'silly rules' is pointless.

Perhaps the only concern the Egoist might have is the effects on society of a much more open approach to sexual behaviour. If they thought this might lead to a more dangerous, careless society, which could lead to harm for them, then they might want some kind of 'rules' to be in place about sexual behaviour.

The **Utilitarian** view of sexual behaviour could be seen as a more selfless version of the Egoist approach. Utilitarians would generally support personal freedom in this area provided that the benefits this brought to the individual did not harm society as a whole. If changes in attitudes about sexual behaviour led to a more thoughtless or unstable society, then that could mean the drawbacks outweighed the benefits. For example, if sex without marriage meant fewer long-term stable relationships, then this could harm overall social stability. If casual sex led to increased rates of disease, more unwanted children, or greater instability in human relationships, then this could affect everyone. Utilitarians want sexual freedom, but a freedom that involves wider interests than just your own pleasure. Homosexuality isn't wrong, unless it harms society. It could, for example, lead to drops in birth rates, leading to imbalance in the population. The age of consent should respect the individual while giving protection. Too young an age of consent could lead to abuses, which would cause unhappiness, and too old an age of consent could lead to frustration of pleasure. Utilitarians would want to ensure that there was a balance between the happiness of the individual (as well as minimising unhappiness through laws designed to protect), while looking after the needs of society as a whole.

ACTIVITIES

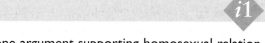

Knowledge & Understanding

1 What is a taboo?

2 What did the research with Ayrshire 15-year-olds discover?

3 How might someone argue that pornography is easier to get hold of nowadays?

4 What is the age of consent in Scotland and why was this age chosen?

5 Give one argument in favour of lowering the age of consent and one against.

6 What was the 'Section 2A' issue all about?

7 Give one argument supporting homosexual relationships and one against.

8 What reasons might be given by people who say that sex should only take place within marriage?

9 Why might someone think 'casual sex' is wrong?

10 What does the Church of Scotland believe about heterosexual sex?

11 What reasons might be given by religious people for opposing homosexual practices?

12 Why might the Egoist think that, with sex, 'anything goes'?

Analysis

1 Write your own problem page – including answers from the agony aunt – on a range of issues related to sexual behaviour, which might apply to people your age.
2 Prepare your own display board using materials available to people of your age – entitle the display board 'Pornography?'. You should use magazine images and newspaper images – though be careful what you use and think about who might see it.
3 Write your own speech in favour of lowering the age of consent. Decide how low it should go and set out your arguments as appropriate. Someone else in your class should devise some questions to challenge your beliefs – be prepared to answer them.
4 A friend of yours admits to you that he/she is gay. Write the discussion you might have.
5 Have a class debate: 'This house believes that sexual behaviour is about freedom of choice – no-one else's business'. Include views that represent religious viewpoints, as well as Egoist viewpoints, in your debate.

Evaluation

'Sex should only take place within a long-term relationship'.
Do you agree? Give reasons for your answer.

Assessment question

Outcome 2 The age of consent has been lowered to 12 years old. This has made opponents go round people's doors asking them if they agree. What would an Egoist and a religious person say?

Homework

Design and carry out your own survey asking the question: 'At what age should sexual activity be legal?'. Ask as wide a variety of people as possible.

ACTIVITIES

Knowledge & Understanding

1 Do you think there are any taboos in the society you live in? What are they?
2 What do you think the benefits and drawbacks of school nurses handing out the 'morning-after pill' might be?
3 In your opinion, is the greater availability of 'pornography' a good or bad thing? Explain your answer.
4 What should the age of consent be? Explain the reasons behind your decision.
5 Do you think that homosexuality is 'unnatural'? Give reasons for your views.
6 In your opinion which argument is strongest – that sex should be part of a long-term relationship, or that it's just for pleasure and no relationship is needed? Explain your answer as fully as you can.
7 In what ways are Christian and Muslim views about sexual behaviour similar?
8 How could the Egoist be persuaded to have some 'rules' about sexual behaviour?
9 What might a Utilitarian think about lowering the age of consent?

Analysis

1 Carry out your own research on issues raised in this section and present your findings to the class. Remember to keep the responses anonymous.
2 Put together a selection of video clips that demonstrate the idea that sexual imagery is more evident now than in the past. You could write your own commentary to go with the collection of clips.
3 Write an article for a newspaper where you propose that the age of consent is raised to 19.
4 You are a 14-year-old and you believe that you are ready for a sexual relationship. You want to discuss this belief with your (open-minded) parents. Act out the discussion as a role play.
5 Using your imagination, write a story about someone your age who 'comes out' as a homosexual in his or her school.
6 Your boy/girlfriend believes that sex should only take place in a long-term relationship. You don't agree. Write the dialogue you might have.
7 A religious person tries to convince an Egoist and a Utilitarian that homosexuality is wrong. Write the discussion they might have.

Evaluation

To what extent do you agree that a sexual relationship needs both partners to be 'mature'?

Assessment question

Outcome 3 'Sex is a gift from God, to be kept only for marriage.'
How far do you agree?

Homework

Write an explanation of your own views on the age of consent. Should it be lowered, raised or kept the same?

MARRIAGE AND ITS ALTERNATIVES

Anne is 24, John 28. They recently got married. How typical is their story? Anne says:

CASE STUDY

We met at work and enjoyed each other's company when we went out with work colleagues. We'd find ourselves spending most of these social occasions just talking to each other. Of course, we started to go out. It was funny how we had so many things in common. We found that our childhood experiences were very similar too. People at work began the 'nudge nudge, wink wink' stuff – wondering 'how far we'd gone'. As our relationship grew over ten months, we eventually reached the decision to get engaged. A year later we got married. We didn't live together first and we didn't have sex before marriage. We had a traditional marriage in a Church – although neither of us are very 'Christian'. We fall out sometimes but are good friends as well as partners so that helps fix problems. We plan to start a family soon. When that happens, I'll give up work (John earns more than me) to look after the children. I'll maybe go part-time when they're at school. We still have our friends – though we're probably not as close to them now as we were. We're glad we got married and didn't just live together – it's a clearer statement about our feelings for each other.

WHAT IS MARRIAGE FOR?

Marriage means many things, not just the joining of two people who love each other. It is seen by many as something which is the mark of a stable society, by others, as something that has had its day and should now be ignored. Supporters of marriage argue that its value is in the strength and stability it gives to a relationship. This is because:

◆ Two people make a public declaration that they love each other and want to spend the rest of their lives together. This is quite a promise and makes going back on it difficult. It is a very public statement of commitment (especially if you're a religious person and you've made your declaration of commitment 'before God').

◆ Marriage also involves a legal contract, which makes separation more difficult. This makes a couple 'work at their marriage' and not give up when things are difficult.

◆ It also involves the 'joining' of the two families. Whether they like it or not, they will have to interact from now on. It means too, that both partners' families will be able to support them through any difficulties.

◆ Bringing children up involves a lot of hard work and effort. This is easier to do if two people are sharing the task. The stability of marriage helps make the job easier. It also gives legal protection to the children, as well as giving them role models of each gender.

◆ It gives a focus for sex. This is a powerful emotion, which needs to be controlled. In a marriage relationship this can be achieved.

Some people have suggested that a modern version of marriage for the 21st century is what is called the 'open marriage'. This is where two people are married but agree that they can both have short-term relationships, or just sex, with other people while they are married – provided that they are 'open' about it with each other. Critics of this say that it misses the essential point about marriage – that it is about single-minded commitment to one person.

DISCUSSION POINT

What might be the advantages and disadvantages of an 'open marriage'?

JUST A PIECE OF PAPER?

Many argue that all these benefits of marriage are equally possible in a long-term unmarried relationship (co-habitation). The law now gives recognition to people who co-habit, as well as rights for their children. Many people argue that such unmarried relationships can be just as stable and secure as 'official' marriages and that the level of commitment involved from both parties is just as much as in a formal marriage.

Those who disagree say that the relationships of people who live together don't last as long, and break down more often than those of people who are married. They argue that most cohabitees see their relationship as a 'trial' before making the complete commitment of marriage (co-habitees see this as a strength). Because of this, such relationships are 'second-best'. However, supporters of cohabitation might argue that being married just means that people stay together even when they no longer want to because splitting up is so complicated and involves so many difficult stages to go through.

DISCUSSION POINT

Do you think that living together shows less commitment than marriage?

MONOGAMY = MONOTONY?

In most world cultures, monogamous relationships are normal. This means you marry only one person at a time. Some cultures accept polygamy – having more than one married partner at a time. Male Muslims are allowed to have more than one wife, provided that they

DISCUSSION POINT

What might be the advantages and disadvantages of polygamous marriage?

can all be treated equally. In a small minority of Christian communities, polygamy is practised. Those who do so argue that it is a good way of making sure that women are supported throughout their lives – opponents criticise it for many reasons.

FIGURE 3.3 *A church wedding*

PLAYING THE FIELD

Some believe that any long-term relationship is unnatural or undesirable and that the best option is to remain single and enjoy short-term relationships ranging from a few years to one-night stands. This kind of lifestyle means that you have less (or none) of the commitment of a long-term relationship and fewer (if any) of the responsibilities. Such people might claim that the stability of society isn't harmed by this because if people are happy with it then they'll function well in society – better that than suffering a loveless long-term relationship or marriage. Opponents argue that such relationships lead to a more unstable society, as well as leading to more emotional and physical hurt for those who are involved in them. Opponents would say that this way of life lacks the safety and security of marriage; yet some people choose to be alone and not engage in long-term relationships.

GAY MARRIAGE

In Holland, gay marriages are legal and are carried out in the same way as heterosexual marriages. Gay people argue that their relationships should be able to benefit from the same kind of public declaration of commitment as any other – and should also have the protection of the law like any other. Lesbian couples have had a family by using donated sperm, while male homosexual couples have either adopted (not always permitted) or produced their own families using donated eggs and surrogate mothers. People opposed to gay marriages argue that marriage should only take place between

FIGURE 3.4 *Gay marriage*

FACTS AND FIGURES

- In 1990, over 25% of births in Scotland were to unmarried mothers.
- It is estimated that between 50% and 75% of men will have at least one affair while married. In 1989, a MORI poll found that 70% of people interviewed placed 'being faithful' as the most important quality in a marriage.
- In 1990, 55% of Scottish people were married; there were 34,600 new marriages that year.

DISCUSSION POINT

Is gay marriage 'acceptable'? Should gay couples be allowed to adopt?

members of the opposite sex. However, supporters say that, where a couple are prepared to publicly state their intention to be committed to each other for the rest of their lives, it shouldn't matter what gender the couple is.

ARRANGED MARRIAGE

In many cultures of the world, the arranged marriage is quite normal and accepted. Here, in the UK, many people find the idea hard to understand because they believe that:

◆ Marriage should begin with love. To have someone chosen for you means that love wasn't there from the beginning.
◆ Choosing your own partner is a basic human right. Anything else harms your personal freedom.
◆ A marriage is about the two people who marry – their families have to adjust to it and accept it, even if they don't like it.

However, supporters of arranged marriages argue:

◆ Beginning a marriage with 'love' isn't always the best way. What we think of as love is often just physical attraction. The first, passionate, stage of a relationship soon fades away. If the couple have nothing more in common than their attraction for each other, this might not be enough to see them through a lifelong relationship. Love can 'grow' after you're married.
◆ Parents have more life experience – they can judge whether or not a potential marriage partner is suited to you better than you can yourself. When choosing your husband or wife they can take everything into account in a calm and rational way. Besides, in most cases, you can still reject their choice if you think it's unsuitable.
◆ Marriages are not just between individuals, they're between families. It is important to make sure that the families will get on well. This makes society as a whole more stable. It also helps to make sure that the married couple are supported throughout their relationship. It also creates support for bringing up children and looking after family members in their old age.

DISCUSSION POINT

In your opinion, what are the advantages and disadvantages of having your marriage arranged?

THE FUTURE

Some people say that the practice of marriage will soon die out and that more people will just live together. Others that marriage will become fashionable again because it is the best way to keep a relationship going in a world that is becoming more complex and more pressurised.

DISCUSSION POINT

Do you think marriage is out of date?

MORAL RESPONSES

The **Christian** view is that marriage is the best option for any relationship. In 1992, the Church of Scotland produced a report called, The Future of the Family: A Crisis of Commitment. This looks at all the alternatives to marriage and concludes:

We believe that marriage is best because:
- *God's will is for love to be expressed between people in long-term relationships.*
- *God keeps his promises and expects people to do so.*
- *God made men and women for each other – to help each other through life.*
- *Sex is a powerful instinct – marriage gives it a focus.*
- *Jesus shared in the joy of a wedding (John 2) – so supporting the idea.*
- *The apostle Paul supports marriage continually (eg in 1 Corinthians 7).*

An evangelical Christian, John Stott, uses Genesis 2:24 to show that marriage should be an exclusive agreement between a man and a woman, sealed by God, preceded by leaving your parents and resulting in a lifelong commitment, which may result in children.

Some Christian groups accept that people will live together as a 'trial marriage'. Others reject this because it doesn't show the same level of commitment and is more likely to break down. Christians are almost entirely monogamous, (1 Cor 7:2–4) and generally oppose both gay marriage and arranged marriage (although Salvationists often limit who you can marry). In Roman Catholic teaching, marriage is a sacrament. While it can be ended according to the law, once consummated it is everlasting.

A man will leave his father and mother and unite with his wife, and the two will become one flesh. So they are no longer two, but one. Man must not separate then, what God has joined together.

Mark 10:6–9

Muslim teaching also places a high value on marriage. It gives security to the couple, with special protection for the woman, as well as a sound basis for bringing up children (see Surahs 4:25; 7:189; 2:221; 30:21). Marriage shows your commitment to each other. It is social as well as individual – arranged marriage is therefore very common in Islam. Muslims believe that this keeps Islamic society strong. Some Muslims believe that the 'freedom' of 'love marriages' in the West is a weak basis for a lifelong relationship. They occasionally argue that this is one of the reasons why western society is so 'immoral'. They point to the success of arranged marriage. However, individuals must be allowed to reject their parents' suggestions if they want (Surah 4:3). Muslim teaching also allows polygamy. Muhammed himself had ten wives. Many Muslims argue that this practice was allowed as a way of looking after women whose husbands had died. It was better for them to have a husband – even if they had to share him with others – than to live alone. In Surah 4:129 it states: 'You will never be able to treat all your wives equally'. Because of this, many Muslims believe that monogamy is the ideal and oppose polygamy today. Muslims generally reject the idea of living together because it is seen as an 'unstable' basis for any relationship. As Muslim teaching forbids homosexual practice, gay marriages would be considered wrong.

The **Egoist** position is based on self-interest. This means that Egoists might either support marriage or reject it as it suited their own needs. If, for example, marriage could be shown to result in more stable long-term relationships then you would support it. You might also feel that marriage gave you legal protection, which living together did not. You might also feel that marriage is more likely to keep your partner faithful. However, if it just meant restrictions on personal freedom, then you might not want to be married. Egoists would want to be able to exercise personal freedom whenever it suited them. For example, if you got bored with your partner and wanted a new one, you might feel that all the legal 'ties' of marriage were just a nuisance. With arranged marriage, it might depend on whether you were arranging it or having it arranged for you. As an Egoist parent it might be in your best interest to arrange your child's marriage so that it will suit you best, by ensuring that you'll be looked after in your old age, for example. If you're an Egoist, you probably wouldn't want an arranged marriage because this limits your own freedom of choice. Of course, you might be happy with it because it saves you the 'bother' of having to find your own partner!

As Egoists would think homosexuality is a matter of your own choice, they would have no problem with gay marriage. In fact, the Egoist would probably not think that gay marriage was any different to any other kind. If that's what you want, why should it not be allowed?

For the Egoist, rules and laws about marriage are only acceptable where they promote your own well-being.

The **Utilitarian** would want to judge whether or not marriage was of more benefit to society generally than living together. If marriage led to greater happiness for society as a whole then it should be supported. Currently marriage does give some protection to individuals, and therefore society, which living together does not. However, perhaps this should just mean that the law should be changed so that couples living together (and their children) should have the same legal rights as married couples. The Utilitarian would probably place a high value on equality of treatment within marriage. Some might argue that marriage is biased in favour of the rights of the man and that this imbalance in the relationship will not be a source of happiness. However, if marriage evens out the rights between both partners, then it is a good thing. Arranged marriages are acceptable provided that they work. If they do result in more stable relationships, then they might actually be preferable. If, however, arranged marriages involved pressure on the couple, then this might lead to longer relationships, but there might always be resentment there, which means that there will be more 'pain' than 'pleasure'. Gay marriages would be acceptable to the Utilitarian, provided that they didn't somehow cause social imbalance (for example, unwanted changes in population). There is no automatic preference for or against marriage in Utilitarianism – it depends on what the likely effects of marriage or living together would have on society.

ACTIVITIES

Knowledge & Understanding

1 Do you think John and Anne's story is typical?
2 In your own words, give **two** arguments in favour of marriage.
3 Why do some people think 'open' marriage is wrong?
4 What do you think are the 'strengths' and 'weaknesses' of co-habitation?
5 What reasons might someone give for opposing polygamy?

6 What reasons might someone give for not having any kind of long-term relationship?
7 Give **two** arguments in favour of gay marriage.
8 What would be **one** advantage of an arranged marriage?
9 State **two** reasons why the Church of Scotland thinks 'marriage is best'.
10 Give **two** reasons why a Muslim might support arranged marriage.
11 How might an Egoist argue that marriage is best?

Analysis

1 Many people believe that marriage works best when both partners have a lot in common. Devise a 'match-making' questionnaire that could be used to match potential marriage partners. Try it out in your class – how useful is it?

2 Devise a set of 'guidelines for married life'. What should each partner in a marriage be prepared to do or accept? Should there be different roles for men and women?

3 You and your partner decide to live together instead of getting married. Your Christian parents don't agree with this. As a role play, act out the discussion that might take place.

4 Design a poster – Marriage is Best.

5 Carry out your own survey of attitudes to the issues in this section – is marriage still popular?

6 Imagine that you are Muslim parents arranging a marriage for your child. What kind of person would you be looking for?

7 An Egoist and a religious person decide to get married. They discuss what each thinks marriage should involve. Write the discussion that takes place.

Evaluation

'Marriage is still important.'
Do you agree? Give reasons for your answer.

Assessment question

Outcome 2 How might an Egoist and a religious person argue that marriage is still important? What reasons would they give for their views?

Homework

Carry out your own interview with either a married couple or a couple living together. Why did they choose this form of long-term relationship? Write a brief report of your findings.

ACTIVITIES

 *i*2

Knowledge & Understanding

1 How might someone argue that John and Anne should have lived together first?

2 In your opinion, does marriage show more commitment than co-habitation?

3 Is monogamy better than polygamy? Explain your answer.

4 What are the benefits and drawbacks of 'playing the field'?

5 Do you think homosexual marriages are a good idea? Explain your answer.

6 Choose **one** argument for and **one** argument against arranged marriage. For each, state your own view of this argument.

7 Do you think marriage will become more or less popular in the future? Explain.

8 How might a religious person argue that co-habitation is acceptable?

9 In what ways might the Utilitarian support or oppose gay marriage?

Analysis

1 Write a short speech supporting the idea of marriage.

2 You are an agony aunt in a magazine. Someone who is about to get married asks your advice about 'making the marriage work'. What would you say in reply?

3 It has been decided to change the law so that co-habitees have *none* of the rights of married couples. You are opposed to this. Write to your MP/MSP explaining your position.

4 You are a religious person with one wife. You decide to take another. How might you explain your decision to your wife?

5 Design a short information leaflet explaining the practice of arranged marriage.

6 Have a class debate: 'Marriage is out of date'. Include representatives of the various moral stances you have studied.

7 Devise your own table showing the points of agreement and disagreement between the various moral stances on: marriage; polygamy; co-habitation; gay marriage; arranged marriage.

Evaluation

'Living together as a trial marriage is always a good idea.'
How far do you agree?

Assessment question

Outcome 3 'Marriage is for life.'
To what extent do you agree?

Homework

Write a brief summary of your own views on marriage/co-habitation and arranged marriage.

DIVORCE

CASE STUDY

An independent study carried out for the Scottish Executive suggests that parents need education about the best ways to help their children through the trauma of divorce. The report suggests that children often blame themselves for their parents' divorce. One child said, 'If I'd tidied my room, dad wouldn't have left.' Around two in every five marriages in Scotland end in divorce. The study found that parents don't explain the process of divorce with their children. Some children only found out that a divorce was taking place long after their parents had split. A Lanarkshire teenager said, 'My father said, "I have to go away for a while" and then he never came back'. What most children in the study said what they needed most was to know that both their parents still loved them.

Sunday Herald, 27 August 2000

CAUSES OF DIVORCE

Divorce rates have risen gradually in the last decade. This might be due to the greater pressures on relationships in the 21st century, or it could be because people treat marriage as a more flexible and less permanent arrangement than it was in the past. In Scotland, the only ground for divorce is the 'irretrievable breakdown of the marriage'. What are the most common causes of divorce?

- Infidelity/adultery – where one partner has a relationship with someone else. One partner suspecting that another is unfaithful could even be enough to tip the balance of a relationship, even if no actual infidelity has taken place.
- Change – as we go through life, we change our interests, likes, views. The people you both are when you marry may be different to the kind of person you are ten years later. You both might 'grow apart'. The love and friendship you once had could 'die'. This is often the case among those who marry when they are young. As they grow older they change. If their relationship doesn't change too it might end.
- Pressures – as you get older you face more pressures in life. Work, family and financial concerns can all add up to putting a strain on your relationship.

In Scotland, a divorce is allowed for:
- unreasonable behaviour (which depends upon whether the court thinks it's unreasonable or not)
- adultery
- desertion (after two years)
- two years' separation agreed by both partners
- five years' separation which has not been agreed by both partners.

Most people agree that married relationships have their 'ups and downs'. The initial fiery passion usually mellows to something less intense but sometimes even stronger. One viewpoint puts it like this:

Marriage is an emotional rollercoaster. You've got to cling on to each other through the really difficult bits and make sure you keep your wits about you. If you don't give it the attention it needs, your grip on the ride will loosen and you won't enjoy the experience. Too loose and you'll be thrown right off ... very messy.

For many people, there comes a point where living together as a married couple is no longer possible or desirable and so divorce becomes the only option.

DISCUSSION POINT

What do you think are the most common causes of the 'irretrievable breakdown' of marriages?

Form of extract decree of divorce

EXTRACT DECREE OF DIVORCE

Sheriff Court	Court Ref No
Date of Decree	*In absence
Pursuer	Defender

Date of parties marriage   Place of parties marriage

The sheriff granted decree

(1) divorcing the defender from the Pursuer;

*(2) ordering that the following child(ren):

       Full name(s)   Date(s) of birth

Reside with the *pursuer/defender and finding the *pursuer/defender entitled to be in contact with the following child(ren): as follows:

All in terms of the Children (Scotland) Act 1995.

*(3) ordaining payment
  *(a) by the   to the   of a periodical allowance of £ per
  *(b) by the   to the   of a capital sum of £
  *(c) by the   to the   of £   per   as aliment for each child until that child attains years of age, said sum payable in advance and beginning at the date of this decree with interest thereon at the rate of per cent a year until payment;
  *(d) by the   to the   of £ of expenses;

*(4) finding the   liable to the   in expenses as the same may be subsequently taxed.

This extract is warrant for all lawful execution hereon.

Date: (*insert date*)   Sheriff Clerk (depute)
    *Delete as appropriate.

FIGURE 3.5 *An extract decree of divorce*

HANG IN THERE

There are many ways in which people and organisations try to avoid divorce. Most courts will expect that some attempts at reconciliation have been made before a divorce is granted. There are groups which give marriage counselling, aiming to avoid divorce. They focus on bringing out into the open, in as calm and reasonable a way as possible, the reasons for the couple drifting apart. During divorces, reasonable discussion is often difficult. Once this is done, couples can begin working on putting things right. They try to focus on the next steps as well as identifying the reasons for the breakdown in the first place. Most marriage guidance counsellors say that most divorces happen because partners aren't open enough with each other. Communication problems seem to play a big part. Some say that many couples only speak truthfully to each other about their feelings when it's too late. Organisations like The Scottish Family Conciliation Service offer advice to separating and divorcing couples and their families.

Many people argue that divorce should never be seen as an option. Marriage vows state that you will be committed to the person you're marrying 'till death separates us'. Your vows also recognise that life will be full of ups and downs – you'll be 'richer, poorer', 'sick and in health'. All of this means that you should stick to your marriage vows no matter what happens – that's what commitment is all about.

THE 'COST' OF DIVORCE

Personal

When divorces are finally granted (which can take between two and five years), it is the end of a long process of often painful negotiation. Of course, some divorces are 'amicable' – achieved in a 'friendly' way – but others are not. Marriages involve powerful emotions. They also require a lot of 'investment' – this could be financial, emotional, personal or social. Sharing a home and a life together can be difficult to take apart in the cold light of a legal process. The business of splitting up what you have built up over the years as a couple can be messy.

Family

It's even more complicated when there are children – especially under 16 years old. Here, custody of the children is awarded to one of the divorced partners, and the court also decides how much access to the children the non-custodial partner receives. The issue of financial support for the children is also decided.

All of this can be difficult both for the parents and the children. It can lead to 'tugs of love' where the children may feel that they are being used as ammunition in a battle between their parents.

Children often suffer greatly during divorce. The powerful arguments and adult issues involved are often difficult for them to cope with – especially as it involves people so close to them who they might only ever have seen getting on with each other.

What factors should be taken into account when making decisions about the custody of children?

In May 1974, the organisation Families Need Fathers was set up. This organisation believed that in divorce cases, there was a bias in favour of giving custody of children to the mother. Alick Elithorn and Keith Parkin, founder members, believed that this was wrong. They wanted to raise people's awareness about the rights of fathers to continue being involved in their children's lives after divorce. They believed that this is also best for the children themselves. Keith Parkin wrote at the time: 'It is time society decided that children need two parents. Irrespective of whether the natural parents are married, separated or divorced'. The group continues to press for the need for children involved in divorces to have the 'full benefits' of both parents' attention afterwards.

Social

Divorces may have effects on society generally. There are pressures on the divorced single parent bringing up children alone. Some people argue that this produces an instability – for example, children without role models of both gender may lack guidance in some areas. The pressure of work on single parents might mean that children don't grow up with the emotional support they need. All of this could lead to wider social problems. Divorces may also lead to people being more wary of making commitments in a marriage themselves.

However, many will argue that a divorced couple or single parent will be able to give a child all the love and attention he or she needs. Anyway, it'll still be better than a child living with two parents who no longer want to be together.

MAKE IT EASY ON YOURSELF

If both partners agree to divorce, it can be completed in two years. Some argue that divorces should be 'processed' more quickly. The 'quickie divorce' is seen as having benefits:
- It means that the trauma of the whole event doesn't drag on for a long time.
- It means that people are able to get on with their lives more quickly after a failed relationship.
  On the other hand:
- It might not give people enough time to really think about what they're doing and change their mind if need be.
- It could lead to a weakening of the original commitment as people know they can get out of it quickly and painlessly if they want to.

DISCUSSION POINT

Should the law make divorce easier to obtain?

Some people argue that rising divorce rates are a symptom of a society where commitment is not taken as seriously as it once was. Others say that it is a 'good sign' because it means that people are no longer prepared to suffer failed relationships.

FIGURE 3.6 *Marriage guidance counselling*

FACTS AND FIGURES

◆ Although the overall divorce rate in Scotland fell slightly between 1993 and 1998, for marriages of 25–29 years' duration the figure increased by 35%.
◆ In 1998, around 150,000 children experienced the divorce of their parents.
◆ The annual cost of family breakdowns is estimated at around five billion pounds

Family Policy Studies Centre Report, March 2000

MORAL RESPONSES

Christians have different opinions about divorce. The principal teaching is that of Jesus in Matthew 19:3–12:

What God has joined together, let not man separate ...
I tell you that anyone who divorces his wife, except for marital unfaithfulness, and marries another woman commits adultery.

The Roman Catholic Church follows the first part of this teaching closely. Divorce is not accepted. However, there can be annulment of marriage. This suggests that the couple's marriage was never valid in the first place. Many Christians focus on the second part of this text and so believe that Jesus' teaching upholds the special status of marriage but allows divorce in certain circumstances. The other Biblical teaching comes from Paul in I Corinthians 7:10–16. Here, Paul supports the teaching of Jesus, but adds comment about a relationship between a Christian and a non-Christian. This was probably in reply to a specific question asked, so it is difficult to apply to all divorce. Some Christians argue that the teaching of the Bible on divorce is not clear and, anyway, Christianity stresses love for others and the idea of forgiveness. This forgiveness should mean that people who have to 'go back' on their marriage vows should be supported and cared for, not criticised. Christians should also be careful of judging people too quickly. For this reason, many Christians accept divorce, as well as remarriage in Church. They see this as a non-judgmental caring attitude, which stresses the idea that you can start your life over again if you feel you've made a mistake and want to put it right. In the Church of Scotland, a Minister may carry out a marriage for a divorcee if he thinks this is the best option for the couple and children of any previous marriage. However, he does not have to carry out such a marriage. Some Christians believe that the marriage vows are before God and therefore should last forever. Others might agree but still think it's better to get out of a failed relationship than stay together on a point of principle.

Muslims stress the importance of family relationships in marriage. Divorce (*talaq*) is permitted but must be seen as a last resort. A man can divorce his wife by saying 'I divorce you' three times over a period of around three months (the *iddah*). A woman can divorce her husband, but this is more complicated. She must show that there is a good reason for the divorce and go before an Islamic court, which looks at the circumstances of her case. In each case, the father bears the responsibility for any children. Because most Muslim marriages are between families and not just individuals, there is a great deal of effort put into making sure that the divorce is as amicable as possible. The consequences for the children are carefully considered – particularly that they will continue to be cared for after the divorce. Muslims may remarry after divorce, although a short period of time should be allowed to pass before they marry anyone else. This is to ensure that if the woman is pregnant it will be clear who the father is. Muslim divorcees can also remarry each other after divorce.

Although divorce seems straightforward in many ways, it is still regarded as something that you should try to avoid as far as possible. The Qur'an sets out clear rules about divorce but doesn't suggest that it should be seen as a desirable option (see Surahs 2: 227–232; 65:1–7; 4:35). The rules are designed to protect both parties from hardship resulting from the divorce. Muslims agree that there are times when marriages fail. This shouldn't mean that people have to suffer too.

The **Egoist** view would be that divorce is perfectly acceptable and that you should be able to remarry as many times as you please. The Egoist would want to ensure that he or she came out of the divorce comfortably – both financially and emotionally. A divorce between two committed Egoists could be a nasty affair indeed as both pursued their own self-interest. The Egoist would want divorce to be as easily available as possible, no matter what the cause of the divorce was. He or she would also probably want to have custody over the children – unless of course he or she felt that having to look after the children on your own actually worked against your own self-interests. The Egoist would not really be concerned about the 'costs' of divorce for others or for society generally. They would consider marriage to be between two people only and up to them to sort out when it goes wrong. However, it is probably true to say that an Egoist might find marriage a difficult agreement to make in the first place – because it involves making a long-term commitment to someone else, which could mean having to compromise and make sacrifices. Such a situation is unlikely to be attractive for the Egoist – but if it were, he or she would want the option of divorce readily available.

The **Utilitarian** approach might be that divorce is acceptable provided that its negative effects aren't too widespread. There would be no point in continuing with a relationship where that relationship resulted in a balance of suffering over pleasure. It might be true that marriages have to be 'worked at' but if that means making too big an effort for too little 'reward', then there would be no point in the marriage continuing. The Utilitarian would take into account the part played by children. It might be the case, therefore, that a Utilitarian would continue to live in a failed and unhappy marriage in order to avoid the greater pain and suffering that putting the children through a divorce might involve. The benefits of avoiding divorce by putting up with a failed marriage might actually outweigh the benefits that a divorce could result in – so divorce would be avoided.

Utilitarians would also want to consider the impact of divorce on wider society. If a Utilitarian thought that increased divorce rates might seriously harm social stability for the majority, then he or she might try to avoid getting divorced. For example, if divorce led to more single-parent families and if the Utilitarian thought this resulted in more social problems, then he or she might try to avoid it individually for the greater good.

ACTIVITIES

Knowledge & Understanding

1 State one finding of the study of divorce in Scotland.
2 Why might divorce rates have 'risen gradually'?
3 State **one** common cause of divorce.
4 State **one** thing that you think might be meant by 'unreasonable behaviour'.
5 In what ways might a marriage guidance counsellor help a couple with relationship problems?
6 Why do some people think divorce is always wrong?
7 In what ways might divorce hurt children?
8 What are the benefits and drawbacks of making divorce easier?
9 Why might a Christian disagree with divorce?
10 Why might a Muslim try to avoid divorce?
11 Why might a divorce between two Egoists be especially difficult?

Analysis

1 You are a teacher of primary 4 pupils. The parents of one of your pupils are going through a particularly nasty divorce. The child comes to you in tears one day, asking you to explain what divorce means. What kind of explanation would you give him? Now imagine that you are in the same situation, but the pupil is in fourth year in Secondary school. How might your advice be different?
2 As people get older, they face more 'pressures' in life. In groups, make a list of what you think these pressures might be. Try to put them into an order – the first being the most likely to put strain on a relationship and so on.
3 Devise your own marriage guidance role play based on the following situation.

Ken and Kylie have been married for ten years. Kylie thinks that Ken is 'married to his work'. When he's not working, he's out with the boys. They have two children, Lauren, 6, and Connor, 3. Ken thinks that Kylie no longer has any time for him – and since she's had the children she's 'let herself go'.

4 Design your own information leaflet for couples who are thinking about divorce: 'Divorce – what you should think about'. In this leaflet set out the arguments for and against divorce and also mention practical issues which potential divorcees might not think about.

5 There is a campaign to make divorce easier and quicker. People are being interviewed on the street, by being asked whether they would support making divorce easier. What would a Christian, Muslim and Egoist say?

Evaluation

'You should remain in a failed relationship until the children have grown up and left home.'
Do you agree? Give reasons for your answer.

Assessment question

Outcome 3 'When you make a commitment in marriage, it should be for life.'
Do you agree? Give reasons for your answer.

Homework

Do you think married couples should be *forced* to go to marriage guidance counselling before a divorce is granted? Explain your answer.

ACTIVITIES   ◆ *i2*

Knowledge & Understanding

1 Why do you think some children feel responsible for their parents' divorce? Why do some parents not discuss it with their children?

2 Do you think that unfaithfulness in marriage should always lead to divorce? Explain your views.

3 Why do the courts expect there to have been some attempt at reconciliation?

4 What, in your opinion, are the greatest costs of divorce?

5 Do you think the courts prefer to award custody to mothers? Should fathers have equal rights? Explain.

6 When might divorce be the best option?

7 Why might someone think that increasing divorce rates are a 'good sign'? Do you agree?

8 Why does a Church of Scotland Minister have the right to refuse to marry a divorcee?

9 Why might divorce never be an issue for an Egoist?

10 How might the presence of children affect the Utilitarian's view of divorce?

Analysis

1 Carry out your own survey, which explores people's views about the idea of marriage being a lifelong commitment.

2 Read some of the responses to the children in Intermediate 1 analysis question 1. You are the parent of this child. What reply might you make to the teacher's views?

3 Devise your own information pack for couples who are about to marry. Include information about divorce. What might lead to it, how to avoid it and what to do if it seems likely.

4 You are the judge in Ken and Kylie's case. The divorce has been granted but you have to award custody of the children. Act out the case in the form of a role play. Write a brief report about the decision afterwards.

5 You are a government Minister who has been given the task of deciding whether or not the law should be changed to make it possible to divorce someone in a matter of weeks, not years. You chair a committee to look into it. You call for 'evidence' to be submitted from various viewpoints. You receive written replies from a Christian, Muslim, Egoist and Utilitarian (among many others). One group should write the submissions. Your group should consider them and make its decision.

Evaluation

'Divorce is personal. It has nothing to do with anyone other than the two people getting divorced.'
How far do you agree?

Assessment question

Outcome 2 Outline the viewpoints of the religious person, Egoist and Utilitarian on whether or not divorce should be 'allowed'.

Homework

The government Minister in Analysis question 5 above has decided to make it possible for a divorce to take only two weeks from beginning to end. Write him a letter outlining your views on this decision.

4 HUMAN RIGHTS

CASE STUDY

Jeffery Dillingham was executed by lethal injection in Texas in February 2000.

His last meal request was: 1 cheeseburger with American, Cheddar and Mozzarella cheese, without mayonnaise, mustard or onions; large French fries; bowl of macaroni and cheese; lasagne with 2 slices of garlic bread; 4oz of Nacho cheese; 3 large cinnamon rolls; 5 scrambled eggs; 8 pints of chocolate milk.

Texas Department of Criminal Justice

In his final statement Dillingham said he was sorry. 'I would like to apologise to the victim's family for what I did.' He spoke to his family before his execution, 'I thank you for all the things that you have done in my life, for the ways you have opened my eyes, softened my heart, for teaching me how to love, for all the bad things you have taken out of my life. For all the good things you have added to it.'

Dallas Morning News, 11 February 2000

Electrocution: produces visibly destructive effects as the body's internal organs are burned; the prisoner often leaps forward against the restraining straps when the switch is thrown. The body changes colour, the flesh swells and may even catch fire. The prisoner may defecate, urinate or vomit blood. Witnesses always report that there is a smell of burning flesh.

Hanging: the prisoner is weighed prior to execution. This weight is divided into 1260 to arrive at a drop in feet. This is to assure almost instant death, a minimum of bruising, and neither strangulation nor beheading. Properly done, death is by dislocation of the third or fourth cervical vertebrae. The noose is placed behind the left ear so as to snap the neck upon dropping.

Amnesty International

WHAT IS IT FOR?

There are probably very few people who are not truly revolted by the details of an execution as a form of punishment. However, in thinking about the moral issues, we must separate the emotional response from the arguments. Some people argue that although the texts above are quite gruesome, those executed have deserved what they got.

Does the state ever have the right to take away someone's life as a punishment? Capital punishment still exists in many countries, including the USA. It was abolished in the UK in 1965 (although was still a possible punishment for treason and piracy until 1998). It is almost always a response to a crime where life has been taken.

There are generally thought to be three aims of punishment. How do these relate to capital punishment?

Revenge

This is the idea that punishment should 'pay back' for what was done. It is sometimes thought of as leading to the 'satisfaction' of those who have suffered the crime. With capital punishment, it might mean that the relatives of those killed are 'satisfied'. However, can we ever really say that this happens? What might it mean to say that the relatives of murdered people are really satisfied by yet another death?

Deterrence

Punishment should be serious enough to put people off committing the same crime in the future. Capital punishment is so undesirable that it should stop people ever committing crimes where it will be the punishment. However, it is not clear that this is so. Countries with capital punishment don't seem to have any less crime than those without. Besides, should people be used as an 'example' in this way?

Reformation

Punishment should involve the chance for wrongdoers to see that they've done wrong and learn not to do so again. They can return to society after their punishment and make society better. Capital punishment does not allow this. It takes away any opportunity for reformation.

DISCUSSION POINT

What do you think is the most important function of punishment?

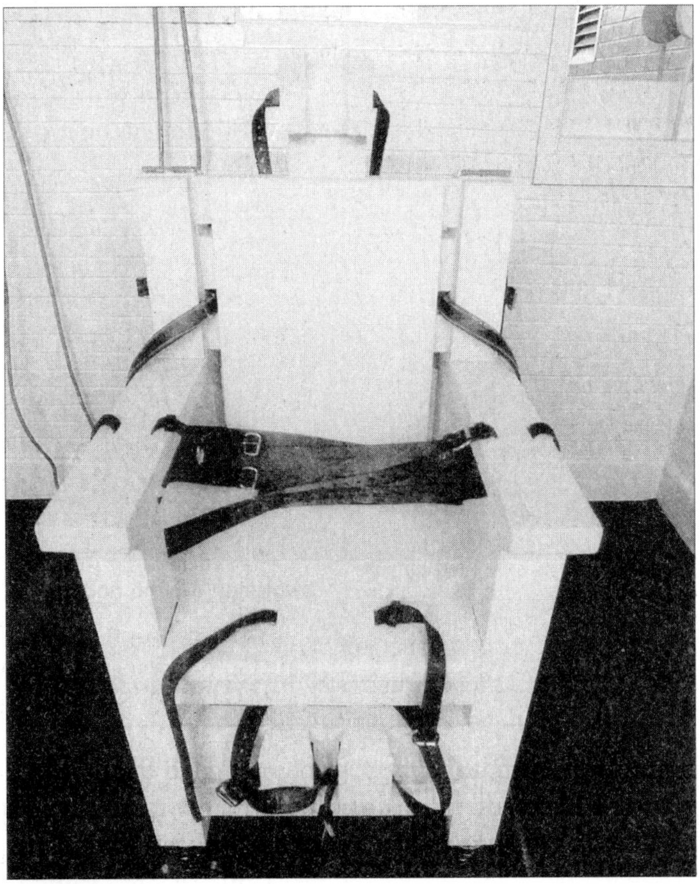

FIGURE 4.1 *The electric chair*

WHOSE FAULT?

When someone commits a crime, is the responsibility for it theirs alone? Some people argue that, in today's complicated society, the idea of completely individual responsibility for wrongdoing is difficult to accept. Many wrong actions are the end result of a series of complicated linked factors. Some people, because of their circumstances in life, might actually have less real choice than others. For example, if you are poor and hungry or if you had abusive parents, then your actions in life could be different to someone who has had every advantage. Why then, should you be punished in the same way? Opponents of capital punishment say that most people who are put to death as punishment are poor or socially disadvantaged in some other way. Therefore, there must be a link between serious crime and social problems. If that's so, then, in a way, these serious crimes are everyone's responsibility – not just the person who does them. Others disagree, they say that everyone has to take responsibility for their own choices in life – no matter what the circumstances of their life have been.

DISCUSSION POINT

How much is personal choice affected by what kind of life you have?

IN SUPPORT OF CAPITAL PUNISHMENT

♦ It deters. If you know that you will lose your life for taking someone else's, you'll avoid killing. When people are executed it sends out a message to others – 'this will happen to you too if you do what this person has done'. In the USA in 1960, there were 56 executions and 9,140 murders. In 1975, with the death penalty suspended, there were 20,510 murders.
♦ Capital punishment shows that innocent life is highly valued. It is society's way of showing how important safeguarding life is and how seriously it responds to murder.
♦ It protects society. Murderers, once executed, can't escape and commit the same crime again. Besides, 'life' in prison usually means less than the person's whole life.
♦ It is less costly. Keeping someone in prison for life costs society a lot. Why should society have to bear this cost?

THE ABOLITIONIST ARGUMENT

♦ It leaves no room for error. Often new evidence comes along, which results in the conviction of a murderer being dismissed. Once executed you cannot be released. Many cases in the recent past have been shown to be 'miscarriages of justice'. With capital punishment, society cannot put its mistake right.
♦ The state should not put its authority above the individual's. If it is wrong to murder, then it is equally wrong to 'murder' in the form of execution. This sends mixed messages to people about the value of life. Some believe execution is worse than murder. Many

FIGURE 4.2 *Death row cells*

Is capital punishment worse than life imprisonment?

- 98 people were executed in the USA in 1999 – on average one execution every 3.72 days.
- The law in the USA allows child criminals and the mentally ill to be executed.
- There are at least seven methods of execution in use around the world today: hanging, electric chair, guillotine, firing squad, gas chamber, lethal injection, stoning.

murders are committed in the heat of the moment. Execution is cold, calculated and ritualised. It is also extremely inhumane.

- Capital punishment rules out the possibility of reform. Many death row prisoners are executed long after their crimes. Sometimes, during that period they have changed or just 'grown up'. Some people have changed so much that they would not have been a threat to society even if they had been released.
- It does not work as a deterrent.
- People murder for all sorts of reasons. However, most death row prisoners are from disadvantaged backgrounds. This can't be coincidence. Capital punishment is just the easy way to deal with social problems, rather than going to the trouble of trying to work them out and so give people less 'reason' to commit serious crime.

CASE STUDY

One of Scotland's most notorious criminals was Jimmy Boyle. In the 1970s and 80s, he was a Glasgow 'hardman' living in the Gorbals. Convicted of murder, he was kept in some of the country's highest security prisons – spending most of his time in solitary confinement. Even here, he managed to cause all sorts of mayhem, and was regarded by the prison officers as one of the worst, most violent criminals they had come across. Eventually, he became an inmate at the Barlinnie Prison Special Unit. This was set up as a new approach to dealing with 'lifers'. The idea was not just to punish but to try to reform. Here, Jimmy discovered a talent for art, in particular, sculpture. Eventually, Jimmy was considered by the parole board as reformed. He was released and set up the Gateway Exchange Trust in Edinburgh. This would help youths avoid getting into the kind of trouble that had got him into prison. In some countries, Jimmy might have faced the death penalty.

THE VALUE OF LIFE

Capital punishment is a response to someone ignoring the value of another person's life. In many belief systems, life is seen as sacred. This means that no-one should have the right to take the life of another. However, some balance this by saying that, although life is sacred, there are times when it is right to take it from someone. Sometimes, life's sacredness has to be 'sacrificed' for the greater good (as in war, for example). When someone kills another person, they 'give up' their right to life. We have to balance up the sacredness of life with what is right and practical to do in response to the taking of life. Some people argue that capital punishment is actually preferable to life imprisonment. Why should ending someone's life be worse than taking away their freedom forever? Both are, in fact, a form of 'death' so maybe the quickest option – capital punishment – is the least cruel.

MORAL RESPONSES

Many of the states in the USA where capital punishment is favoured are states where **Christianity** is strong. In the Old Testament, there is a clear case for supporting capital punishment:

Eye for eye, tooth for tooth, burn for burn, wound for wound.

Exodus 21:24–5

Man was made like God, so whoever murders a man will himself be killed by his fellow-man.

Genesis 9:6

Humans are made in God's image, therefore their life is sacred and not to be taken. The punishment for a crime should match how severe the crime was. This idea of revenge or retribution is used by many Christians to argue that when someone takes a life, they give up their own right to life. The state, as God's chosen rulers, has to act on his behalf and take away the murderer's life. However, the Old Testament allows capital punishment for many things other than murder: (Leviticus 20:9). It also allows people to kill their slaves in some circumstances with little or no punishment at all (Exodus 20:20–21). Many Christians argue that this support for capital punishment has to be seen in light of life in Bible times. In a tribal society, instant death as a punishment for murder probably avoided endless retribution and revenge – which would result in even more deaths. Jesus seemed to oppose the death penalty when he said:

You have heard it said, 'eye for eye, tooth for tooth...' But now I tell you: do not take revenge on someone who wrongs you.

Matthew 5:38–39

Paul also adds:

Never try to get revenge: leave that to God's anger.

Romans 12:19

Many Christians oppose capital punishment because it does not allow for forgiveness. Also, it doesn't give the person the chance to change for the better, which Christians believe everyone can do.

Many **Muslims** also support capital punishment. In strict Islamic states, it is still practised. The Qur'an seems to say that you should punish someone in a way that matches the crime.

If you punish your enemy, then punish them with the like of that with which you were afflicted.

Surah 16:126

Shariah law also teaches that punishment should be severe enough to provide satisfaction for the family of people who have been murdered. It should also act as a deterrent for other possible wrongdoers.

However, in Islam, the idea of mercy is also very important. In practice, this means that in some Islamic countries, the relatives of murder victims may ask for the life of the murderer to be spared. They sometimes receive payment instead to make up for their loss. This blood-money is not seen as buying your way out of capital punishment. Instead, it is a symbolic way of giving forgiveness, which means that everyone is satisfied and no-one owes anyone anything. This helps to put an end to the whole sad business. Muslims believe that Allah shows them mercy for their wrongdoings and forgives them – so they should act in the same way towards their fellow humans if they can.

If the killer is forgiven by the brother, or relatives, of the killed against blood-money, then adhering to it with fairness and payment of the blood-money to the heir should be made in fairness.

Surah 2:178

The **Egoist** could either support or reject capital punishment depending upon the circumstances and also whether he was the person about to be executed or not. If he was a convicted killer, then he could have two responses:

◆ Death is final and puts an end to any opportunity for personal satisfaction. Besides, doing a life sentence might provide you with some opportunities for self-satisfaction. You might also escape or be released early. So he might oppose capital punishment.

◆ Death is preferable to life imprisonment where there would be very little chance of looking after your own self-interest. At least there would be no suffering afterwards. So he might support capital punishment.

If the Egoist wasn't someone about to be executed, then again he might have different responses:

Supporting capital punishment

◆ Capital punishment ensures at least one fewer killer is roaming the streets and will never be released to commit the crime again. This is in the Egoist's self-interest.

◆ It means that the Egoist's taxes don't have to go towards keeping someone in prison for life.

◆ If it works as a deterrent, it makes society a safer place to live in, which is good for the Egoist.

Opposing capital punishment

◆ There's always the risk that the Egoist might be wrongly accused of a crime and lose his life unjustifiably

◆ Perhaps capital punishment makes society a harsher place. If we're prepared to put people to death, what next? This might make life more risky for everyone.

In a speech given in 1868, the **Utilitarian** philosopher, John Stuart Mill, argued in favour of capital punishment. He argued that the taking of an innocent human life was so much in opposition to the pleasure principle that a murderer should have his life taken from him, 'to blot him out from the fellowship of mankind'. He also argued that a life sentence was actually more cruel than the death penalty. This was because it was an endless form of suffering, whereas death at least was quick. He also argued that whether or not it was a good deterrent wasn't the point. He claimed that 'hardened criminals' learned to ignore its possibility in the same way that a soldier learns to ignore death on the battlefield. That didn't make it useless though. He did think that if it was around, it might put people off murder from their 'earliest days'. It would help them to grow up wanting to avoid such a punishment. He argued that although it might seem odd to say that killing is wrong by killing yet again, it isn't that unusual. He argues that any form of punishment is responding to crime with yet 'more crime' – the death penalty is no worse in this respect.

Utilitarians might support capital punishment if they thought its existence reduced murder rates and so brought greater safety to the majority. However, they could also oppose it if they thought that it led to a more cruel society, where human life was treated carelessly. This could make life more unpleasant for everyone.

ACTIVITIES

Knowledge & Understanding

1 Why do you think Amnesty International has collected such gruesome descriptions of executions?

2 When was capital punishment abolished in the UK?

3 What does it mean to say that capital punishment acts as a means of revenge?

4 What is deterrence?

5 How might some people argue that we're all responsible for crime?

6 State **one** argument in support of capital punishment and **one** against.

7 How might someone be able to use the Jimmy Boyle story to argue that capital punishment is wrong?

8 How can someone who believes that life is sacred still support capital punishment?

9 How might a religious person support/oppose capital punishment?

10 How might an Egoist support/oppose capital punishment?

Analysis

1 Design a display board for your classroom, which covers the arguments for and against capital punishment. Your class should split into two, one group taking each viewpoint.

2 You are the leader of an organisation which is opposed to capital punishment. Design a short information leaflet outlining your argument.

3 Carry out a survey in your school on the capital punishment issue. How many people support it? What crimes might they support it for?

4 You are governor of the State of Texas (the real governor of Texas was once George W. Bush, the president of the USA). Someone has just read about the execution of Jeffery Dillingham – including his last words to his parents. They have written to you asking how you could have gone ahead with the execution. Write your reply.

5 Occasionally, bringing back capital punishment is raised in parliament. Have a debate in class and decide at the end of it by vote whether 'your parliament' would bring it back. Include representatives of religious views and Egoism in your debate.

Evaluation

'Capital punishment is never right.'
State whether you agree or not and give at least **two** reasons for your answer.

Assessment question

Outcome 2 Someone is about to be executed for a murder that they claim they didn't commit. Outside, both protesting against the execution, a religious person and an Egoist are in the crowd. How might each one explain their reasons for being there, based on their moral stance?

Homework

The Scottish Parliament is to debate bringing back capital punishment. Write a letter to your MSP outlining your views.

ACTIVITIES

Knowledge & Understanding

1 The last meal requests of death row prisoners have been posted on the internet. Why do you think this has been done?

2 Do you think the family of someone murdered would be satisfied by the execution of the murderer? Explain.

3 Why do some people think that capital punishment is a weak response to society's problems?

4 Choose **one** argument in support of capital punishment. Write a criticism of it in your own words.

5 Choose **one** argument opposing capital punishment. Write a criticism of it in your own words.

6 Some people argue that life imprisonment should be for life. Explain your views on this.

7 Do you think there's any specific problem with executing child criminals and the mentally ill? Explain.

8 In what ways are the ideas of mercy and forgiveness important for religious people in relation to capital punishment?

9 How might a Utilitarian support/oppose capital punishment?

Analysis

1 Carry out a class debate: 'This House believes that Scotland should re-instate the death penalty'.

2 You are the parents of Jeffery Dillingham. You've been invited on a chat show (like *Oprah*). What might you say? What questions might the audience ask? Act out this role play and write down any interesting issues raised. Try to include representatives of each of the moral stances in your audience.

3 Write and give a short speech outlining your own views on capital punishment.

4 Do you think some murders are 'worse' than others? Should there be different levels of punishment for each 'kind'? Write your views and discuss them in class.

5 In pairs. One of you is on death row waiting execution in a month or so. The other is someone who has been writing to the prisoner. Write a series of two or three letters that you might send each other.

Evaluation

'Capital punishment is no worse than spending the rest of your life in prison.'
How far do you agree?

Assessment question

Outcome 2 What might a religious person, an Egoist and a Utilitarian say in response to the question:
'Would you support the re-introduction of capital punishment for murder in Scotland?'

Homework

Find out where capital punishment is still carried out. If you have access to the internet, you should also try to find out how often it has been carried out recently and for what crimes. What reasons do these countries/states give for continuing its use?

RACIAL PREJUDICE

CASE STUDY

In December 1997, the UK government announced a new Crime and Disorder Bill, which made anti-English activity illegal in Scotland. This may have been partly in response to the growth of groups like 'Scottish Watch' and 'Settler Watch'. These groups claimed to exist to combat the increasing numbers of English people who were moving into the country. They argued that because these people were generally wealthy, their purchasing power was pricing locals out of their 'own lands'. They also argued that this would lead to an 'Englishing' of the Scottish way of life. Scottish Watch states: 'We will resist the continued English settlement of Scotland and the presence of an ethnic elite in positions of power and influence ... .' However, it also states: ' We reject any form of racism ...'.

Opponents of groups such as these think their very existence is racist.

An Englishman, who ran a pub in the borders, recently went to court, accusing locals of harassing him and his family out of town because they were English.

DISCUSSION POINT

Is 'anti-English feeling' racist?

PREJUDICE

Prejudice occurs when judgements are made without accurate facts or based on stereotypes or assumptions. Racial prejudice may be based on colour of skin or some other feature of an ethnic or minority group. The Scottish Ethnic Minorities Research Unit interviewed 150 people who were of Indian, Pakistani and Chinese origin in Glasgow. They found that more than 80% had been subjects of racist abuse, 20% attacked and 50% had had their homes or property damaged.

Worldwide, racism results in violence and death. Treating people badly on the basis of their racial origin was one of the most depressing features of the 20th century and, as we begin the 21st century, it looks as if little has changed. 'Ethnic cleansing' in the recent conflict in the Balkans was prominent. A Europe that hadn't seen concentration camps since World War Two witnessed them again.

FIGURE 4.3 *A Scottish Sikh*

WHAT'S BEHIND RACIAL PREJUDICE?

- Mistreating an ethnic group may be seen by some as an easy way to 'escape' from your own problems. If you can blame someone else, then this gives you a *scapegoat* to take out your frustration on. Easily identifiable groups, like those with different skin colour, are often used in this way. You can 'blame' them for your own problems, by claiming things like 'they' take all 'our' jobs'. Because ethnic groups are minorities in a society, they are easier 'targets'.

- Treating someone badly on the basis of their race may make you feel superior. It may be that the most racist people are socially 'weak' themselves. They might have low self-esteem because they have a job that they think is 'lowly' or because they haven't achieved what they wanted to in their life. Acting in a racist way gives them a sense of power. This kind of racism can often start quite subtly, for example, by the use of racist 'jokes'.

- Behaving in a racist way means that you never have to go to the 'trouble' of finding out anything about people with cultural origins which are different from your own. You just treat them as 'all the same' (stereotyping). By doing this, you conveniently ignore the fact that within any racial group (including your own),

DISCUSSION POINT

What racial stereotypes are you aware of? How justifiable are they?

there are many differences, as well as similarities. Racial groups are made up of individuals. To lump them all together on the basis of their racial origin doesn't make sense. It would be like saying that all Scots like haggis – or that they are all mean with their money.

EXPLANATION OR EXCUSE?

Most people fortunately do not agree with racism, especially when it leads to violence or making life uncomfortable for ethnic groups. However, there have been attempts to explain racism:

◆ Humans are most likely to survive where people stick together in groups. This kind of grouping may be based on ethnicity, culture or race. This kind of arrangement might set up antagonisms between groups. The tension between integration and remaining separate is there in every human society. Where integration of groups within any society is weak, racism will be strong.

◆ Racism, when used as a way to 'escape' a life of powerlessness or poverty, points to the need to make everyone's social conditions as pleasant as possible so that racism never arises. Nazi Germany before World War Two provided the ideal conditions for the growth of racism – a general population that was poor and a ready scapegoat in the form of the Jewish population. Clever leaders can manipulate these conditions to their own benefit.

◆ Racism is based on ignorance. Racist people may have been poorly educated or 'indoctrinated' from childhood into racist views. It is very difficult to put aside what you've been brought up to think. The challenge there is to re-educate.

◆ Some people feel that racism is an expression of their need to protect their own 'way of life'. They might see ethnic or minority groups as some kind of threat and so act in a way that they think will lessen this threat. Perhaps humans are 'naturally' wary of anything different. Maybe it is just human nature to treat with caution anything that is not like you. This is another way to survive.

◆ Some people who suffer from the effects of racism might behave in what to another person may seem like a racist way themselves. For example, a minority group might not allow members to marry outside their own ethnic group. The aim of this is to preserve their own way of life, culture and traditions. However, the racist might see this as a form of discrimination itself. This could lead to the racist feeling 'justified' in his or her views. At the same time he'll probably conveniently ignore similar practices of their own.

◆ Racist views may be the result of people conforming to the views of others. Psychologists like Asch (1951) have shown that people will do the most strange things not to be different to others in a group. Perhaps when racist actions begin, people get 'caught up in it' and don't really think about what they're doing until it's too late. Some people are able to hide behind the action of a group.

DISCUSSION POINT

What do you think of these 'explanations' for racism?

THE DAMAGE

Racism causes individual pain and suffering for those who experience it. It can also lead to people feeling of less worth than others. It can lead to society in general being a harsher, more unstable place. It may lead to further violence as those at the receiving end fight back. Maybe one of the most unpleasant features of racism is that it is a prejudice based on something you can't change. Being born with a particular colour of skin is no more under your control than being born with a particular colour of eyes. Also, do we really want a world where everyone's culture and way of life is the same? Doesn't a world full of variety make life more interesting?

FIGURE 4.4 *Groups like these may believe they are 'only protecting their own way of life'*

RESPONDING TO RACISM

- The treatment of groups like Jews and Gypsies during World War Two led to widespread atrocities – in particular, the concentration camps. Ever since, groups like the Anne Frank Institute in Amsterdam have tried to remind people what racism can lead to.
- The Indian leader Mahatma Gandhi carried out a programme of non-violent resistance which resulted in the British pulling out of India, where they had oppressed the indigenous population.
- Martin Luther King in the USA followed this pattern in the 1960s, achieving many rights for black Americans. He was, however, assassinated.
- At the same time, Malcolm X supported the use of violent retaliation to achieve equality for black Americans.
- In South Africa, activists such as Nelson Mandela spent many years in prison for opposing the racist system of apartheid. Eventually, equality was peacefully achieved and Mandela became the new South Africa's first president.

In Britain, racial discrimination is prohibited by law. Organisations such as the Commission for Racial Equality and local community relations organisations keep a watch on the treatment of ethnic groups.

DISCUSSION POINT

What do you think of this poster? Do you think it is likely to be effective?

FIGURE 4.5 *Anti-racist campaign poster*

FACTS AND FIGURES

◆ One of the original members of Settler Watch was a German, Sonja Vathjunker.
◆ The event 'Threads in the Tartan' took place in Glasgow in September 2000. The aim was to celebrate racial and cultural diversity in Scotland.
◆ Around 1.2% of the Scottish population is classed as 'non-white'.

MORAL RESPONSES

In the creation story, **Christians** are taught that God creates humans in his own likeness (Genesis 1:26). It isn't suggested that he makes some kinds of humans better than others. Many Christians take the word 'likeness' to mean that all humans share something of God's nature, whatever race they belong to. This makes racism impossible. Jesus' story of the Good Samaritan (Luke 10:25–27) could be understood as a direct attack on racist views. The Jews and Samaritans mistrusted each other, although Jesus tells this story – (where the Samaritan is the hero) – to a group of Jews . He seems to suggest that our treatment of each other should be based on our common humanity, not racial differences. Jesus goes further when he says that the most important commandment involves 'loving your neighbour as much as yourself'. This teaching makes it quite clear that treating someone badly on the basis of their race is wrong.

Paul picks up this idea in his letter to the Galatians. Here he states:

There is no difference between Jews and Gentiles, slaves and free men, between men and women; you are all one in union with Christ Jesus.

Galatians 3:28

This is taken by most Christians to be an absolute ban on racist views and actions; although, a minority of Christians, however, believe that these teachings should only be applied within the Christian family. Again, for many Christians, their faith isn't about picking out particular Bible passages and applying them as they see fit, it's about a whole approach to life. Christianity stresses love for everyone and treating everyone fairly no matter who they are. This makes racism very difficult for a Christian to justify.

Muslims also stress the shared nature of humans. Everyone is a creation of Allah and so all deserve respect as his children (Surah 49:13). Muhammed himself said:

Your God is one and your forefather Adam is one ... an Arab is not better than a non-Arab ... a 'red' person is not better than a black person

Narrated in Mosnad Ahmad #22978

The only distinguishing feature between people is their faith and piety. The Qur'an seems to celebrate diversity:

Among His wonders are the creation of the Heavens and the earth, the diversity of your tongues and colours.

Surah 30:22

According to Islam, all human beings are part of the same family. This idea of brotherhood (*ummah*) is very important in Islam. At the annual Hajj, one of the five pillars of the faith, Muslims dress in the white seamless *ihram*. The idea is that all are dressed equally before Allah, outwardly showing that they are all equal before Allah, whatever their race or social status.

Believers are but brothers.

Surah 49:10

Muslims are also expected to treat non-Muslims kindly and fairly. In particular, they should treat 'people of the book' with particular warmth. In practice this means Christians and Jews, with whom they share many beliefs and ideals.

Of course, in the UK, Muslims may be more likely to be the victims of racism than the source of it. This is because in Britain, the Muslim community is an ethnic minority. Even so, although Muslims should protect their way of life and belief, they would consider it wrong to act in racist ways themselves. *When the foolish address [the faithful], reply back with mild words of peace* (Surah 25:63).

An **Egoist** might be quite content with racism, particularly if it served his own ends as someone who was not a member of an ethnic minority group. For example, if racist attitudes led to some jobs only being available to people of his race, then this increases the chances of him getting such a job. This is obviously beneficial. He could oppose laws aimed at producing equality of opportunity because this might adversely affect him. He might also support racist attitudes because he might think that such an approach is more likely to protect what he thinks is his own way of life. He might also like the idea that racism gives him a ready excuse for his own troubles, because he can use others as scapegoats to take attention away from his own failings. The Egoist wants to look after what is 'his own'. Racist attitudes and actions are a classic example of protecting your own interests at the expense of others.

Of course, it would be different if the Egoist was a member of a minority group. However, again, he might use race issues as a way of protecting his own interests – for example, he might claim that an individual or institution is being racist, even when they are not.

Egoists might also oppose racism because of its negative consequences for society. If it does make society less stable and secure, then this isn't good for the Egoist. Also, if society accepts racial prejudice, then prejudice based on other factors might become easier to accept too.

The **Utilitarian** could find some difficulty with racism. Utilitarianism argues that the best course of action is one where the interests of the majority are served, even if this sometimes means that minority interests take second place. There is a tension here. On the one hand, making moral decisions based on Utilitarianism might sometimes mean that practices which might be considered 'racist' may occur. On the other hand, the unhappiness caused to the minority by such actions might be so great that it rules out the actions in the first place. The Utilitarian therefore has to strike a delicate balance between the rights of the individual, the rights of minority groups and the rights of the majority in any society. This means that the Utilitarian has to be sure about the possible consequences of any decisions and how they might change the overall balance of pain and pleasure. Few Utilitarians would support outright racism because this obviously causes suffering. Even fewer would support direct discrimination or violence against racial minorities because this would lead to suffering in society generally and to making society a harsher place. However, Utilitarians could end up supporting actions that were indirectly racist or that had subtle racist outcomes. There may be some times where trying to achieve what's best for the majority means that you can't avoid causing harm to a minority.

ACTIVITIES

Knowledge & Understanding

1 What do Scottish Watch and Settler Watch aim to do?
2 What does the word 'prejudice' mean?
3 What did the Scottish Ethnic Minorities Research Unit find out?
4 What does it mean to use someone as a 'scapegoat'?
5 What does it mean to say that racism is based on ignorance? Do you agree?
6 State **one** thing a racist might say in support of his views.
7 What are the possible effects of racism?
8 Do you think people are more likely to be racist in a group or on their own? Give a reason for your answer.
9 What do Christians think the idea that God created people in 'his own likeness' teaches about racism?
10 What is *ummah*?
11 How should a Muslim respond to racism?
12 How might an Egoist support racist views?

Analysis

1 What it means to belong to a particular racial group is often difficult to define. Discuss the following question and note down your group's conclusions. Who is and who isn't 'Scottish'?

2 Find out more about racism in your own country. What kinds of things happen, to whom and why? Prepare a short report on your findings using newspaper and magazine cuttings etc.

3 Someone in your school is telling racist jokes. You disagree with this. Write what you would say to the person to explain your disagreement. What arguments might the person make in response?

4 Draw up a set of anti-racist guidelines for your school. What practical steps might you take to keep racism out of your school?

5 Design a display on the life and work of one of the following: Gandhi, Malcolm X, Martin Luther King or Nelson Mandela.

6 There has been an increase of racist abuse in your town. A group of religious people get together to draw up a statement of their feelings about this. Write a brief speech which might be made on their behalf.

Evaluation

'Racism is always wrong.'
Do you agree? Give reasons for your answer.

Assessment question

Outcome 3 'Racists just want to protect their own way of life'.
Do you agree? Give at least **two** reasons for your answer.

Homework

Make a list of **five** things you think the Scottish Parliament could do to end racist attacks in Scotland.

ACTIVITIES

Knowledge & Understanding

1 **What** do you think Settler Watch means by the **'English**ing' of Scottish life? Do you agree that this is happening? Is it wrong?

2 In what ways might ethnic minorities be 'easier targets' for people's anger?

3 Why does it not make sense to treat members of a racial group as 'all the same'?

4 What might be the link between poverty and racist views?

5 State one 'justification' for racist views and give **one** argument against them.

6 What damage might racism cause society in general?

7 What does it mean to 'celebrate diversity'?

8 In what way is the story of the Good Samaritan anti-racist?

9 How does the Hajj show the ideal of *ummah*?

10 How might an Egoist explain his opposition to racism?

11 In what ways might Utilitarianism 'support' racism? Do you agree that Utilitarianism is racist?

Analysis

1 Carry out a class debate where each of the moral stances is represented: 'This house believes that racism is an unavoidable part of human nature'.

2 Design your own anti-racist poster.

3 Do some further research on the facts and figures and write an article for a newspaper entitled: 'Scotland the brave; and we thought we weren't racist?'

4 You have been given the responsibility of organising an event to combat racism in Scotland. What would you include? Design a programme of events, which would take place over one day. How would you best get across the message about the value of cultural variety?

5 Find out more about **one** of the situations in the 'Responding to racism' section. Write a short information booklet on it.

6 Design information leaflets outlining religious views on racism.

7 As a Utilitarian, you must make a speech about the rights of minorities. Write a series of headings you would use to build your speech around.

Evaluation

'There can never be good reasons for racism.'
How far do you agree?

Assessment question

Outcome 2 How might a representative of each of the moral stances argue that racism is wrong?

Homework

Someone in your class is continually telling racist jokes. Write a short story describing what you do about it.

FREEDOM OF SPEECH

CASE STUDY

Every year in Scotland, around the 12th July, the Orange Marches take place. Depending upon your point of view, these are either celebrations of a way of life, demonstrations of loyalty to a cause, or provocation of one side by another. In Northern Ireland, the Drumcree Marches follow a similar pattern, but often end up in more serious trouble. Each time one of these marches is planned, the organisers have to apply to the local authorities for permission. The local authority takes advice from the police about how likely the event is to end up causing trouble and then make their decision. Some people think that such events should never take place because they represent extreme viewpoints and give 'respectability' to what is not 'respectable'. Supposing it was a march by neo-Nazis, or a group supporting paedophiles?

FIGURE 4.6 *Orange March parade*

I CAN DO ANYTHING

There are tensions between allowing people to say and do whatever they want (absolute freedom) and saying that some things are not acceptable and so should be kept to yourself (relative freedom). There should be a balance between absolute freedom and relative freedom to protect the rights of others. Most societies value freedom of speech – up to a point. Where that point lies is the subject of this moral issue.

Censored

Most schools where pupils are allowed access to the internet have a 'firewall'. This prevents pupils gaining access to inappropriate websites. What these are is usually decided by the school or local authority. There have also been attempts to regulate the internet for adults, so that unacceptable sites are banned. This has been resisted by many internet users because they want to decide for themselves what's acceptable and what isn't.

What things are usually censored?

Pornography

In Britain, the (informal) 'Kintyre peninsula' rule is often used as an example (usually by supporters of free access to pornography who think it's a bit silly) of what is and isn't acceptable. In short, British pornography laws do not allow the penis to be shown (in any publication or film) any more erect than roughly the angle of the Kintyre peninsula (although female genitalia may be shown freely). Films and magazines must be submitted to censorship boards, which classify them according to the age group for which they are suitable (up to 18, although there are R18 videos as well, which can be sold in licensed sex shops). Sex involving animals or children (anyone under 16) is also not permitted. Sexual acts involving violence may also be subject to censorship. TV programmes are also subject to vetting by censorship organisations. They are also expected to regulate themselves. For example, certain programmes should only be shown after 9pm – the 'watershed'.

Violence

Again, films must go through censorship boards, which will only pass them if any violence in them is at an 'acceptable' level. Also, TV tends to regulate itself here, although there are TV watchdog organisations that supervise this self-regulation (like the ITC).

Freedom to express your views

In Britain, you may be prosecuted if you say (or imply) something about someone which puts their character in doubt and for which you have no evidence. These laws of libel/defamation are designed to protect people from malicious rumours and half-truths being passed off as the truth. You're free to express your opinion, if it is just an opinion (as long as you're not using a position of power to give that opinion extra 'weight'). This freedom does not exist in all countries. In some countries, freedom to express your viewpoint may be severely limited.

Propaganda

In wars, for example, many governments don't tell their people the whole truth because if they did it might lower morale or give away things that need to remain secret for the safety of those involved in battle.

Other 'unacceptable' views

Sometimes views are censored because they oppose what the government says. In Britain, this rarely happens (although some individuals and groups might disagree). In many countries, speaking against the government is subject to censorship. You may also have to conform to certain rules of behaviour or suffer the consequences. For example, in some countries women may be expected to dress in a particular way or be punished. In Britain, however, this conforming usually means being careful about what you say about groups within society, for example, not making fun of people because they are disabled or because of their race.

THE VALUE OF CENSORSHIP?

- It should protect society. In any society, we accept that we're not entirely free. For example, we are not free to kill other people just because we want to. It is also difficult to say just how 'free' people are about their choices and how free they should be. Censorship is a way for the 'strong' to save the 'weak' from having to make difficult choices. For example, suppose a group got together to argue that all black people should be forced to leave Britain. Should we calmly listen to their arguments and let them advertise their message? Perhaps some 'weak' people should be protected from this kind of message?
- It protects individuals. Censorship is society's way of looking after its members, in particular, the most vulnerable ones. With complete freedom of speech, people may be harmed by its consequences. Words may not break your bones but they could cause serious harm. If you say things which aren't true or which are only half-true, they could stick. Once a view is expressed it is difficult to take back.
- Censorship avoids exploitation. Opponents of pornography argue that it exploits women and other vulnerable people. It also sends out the wrong signals to men about women in general.
- Censorship prevents imitation. One of the arguments against pornography and violence on TV, for example, is that seeing it is more likely to lead to copycat behaviour. For example, there may be links between pornography and violence against women, and between violence on screen and violence in real life. Censoring more extreme forms of either on TV or in films could cut real-life cases.
- Censorship keeps society stable and sends out clear messages about what is 'right' and 'wrong'. In some countries, criticism of the government is punished because it shows 'disloyalty' and could lead to unrest. These countries say that their censorship practices are doing everyone a favour because they are keeping a government 'strong'. It also keeps 'undesirable' views from gaining support – by depriving the people who have them of the publicity they need to get their message across.

DISCUSSION POINT

Who should decide what is censored and what isn't? Based on what?

NO CENSORSHIP

- Everyone should be free to think and act as they like, especially if they are an adult and not likely to harm anyone by their views or actions. Everyone can make their own decisions about what they watch or do. Everyone's TV has an 'off' button. We should just use it if we don't like what we see. Besides, deciding what to censor and who should do it just means making one set of choices instead of another. Where would women be today if the views of the suffragettes had been successfully outlawed?
- There is no clear link between watching pornography and sexual abuse or between violence on screen and in real life. There's just as much serious crime in countries with strict censorship as in countries without.
- Exploitation of individuals will take place whether censorship is around or not. In fact, the more something is banned the stronger you make it. If, for example, all forms of pornography were banned tomorrow, then it would just 'go underground' illegally. This would make it more difficult to regulate and probably lead to even more abusive and exploitative material than is around today.
- Criticism and satire is a good way to keep a government and society's 'institutions' on their toes. If we blindly accept 'the way things are', then this could lead to all sorts of horrors. Many argue that Hitler wouldn't have been able to do some of the things he did if more people had spoken out against him. Besides, who decides what is acceptable and what isn't? One person's terrorist is another person's freedom fighter. Amnesty International always classified those in prison for crimes related to the troubles in Northern Ireland as 'political prisoners', although many British people wouldn't have seen them that way. Again, maybe the more you try to ban people's viewpoint, the more people will want to hear it and the stronger it will become.

DISCUSSION POINT

Does censorship just make a viewpoint stronger?

Children who disobey their parents may have been influenced by TV characters such as Bart Simpson, a new report by the Independent Television Commission (ITC) says. Its research found that adverts and programmes with disobedient characters often inspired copycat behaviour in children.

Times Educational Supplement, 10 November 2000

FACTS AND FIGURES

- The Obscene Publications Act (1959) bans materials which are 'likely to corrupt or deprave'. Whether material does this is decided by the courts.
- When the word 'f∗∗∗' was heard on TV for the first time, National Viewers and Listeners Association chief, Mrs Mary Whitehouse, wrote a letter to the Queen in protest.
- Article 19 of the UN Declaration of Human Rights states that 'Everyone has the right to freedom of opinion and expression.'

FIGURE 4.7 *South Park characters. Do you think characters in cartoons like this one can influence people's behaviour?*

MORAL RESPONSES

Christians have traditionally supported censorship where the aim was to protect weaker or more vulnerable members of society. This might mean supporting or campaigning for stricter laws about pornography or violence. Christians believe that life should be lived in a spirit of concern for other people (Romans 13:9). Sometimes, this might mean that we stop others doing certain things so that people are protected. Although Christians believe that everyone is individually responsible for their own choices in life, they also argue that society has a responsibility to act in a sensible way, by setting good examples for others to follow. Christians also believe that Christian teaching is the first thing anyone should obey and if this comes into conflict with 'human' law then there could be problems. For example, a government may be oppressing its people, so Christians would want to speak out against that even if doing so was illegal. Christians also believe that order and good government are the will of God. This means the government has the right to protect its people as it sees fit – even if this means clamping down on individual freedom. The Christian has to treat this situation with care, because of the conflict involved between supporting the government and doing what the Christian thinks is right (Matthew 22:15–22). The Old Testament prophets often criticised the government of the day (eg Jeremiah 21:11–12) and Jesus regularly challenged the beliefs of the powerful groups in society (eg Matthew 23:1–12). Christians should therefore feel free to speak out about what they think is wrong. However, Jesus also asked people to make up their own minds about his teaching – so perhaps people should be free to respond however they like to the issue of censorship.

In **Islam**, the teaching is similar. Muslims have a duty to put the teachings of the Qur'an into practice. This means opposing injustice wherever it takes place – even if it is being carried out by a government. This might mean speaking or taking action against a government to remind it of what is right (Surah 26:150–152). Muslims also believe that the community has a responsibility to its members to help people keep up certain standards of behaviour. In practice, this might mean supporting censorship, as one way to stop unwanted images or ideas reaching people who can't cope with them. In Islam, it is common, for example, for Muslim women to wear a covering for the body (the *hejab*). This is seen as a way of protecting the woman from the lustful thoughts of men as her 'womanly curves' are hidden away. This protects her but also protects the man from thinking wrong thoughts about a woman (Surah 33:59 and 24:30–31). Some argue that this is an example of censorship or taking away of personal freedom. Muslims respond that sometimes people need help to be the best they can. This shows that Muslims accept limits on personal freedom when it's beneficial. Muslims often point to 'Western' pornography as an example of what happens when you have too much freedom. Many Muslims also believe that complete freedom of speech is wrong if it leads to wrongdoing or insult, as the Salman Rushdie case showed. When you speak, it should be the truth and not likely to harm others (Surah 22:30).

An **Egoist** could take one of two approaches:
- Egoists believe that, in most situations, personal freedom should be absolute. This means that the Egoist would want to be able to say, do, watch or read whatever he wants. The Egoist alone should have the choice about this; it shouldn't be censored by someone else based on their idea of what is right and wrong. The Egoist's self-interest is most likely to be served where he has complete freedom over everything he does. To have someone else stop him doing (or seeing) it in the first place obviously doesn't make sense.
- On the other hand, Egoists would want above all to be sure that their own self-interest was protected by laws and social rules generally. This could mean that the Egoist would support censorship if it seemed to be in his own interest. For example, say watching TV violence was clearly linked to real-life violence. If the Egoist were on the receiving end of this violence, then he might feel very strongly that TV violence should be censored by the government. In this way, clamping down on people's freedom of speech (and action) might be the Egoist's best chance for self-protection. Although the Egoist values his own personal freedom of choice highly, he may not value other people's freedom of choice at all. If their decisions led to problems for him, then he'd want their choices limited.

Utilitarians value personal freedom highly. This is because anything else would result in unhappiness. A society full of people who were being watched over by some kind of 'big brother' would probably not be a happy one (like the society in George Orwell's book *1984*). Censorship would have to be used lightly. It is important that people are allowed to make their own free decisions about what they say, watch etc. However, Utilitarians would support censorship where it would be beneficial for society in general. For example, if violence on TV was shown to lead to more violence in real life, this would be a good reason for censoring TV violence. If pornography was likely to lead to poor attitudes towards women or violence against them, then this would lead to suffering. If you can stop this happening by censorship, then perhaps you should. The Utilitarian would argue that censorship is valuable because it protects the majority at the expense of the freedom of a minority. When people exercise their freedom, they might not always make decisions that show concern for others. This might mean that the decision has to be made for them, by not allowing them the choice in the first place. Also, people might not be completely free in their choices. For example, the more violence there is on TV, the less there is real choice about what to watch.

Utilitarians also support the need for a government to rule in the best interests of the majority. This might sometimes mean clamping down on people's freedom to speak out against government action. However, where the government's actions were unfair, the Utilitarian wouldn't support their right to stop people speaking out against the unfairness.

ACTIVITIES

Knowledge & Understanding

1 What happens in Scotland around the 12th July each year? Why do some people oppose this?
2 What is a 'firewall'? Is it right for schools to have one?
3 State **two** things that would be banned under Britain's pornography laws.
4 What is propaganda?
5 In your own words, state **two** arguments for censorship and **two** against it.
6 What does the research done by the ITC suggest?
7 Why might a Christian support censorship?
8 When might Christians think they should 'speak out'?
9 Why do many Muslim women wear a *hejab*? Is this censorship?
10 When might an Egoist support censorship?

Analysis

1 Brainstorm a list of TV programmes which people in your class regularly watch (aim for about 20). Now think about which of the following categories might apply to each programme (a programme may be in more than one group and may only occasionally fit the category) *racially offensive; 'strong' language; sexually explicit; offensive to women; offends religious beliefs; offends minority groups in society, the disabled; violent; encourages bad behaviour.* Discuss and draw up your own table:
2 Using the categories above, choose one of the programmes and write a short talk for your class explaining why you think the programme should be banned. Someone else should give a short talk opposing your view.

3 Devise a questionnaire that tries to work out if there is a link between watching violence on TV and aggression in real-life. Are aggressive people more likely to watch violent TV programmes? Write a report about your findings.
4 Carry out the following role play.
Nathan is 15, he likes to tell racist and other offensive jokes. You have been asked by your friends to tell him to stop. He doesn't want to because he thinks he has the right to say whatever he wants.
5 A neo-Nazi march is planned for your town. What might a religious person and an Egoist feel about it? Write what you think they would say.

Evaluation

'There should be no violence on TV.'
Do you agree? Give at least **two** reasons for your answer.

Assessment question

Outcome 2 'All pornography should be banned.' How might a religious person and an Egoist respond to this?

Homework

Find out what happened when Salman Rushdie's book, *The Satanic Verses,* was published. Write a brief outline of what happened.

ACTIVITIES
i2

Knowledge & Understanding

1 What's the difference between absolute and relative freedom?
2 Why do you think 'female genitalia' can be shown freely, but male genitalia can't?
3 What is the purpose of libel laws?
4 Why might a government censor free speech?
5 What do you think is the strongest argument in favour of censorship?

6 What do you think is the strongest argument opposing censorship?
7 Do you think that censorship is a good way to protect people?
8 How might a religious person justify censorship?
9 Do you think the Egoist would be more likely to support or oppose censorship? Give reasons.
10 What might a Utilitarian feel about governments 'clamping down' on freedom of speech?

Analysis

1 Use the list of TV programmes drawn up by the Intermediate 1 group. Choose a few and write a defence of them as if you were responsible for them.

2 Draw up a code of practice for the use of the internet in your school. What, in your opinion, should be banned? Would there be a difference for different year groups? Perhaps you could do the same for the use of language.

3 As a class, debate the following issue, ensuring that each of the moral stances is represented. 'This house believes that there should be no censorship on TV.'

4 The book, *1984*, by George Orwell, is based on the idea that everything we say or do is watched and controlled by the government 'Big Brother'. Write your own story where this happens in Scotland.

5 Liberation Theology is a Christian response to injustice. Many governments have tried to suppress it. Find out about it and write a short report about your findings.

6 Act out this role play.
Your girl/boyfriend is an Egoist and intends to be photographed for a pornographic magazine. You consider yourself to be 'religious' and disagree with this action. Act out the discussion you might have.

Evaluation

'A government has the right to control what people say and do.'
How far do you agree?

Assessment question

Outcome 3 'In a fair society, there would be no censorship.'
To what extent do you agree?

Homework

Find out what happened when Salman Rushdie's book, *The Satanic Verses,* was published. Explain whether or not you think the Iranian government was right in its actions.

WAR AND PEACE

NON-VIOLENCE AND PACIFISM

Peace One Day is an organisation working to establish the first ever Global Cease-Fire Day. The founder of Peace One Day, filmmaker Jeremy Gilley, is documenting the entire process. The results will be made widely available so that adults and children of all cultures can become inspired to play an active role in creating peace. Due to the support of the United Nations, governments, non-governmental organisations, Nobel Peace Prize Winners and individuals around the world, Peace One Day has proved that a starting point for peace, a Global Cease-Fire Day, is well within reach. Visit www.peaceoneday.org

DISCUSSION POINT

Do you think that it is likely that the world could have such a day of peace?

PHILOSOPHICAL PACIFISM

Some people believe that taking part in wars is always wrong. Pacifism as an idea developed after the Congress of Vienna in 1814. It gathered strength during World War One with organisations such as the 'Fellowship of Peace' (1914). During World War One, many became conscientious objectors. These people refused to accept their 'call-up' to join the armed forces. They often faced great hardship as people regarded them as cowards or traitors. They could be imprisoned and were usually thought of as unpatriotic. By World War Two, a pacifist stance was less harshly treated, although in the USA, 6000 people were imprisoned for their refusal to join the armed services. Many pacifists compromised, joining the forces as 'non-combatants', where they had duties that supported the forces but which did not involve fighting.

Modern pacifism has two main foundations:

◆ War is wrong in itself because killing is never right in any circumstances.
◆ War solves nothing. Violence breeds more violence. There are more creative and less destructive ways to solve disputes.

FIGURE 5.1 *Kofi Annan, Secretary-General, United Nations, and Jeremy Gilley, Founder – Peace One Day*

Photo by UN DPI

DISCUSSION POINT

What do you think of this kind of pacifism?

RELIGIOUS PACIFISM

In the West, many pacifists have come from within the Christian faith. The basic principle they follow is that taking part in war goes

FIGURE 5.2 *Anti-war demonstration*

DISCUSSION POINT

What might be the advantages and disadvantages of being a pacifist?

against the teaching of Jesus, which stressed love for your neighbour as well as a peaceful response to conflict generally.

Quakers believe that war goes against the teachings of the Bible but they also believe that it is evidence of a fault in people's thinking about each other. The way to overcome this flaw in human nature is to resist it – even if it means your death.

Some people believe so strongly in pacifism that they will not fight back if personally attacked. They call this 'biblical non-resistance'. They believe Jesus' instruction to 'turn the other cheek' must be taken literally.

Many Buddhists are pacifists. They believe that violence is wrong. The principle in life is to cause as little suffering to other living things as possible. This attitude extends to all living things. Violence is a source of bad karma. During the Vietnam War, many Buddhist monks burned themselves to death as a protest against the atrocities of the war.

IDEAL OR IDEALISM?

Most sane people agree that a world at peace is desirable. The problem is how best to achieve it. Pacifists argue that:
- Pacifism is not just empty idealism. It sets an example for others to follow – that there is another way. There are more constructive responses to violence.
- War is not inevitable. It is the end result of a particular set of choices based on particular beliefs about human nature and what is right or wrong.
- Few human conflicts are simple and rarely about 'pure good' against 'pure evil'. Negotiation, compromise and good sense can always lead to the avoidance of violence.

♦ It is morally wrong to maintain peace through the threat of war. Such a 'peace' is unstable and more likely to lead to war as tension builds.

However, pacifism has its critics:

♦ Doing nothing is an odd way to respond to attack. The idea that this will somehow deter the attacker is just nonsense.

♦ War is regrettable but unavoidable. Dictators and the power-hungry will only really understand violent responses.

♦ The threat of violent retaliation is in fact the best way to maintain peace. No aggressor will attack your country if he knows that he will be resisted and perhaps eventually beaten.

♦ Pacifism is a good idea in theory but not in practice. It goes against human nature and so is unrealistic.

FIGURE 5.3 *Peace Camp at Faslane nuclear base*

NON-VIOLENT PROTEST

One example of this is the Peace Camps at the Faslane nuclear base on the Clyde. Groups set up camps next to the base to protest at the existence of the nuclear submarines based there. One of the members of the camp commented:

We are here as silent witnesses to the madness of nuclear weapons, to remind people in Scotland that these weapons of mass destruction are just down the road from their homes. We protest by simply being here. We do not believe in violent protest – it is the potential for violence we're protesting against after all. Anyway violent protest just hardens the resolve of those we are protesting against.

WHAT IS NON-VIOLENCE?

This is a way of protesting against something without resorting to violence. The organisation, Ploughshares 2000, which is involved in protests at the Faslane Peace Camp, sees it as a way of exercising power without the need for violent action. A group associated with Ploughshares 2000, named after the monk 'Adomnan of Iona', outlines what non-violent action is:

◆ *Dramatic action – to catch the headlines*
◆ *Non-cooperation – strikes, boycotts etc*
◆ *Intervention – blockades, sit-ins*
◆ *Providing alternatives to things you think are wrong*
◆ *Creative disorder – demonstrations, marches etc*

Adomnan of Iona Ploughshares 2000 affinity group at Edinburgh University

DISCUSSION POINT

Which of these tactics do you think is most effective? Why?

THE NEED FOR PROTEST

People who support non-violent protest argue that:
◆ There comes a time when everything else has failed and the only thing left is to make your feelings known by marching or civil disobedience.
◆ Protest is therefore a way of exercising your basic right to free speech.
◆ Many people are excluded from the decisions which affect them, or their opinions are ignored or not considered very valuable. Protest gives them a voice. It also enables you to speak for others who can't speak for themselves – for example, people in prison or animals.
◆ Protests enable you to voice your argument with others, often in a dramatic way. Decision-makers are more likely to pay attention than they are when individuals complain.
◆ Some things are so wrong that we have to make our feelings known strongly. When something becomes law it can only be fought by many people protesting against it.

FACTS AND FIGURES

◆ 528,000 soldiers have taken part in UN peacekeeping duties between 1945 and 1992 – this has cost around 8.3 billion dollars. 800 have died in action.
◆ On 1 August 2000, 83 protesters were arrested at the Faslane base.
◆ A peace march organised by Trident Ploughshares was officially welcomed by the Lord Provost of Glasgow on 2 August 2000.

Never doubt that a small group of thoughtful committed citizens can change the world. Indeed, it is the only thing that ever has.

Margaret Mead

No need for protest

Opponents argue that:

◆ In most societies, there are perfectly reasonable ways to make your opinions known without protesting. In Scotland, for example, you can make your opinions known every time you vote, by not voting for people whose views you disagree with.

◆ Protests are too easily 'hijacked' by people who don't really care about the issues but just enjoy trouble-making. So they are not a good way to express your opinions.

◆ Protests don't often influence the decision-makers anyway – they just make them more convinced that they are right and more likely to stick with their decisions than change them.

MORAL RESPONSES

For the **Christian**, there is not much doubt that Jesus placed a high value on peace. He lived in a country which was ruled by a foreign power, the Romans. Many Jews supported armed resistance against the enemy. The Jews expected a Messiah to come who would lead them in battle and free Israel – so for many it seemed unlikely that this peace-loving Jesus could be that Messiah. Jesus stresses love for enemies throughout his teachings. This includes such parables as the Good Samaritan (Luke 10:25–37), where he states that love for others is the greatest commandment. An important pointer to Jesus' desire for peace is that on the cross he prays for the forgiveness of those who are killing him rather than asking for their destruction in revenge (Luke 23:34).

Jesus also comments on the value of those who not only live peacefully but actively try to bring about peace. He says that for such people God will grant the highest rewards (Matthew 5:9). However, Jesus has kind words for the Roman Centurion – he does not tell him to give up his warrior's lifestyle (Luke 7:1–10). He also seems to suggest that in worldly affairs fighting might not be wrong (John 18:36).

Christians have understood Jesus' words as pointing to an ideal. Some believe that we should try to put this ideal into practice whatever the cost, others that in a sinful world we can only put this ideal into action so far.

Blessed are the peacemakers, for they shall be called the Sons of God.

Matthew 5:9

In **Islam**, peace is also the ideal. War is always seen as the last resort in terms of the *Jihad* ideal. Muslims are to protect the faith, but to act defensively not aggressively. The Muslim is meant to respond to the actions of others reasonably – so that if the other desires peace, the Muslim should agree:

> 'But if they incline to peace, you also incline to it and put your trust in Allah.'
>
> Surah 8:61

Muslims are to try to diffuse situations of tension with peaceful responses:

> The Merciful's servants are those who walk on the earth in humility and sedateness, and when the foolish address them (with bad words), they reply back with mild words of gentleness'.
>
> Surah 25:63

Muslims do not generally consider pacifism a realistic option because they believe that you must protect those who need your help. The protection of the weak by the strong is seen as a duty of justice. There is also the duty to protect the faith of Islam, which would be difficult to achieve by responding to aggression as a pacifist. Muslims look forward to the day of judgement when peace and justice will be restored to all by Allah.

> On that day she will tell her news … . On that day men will appear in droves to be shown their actions, and who-ever has done an atom's weight of good will see it; while whoever has done an atom's weight of evil will see it.
>
> Surah 99:1–8

In general, the **Egoist** would be likely to prefer peace to war because living in peacetime is generally safer than in wartime. However, he could respond to peace in a number of ways:

◆ He might support pacifism if he thought that doing so would protect him from harm. For example, the Egoist might be able to avoid being called up to join the forces during a war by claiming that he was a paci-fist. In this way, he would be able to avoid the more extreme possible harm which war might cause him.

◆ Of course, he might think that being a conscientious objector was even more difficult to deal with and so want to avoid that. He might join the forces and be part of a service where he was unlikely to be in any actual combat.

◆ However, if the Egoist were an arms manufacturer or trader he might welcome war because this gives him a market for his products without his having to be involved in anything dangerous. Local wars in far-off countries might be particularly attractive to him.

◆ Also, if the Egoist believed that the war was necessary to protect him, then he might support war – even though he might try to avoid actually being a part of it.

Peace, for the Egoist, is only of value where it is of benefit to him.

The **Utilitarian** is concerned with happiness, in particular the happiness of the majority. Generally speaking, happiness is usually not a feature of war. Utilitarians believe in maximising pleasure and minimising pain. During war, pain is commonplace – whether it is emotional or physical. You would expect Utilitarians, therefore, to avoid war at all costs. In practice, this doesn't happen though. Utilitarians also value freedom (or liberty) very highly. For some Utilitarians, this is the most important feature of happiness. Obviously if there is a threat to people's freedom, sometimes going to war might be the only solution. The Utilitarian would then accept the 'cost' of so much pain and suffering in the short term if it was likely to lead to greater benefits in the long term. Utilitarians usually oppose killing. However, where such killing can lead to a greater happiness, then it is acceptable, although not to be taken lightly. Utilitarians stress quality of life. A good quality of life can only be maintained where people have justice, freedom and basic human rights. Where one country invades another or mistreats minority groups within its own boundaries, then the quality of life of those living in that country are often seriously harmed. Going to war might be the only way to restore their quality of life. Protecting yourself and others is acceptable.

> The sole end for which mankind are warranted, individually or collectively, in interfering with the liberty of action of any of their number, is self protection.
>
> J S Mill, On Liberty (1859)

ACTIVITIES

Knowledge & Understanding

1 What is Jeremy Gilley doing? Why?
2 How did some people feel about conscientious objectors during the World Wars? Do you think this was fair?
3 Give **one** reason why someone might be a pacifist.
4 What reasons might a Quaker give for being a pacifist?
5 In your own words, state **one** argument against pacifism.
6 What is non-violent action?
7 In your own words, state **two** arguments in support of non-violent protest.
8 Do you think Jesus would have been a pacifist? Explain your answer.
9 What should a Muslim do when an enemy wants peace?
10 Explain how an Egoist could be a pacifist.

Analysis

1 If you could speak to the world's leaders, what arguments might you use to persuade them to give up war for just one day?
2 Write a short story about a pupil in your school who is a pacifist. How might he or she deal with playground aggression? How might he or she try to persuade others that this is the right approach?

3 Choose a topic that you would like to protest about non-violently. Explain *how* you would protest.
4 Use your imagination. The Roman Centurion has just met with Jesus. He returns home (to find his servant well). Later that evening, he meets with a follower of Jesus to discuss the events of the day. This follower tells the Centurion that Jesus has come to bring peace. The Centurion begins to think about his lifestyle. Write the conversation they might have.
5 Make a list of 'situations of tension' which regularly arise in your school or community. How might a Muslim respond to each one by following the teachings in Surahs 8:61 and 25:63?

Evaluation

'Some of the last words of Jesus on the cross prove that he was a pacifist.'
Do you agree? Give **one** reason for your answer.

Assessment question

Outcome 3 Your country is at war. You receive your call-up papers. What do you do and why?

Homework

Design your own poster based on Matthew 5:9.

ACTIVITIES

Knowledge & Understanding

1 What does Jeremy Gilley believe the world can learn from a day of peace?
2 What did some conscientious objectors do instead of going to prison? Is this compatible with pacifism?
3 Why are Quakers pacifists?
4 How does a Faslane Peace Camp member justify a non-violent approach to protest?
5 Why was the idea of Jesus as the Messiah difficult to accept for many who lived during his lifetime?
6 Does the way Jesus treated the Roman Centurion contradict what he seems to believe about violence?
7 In what way might justice get in the way of a Muslim being a pacifist?

8 How might the Egoist justify supporting war?
9 Would a Utilitarian be a pacifist? Give reasons for your answer.

Analysis

1 In a group, work out a short presentation you would make to contribute to the Peace One Day film.
2 What reasons might someone give for opposing the Faslane Peace Camp?
3 Find out more about why Quakers are pacifists. Write a brief report of you findings.
4 Give a short talk to your class on one of the following topics: 'Why I am a pacifist' or 'Pacifism, nice but naive'.
5 Read Luke 19:45–48. Now imagine that you have to

interview Jesus. The question is, 'Do these actions show that Jesus supported violence in a good cause?' Write the conversation which might take place.

Evaluation

'A Utilitarian could not be a Pacifist.'
How far do you agree?

Assessment question

Outcome 2 Jimmy's country is at war. He has received his call-up papers to join the forces. Because he is a pacifist he refuses to go. Three of his friends each write him a short letter telling him what they think of his decision. One is a Christian, one a Utilitarian and one an Egoist. Write a brief letter from each to Jimmy.

Homework

Jimmy has been imprisoned because of his refusal to take part in the war. Write him a brief letter outlining your opinion on his situation.

THE JUST WAR THEORY

CASE STUDY

I am a Chaplain in the Royal Navy. According to the Geneva Convention I am not allowed to carry weapons. In a battle situation I assist the medics. Many people ask me how I can be a Christian and yet be part of situations where I know that people will be killed and that the men I work with will do the killing. Well, these men need God's help as much as anyone else – perhaps more sometimes, as their work often brings them face to face with death. Most of the men see themselves not as warriors, but as peacekeepers. They are there to protect the weak. Human nature means that wars will always happen. I'm sure God weeps at human foolishness and wishes that all wars would come to an end, but he gives us the freedom to choose and has to accept our choices.

I'm there to remind people of God's constant love. That's especially important in situations where he appears to have left us to it.

A JUST WAR?

This Chaplain believes that war is a part of life that we, unfortunately, have to get used to.

There have always been wars, however, human society seems to have agreed that even in war there should be rules. The best known version of these rules is found in the *Summa Theologica* of St Thomas Aquinas (1224–74). Here, he explains why wars have to be fought and suggests what we can and cannot do in a war.

A NEED FOR RULES?

Why might rules in a war be helpful?
◆ If there are rules, then it might help to stop the war escalating out of hand or spreading. Local disputes can often draw in other countries and become world wars. So, rules about going to war are helpful.

◆ A government will hope that after a war, however widespread, there will be peace. Whoever wins does not want to face the possibility of acts of revenge from those who were unfairly treated during the war. If there are rules, then such endless retaliation might be avoided – meaning that life can eventually return to normal. So, rules about what you can do in a war are helpful.

◆ If there are rules, then those who break the rules will have to face up to their crimes. If you know this during a war, you might be less likely to break the rules and so fight the war 'fairly'. This will mean that certain groups (for example, children) can expect special protection even in wartime.

Some might disagree and say that war is about winning. How you win doesn't matter.

DISCUSSION POINT

Do you think having rules during war is helpful?

FIGURE 5.4 *A naval battle off the coast of Vietnam, during the Vietnam War*

THE CONDITIONS FOR A JUST WAR

The just war theory can be split into two sections:
◆ *Jus ad bellum* – When it is acceptable to go to war.
◆ *Jus in bellum* – What it is acceptable to do in war.

There must be good reason for the war

One person's idea of a good reason will be different from another's. Wars are generally fought to protect your way of life but how can

DISCUSSION POINT

List what you think are 'good reasons' for going to war.

you tell if that is really threatened? Sometimes wars are fought over land or resources or to stop some interference in your country's business. Generally, wars are supposed to be fought defensively. However, acts of aggression might be your country's way of protecting itself first so that it doesn't have to act defensively; it might think that making the first strike is a good way of avoiding a longer war or losing in the end.

War must be a last resort

All other options should have been tried. Some believe this is easier to say than do. How long do you discuss and negotiate with a potential aggressor? What if another country has already harmed yours? This may also involve the need for a lot of trust. In a situation of conflict there often isn't much of that. There also has to be a balance between political action and military action – perhaps while you are trying out all the options in political discussions, your potential enemy is gaining a military advantage. By the time you decide that all the options have been tried, your enemy is much more prepared for war than you are.

DISCUSSION POINT

What other options are there instead of going to war?

The war should be fought to restore good over evil

Again, this depends upon your point of view. It is said that 'the first casualty in war is the truth'. This means that each side in the war tries to convince its own people that its actions are right and that the enemy is wrong. This propaganda is meant to make you support your own country's war effort. In some conflicts, 'evil' might be obvious and has to be opposed, but in others it is far less clear.

There should be proportionality in the war

The idea of proportionality means that you should do only what you set out to do and use no more force than is necessary to achieve your goal. During the Gulf War, many argued that the forces opposed to Saddam Hussein should march right into Bhagdad and overthrow his government. The Allies argued that this was wrong. They set out to remove Iraq's forces from Kuwait and stopped when they had achieved this. War has costs – financial, emotional and practical. Perhaps it makes sense to have limits and to set out to achieve only a limited goal. The basic idea is that your actions in war should not outweigh the problem you are trying to solve. Again, this can be a matter of opinion. Also, in war, it is sometimes difficult to do the task 'rationally'. Many war crimes take place because people lose their cool and carry out acts of revenge even after the initial objective has been achieved.

Civilian casualties should be avoided

This is one of the most difficult areas of the theory. Most governments accept that there will be some 'collateral damage' – that sometimes civilians will be killed during attacks on military targets. Even modern 'precision bombing', which is supposed to be accurate, has been known to go wrong. The theory suggests that the intentional targeting of civilians is wrong or, for example, the use of civilians as 'human shields' to cover military activities. The question is – how can any civilian be thought of as innocent? Some argue that everyone in the enemy's country is the enemy. You may not be fighting but your efforts support the fighting forces. This means that you are just as much the enemy as those who are actually engaged in combat.

The war can only be started by the government

Types of government vary around the world. You might think some are acceptable and others not. How far you should support the decisions of a government you disagree with is a matter of opinion. In today's world, democracy is held up as the best example of government. Does this mean that wars started by non-democratic governments should not be supported? Also, this raises the important question of the role of the 'international community'. The United Nations, for example, sees itself as the organisation which tries to maintain world peace. Sometimes the international community engages in acts of war against countries which are 'doing wrong'. Is this right or is it unreasonable interference in the affairs of one country by others who have nothing to do with it?

FIGURE 5.5 *Bombing in Yugoslavia*

THEORY INTO ACTION

Rules for war have been agreed by countries and are summed up in practical guidelines, which are meant to be observed during war. Putting the guidelines in these conventions into practice is supervised by various organisations.

FACTS AND FIGURES

- Since the end of World War Two, 14.9 million land mines have been recovered in Poland alone. Land mines kill indiscriminately.
- From 1945 to 1989, around two million people have been killed in wars.
- During the Gulf War, 100,000 Iraqis and 234 members of the Allied Forces died.

The Geneva Convention (1864)

This is an agreement which covers the treatment of prisoners of war, as well as those who are sick, wounded or killed in battle. The idea is to ensure that even in a situation of conflict, some basic human rights remain in force. It covers many aspects of the treatment of the sick, as well as setting out detailed regulations about the proper treatment of the dead.

The Red Cross and the Red Crescent

These international organisations try to ensure that the regulations of this convention are put into practice. The Geneva Convention clearly states that, even in wartime, the flags of these two organisations should guarantee protection for those who travel under them. Both organisations are concerned with the care of the sick, dying and also with the humane treatment of prisoners of war. Other voluntary organisations also help in situations of conflict – for example, charitable organisations like Médicins Sans Frontières. The existence of these safeguards reminds us that even in war, humans are expected to behave humanely towards each other.

MORAL RESPONSES

Christians have different opinions about whether war is right or wrong, although it is seen as a part of human life (James 4:1–2). In the Old Testament, God helps the Israelites destroy their enemies in war. This was usually in response to injustice – where the Israelites were unable to carry out God's work because of the threats of their enemies. This makes many Christians believe that war is acceptable provided that it has the aim of restoring justice and bringing about peace.

Jesus does not seem to have approved of war. He taught that we should 'turn the other cheek' (Matthew 5:39–41), meaning that we should not fight violence with violence. He also taught that we should 'love our enemies'. This would make war difficult, unless you thought that loving your enemy might include punishing them when they did wrong. However, Jesus used aggression and violence when he cleared the temple of traders (John 2:15). Some say that this shows he supports violence in defence of what is right. The idea of protecting the weak is also important in Christianity, leading some to believe that although war is evil, it is a necessary evil.

Love your enemies, and pray for those who persecute you, so that you may become the sons of your Father in Heaven.

Matthew 5:44

Many people think of **Islam** as a war-like faith. This is because the early expansion of Islam may have included forced conversions to the faith, as well as many battles involving conquering others for other reasons. Also, Muslims had to defend themselves and their new faith.

One of the first acts of Muhammed was to win the battle of Badr (AD 624). This was followed six years later when he took charge of Makkah, although no-one opposed him because his army was too strong. It was believed that his military successes were because Allah was with him.

Jihad, or holy war, is another reason why some consider Islam a faith that readily supports war. However, Jihad is mostly seen as a personal struggle against our own desires. Jihad – in the form of armed conflict – is allowed, but it can only be called for by a religious leader, not a political leader and only:

◆ in defence of Islam
◆ to overthrow bad rulers
◆ to preserve the ability to live and worship freely.

Many Muslims believe that the idea of holy war has been abused by some Muslim leaders to further their own desires. It may also have been used by enemies of Islam to suggest that it is a violent faith. Jihad is meant to involve defence, not aggression.

You may fight back against anyone who attacks you, because you have been wronged.

Surah 22:39

An **Egoist** response to the just war theory would depend upon the situation you found yourself in during war. It is likely that an Egoist would want as many safeguards as possible surrounding how the war is fought, so that your own position is protected. Given that war can be a stressful experience for all involved, you would probably want it to be a last resort and to be fought for a good reason, and for reasons that benefit your own lifestyle. You would want to gain something pleasant from the war and avoid the unpleasant. This would be the position if the Egoist were looking at the war from the point of view of how they might be treated by enemy action.

On the other hand, it probably wouldn't matter to an Egoist how much force was used or that the civilians of 'the enemy' were protected. Whatever it took for your side to win the war you might support, provided that this had no harmful effects for yourself. In fact, you might find the existence of rules in war a little irritating, if those rules stopped your side from winning quickly and decisively. You might completely reject the just war theory, if moral thinking got in the way of your side winning.

Utilitarians seek maximum happiness at minimum cost. You would expect a Utilitarian to want to avoid war at all costs, because the suffering and pain involved in war is considerable. The difficulty is that wars involve conflicts of interests and judging how to weigh up those interests is not going to be easy. Perhaps avoiding war entirely will only put off even greater suffering in the future, and not responding to aggression by an enemy might be the best thing to do to strengthen the enemy's position. Also, responding to aggression by an enemy might be acceptable if not doing so would lead to that enemy harming the innocent. Overall, this would mean that avoiding violence in war ended up allowing even more violence to take place. So a Utilitarian would be able to accept the idea of going to war, provided that there were rules attached so that the war could eventually end and not spill over for an unlimited time in acts of revenge by the losers.

On the other hand, the consequences of war in the short and long term are so widespread and so unpredictable that they probably rule out the wisdom of going to war in the first place. It is difficult to justify engaging in a war that has no foreseeable end and perhaps few real benefits for the majority.

The Utilitarian could therefore respond to war in one of two ways, depending on predicting what would happen if the war was not fought and depending that the war wouldn't outweigh the final benefits it might bring.

ACTIVITIES

Knowledge & Understanding

1 What does the naval Chaplain think God's view of war might be?
2 Who first set out the just war theory?
3 In your own words, give **one** reason why rules in war might be helpful.
4 In your own words, explain **one** of the arguments in the just war theory.
5 What does it mean to say that there should be 'proportionality' in war?
6 What is the Geneva Convention meant to achieve?
7 Give **one** reason to support the belief that Jesus would have been against war.
8 State **two** situations where Jihad is allowed.
9 In your opinion, how might an Egoist respond to a war?
10 Why might you expect a Christian to want to avoid war at all costs?

Analysis

1 You are a pacifist. You believe that the Chaplain's point of view is wrong. What might you say to him?
2 Design a table that summarises the main points of the just war theory. You might like to do this in the form of an illustrated poster, using images of war to support your outline.
3 Find out about the work of the Red Cross/Crescent. Design a short information leaflet outlining their work and why they do it.

4 Imagine you are a reporter living at the time of Jesus. Report the events of John 2:15 as you see them. Include your own comment about what message you think Jesus is trying to get across in his actions and how this compares with his other teachings.
5 Design a diagram which outlines and explains Muslim beliefs about Jihad.
6 Give a short speech to your class: 'I'm an Egoist, I'm not fighting in anybody's war.'

Evaluation

'The Chaplain's views on war are an example of him not living his faith, but ignoring it'.
Do you agree? Give **two** reasons for your answer.

Assessment question

Outcome 2 Eddie the Egoist thinks that there should be no rules in war. Based on his Egoist beliefs, what might he say to support his view? What might Claire the Christian say in response?

Homework

Give **two** situations where you think it is acceptable for one country to 'interfere' in the affairs of another.

ACTIVITIES

Knowledge & Understanding

1 How does the Chaplain justify his work?
2 What possible benefits might there be in having rules during war?
3 How might a country justify an act of aggression as a good reason for going to war?
4 Why is proportionality often difficult to achieve?
5 How might someone argue that there is no such thing as an innocent civilian?
6 What do you think is the value of making sure wars are only declared by governments?

7 When might a Christian think that war is acceptable?
8 What reasons might a Muslim give for the successes of Muhammed in battle?
9 How might a Utilitarian support the principle of going to war?

Analysis

1 Outline the arguments for and against having rules and guidelines during war.
2 Choose **one** of the conditions for the just war. Use this as the basis of a class debate.

3 You are at war. You have just placed a set of landmines in a field of your enemy as you retreat. Years later, you meet your enemy after the war has ended. He describes how innocent people were killed by your landmines. You try to justify your actions. Write the dialogue which might take place.

4 How might a Christian justify 'loving his enemies'? Write an explanation.

5 You are a soldier fighting in the battle of Badr. Write a letter home explaining to your children why you are taking part in this battle.

Evaluation

'Civilians should always be protected during wartime.'
To what extent do you agree?

Assessment question

Outcome 3 'It is never acceptable to go to war.'
Outline arguments for and against this view and set out your own conclusion with at least **two** supporting reasons.

Homework

Ask this question of as many people as you can and be prepared to discuss your answers in class: 'Do you think war will always be a part of human nature?'

NUCLEAR WEAPONS

CASE STUDY

Sinister figures in protective suits and visors, flashing lights, flames flickering through clouds of steam and – a few yards away – 10 hydrogen bombs in lorries locked in a traffic jam. With yours truly stuck behind in a red Micra, noticing that my lips have for some reason gone dry, and all of a sudden chasing nuclear convoys doesn't seem such a fun idea.

This wasn't an episode from the X files; it was the nightmarish scene at 12:30 on Tuesday 26 November 1999 on the M77, near the service station at Hamilton. There had been a collision involving lorries carrying chemicals but, like the pony express, the nuclear convoy had to get through. I got held up. So I had to prove that I can with a Nissan, and go like the proverbial bat out of hell (an appropriate simile under the circumstances) to catch up and pass the convoy before we reached Stirling. Your Scottish CND highly trained SWAT team duly sprang into action, and we managed with just seconds to spare.

Scottish CND Magazine

JUST ANOTHER WEAPON?

Robert Oppenheimer, one of the scientists who worked on the early development of nuclear weapons, was standing watching the first test explosion of a nuclear warhead. On seeing its power it is said that he quoted from the Hindu scriptures:

I am become death, destroyer of worlds.

DISCUSSION POINT

What does Camus mean? Do you agree?

After the use of nuclear weapons against Japan in World War Two, Albert Camus, the French philosopher said:

Technological civilisation has just reached its final degree of savagery. We will have to choose, in the near future, between collective suicide and the intelligent use of scientific conquests.

However, many argue that the use of nuclear weapons by the USA against Japan brought the war to an immediate end – so saving many more lives in the long run than were lost in Nagasaki and Hiroshima.

What moral questions are linked to nuclear weapons?

◆ Are they just another weapon, or does their immense power make them somehow special?
◆ Should they only be held for defensive purposes or to deter others from aggression?
◆ Is it ever right to use them?
◆ Should the possibility of accidental use be enough to make us want to destroy them?
◆ Is their production, storage and maintenance too costly and dangerous to justify their existence?

In Scotland, there are or have been nuclear submarine bases, reprocessing plants and power stations, as well as plans to dump nuclear waste in Scottish waters. Scottish CND have recently been protesting at the movement of nuclear weapons around the country (see above).

A poll carried out by Scottish CND on 26 April 1999 asked: 'Should Scotland have nuclear weapons?'. 85% said NO and 15% YES. Nuclear weapons raise strong emotions, but what about the arguments?

DISCUSSION POINT

How reliable do you think this finding is?

THE CASE AGAINST NUCLEAR WEAPONS

◆ It is morally wrong to use nuclear weapons. They kill indiscriminately. Also, the destruction they cause is long-lasting and harms all forms of life as well as humans.
◆ The power of nuclear weapons is too great a responsibility for us. Human society is too complex – little arguments easily get out of hand leading to escalation of conflict.
◆ If one country has nuclear weapons, it makes it more likely that its enemies will want them too.
◆ The technology involved is too complicated. Perhaps a nuclear war could be caused by computer error. Also, someone could hack into a computer system and start a nuclear war accidentally – or on purpose.
◆ Creating and having nuclear weapons is very costly. This money could be far better spent on conventional forces – or on feeding the poor, for example.

FIGURE 5.6 *Nuclear weapons in transit*

◆ Nuclear weapons do not work as a deterrent. The threat of violent retaliation is not a proper or effective way to settle conflict. This kind of threat usually only makes the enemy more determined to win.

Some anti-nuclear campaigners oppose all forms of violence. However, others accept the occasional need for conventional warfare but believe that nuclear weapons are a special case because of their destructive power.

Most wars are fought with the hope that peace and normal life will eventually return – whoever wins. If nuclear weapons were ever used, they would have such widespread harmful effects for the planet, that life as we know it might never recover. Nuclear war could result in what is known as a nuclear winter. This could involve materials in the atmosphere lessening the amount of sunlight which reaches earth. This could result in climate change, including freak weather, ice ages and more. This could make life on earth extremely difficult for everything. It could result in mass extinctions – perhaps including humans.

THE CASE FOR NUCLEAR WEAPONS

◆ Nuclear weapons exist. As long as the technology exists to build them, they'll be built (instructions for building one have been found on the internet). This means that even if a country wanted to get rid of them it couldn't, because it could never really be sure that its enemies – or possible future enemies – would too.

◆ They are a good way to keep the peace by acting as a deterrent. No country will fire first on another country when it knows that it could retaliate using nuclear weapons. The USA would probably not have used nuclear weapons on Japan if Japan had had them too. If everyone has them, then everyone will avoid using them. If one country gave them up then that action itself could have destabilising effects – because it could then trigger a nuclear attack by another country – which would be sure of 'winning'.

◆ Killing is killing. It is wrong to say that the use of nuclear weapons is more morally wrong than the use of other weapons. In a war, everyone in the enemy's country is the enemy. Besides, use of the nuclear option could end a war quickly so avoiding much more pain and suffering in the long run.

◆ Nuclear weapons also affect non-human life, but all warfare does.

◆ Nuclear weapons are costly to build and maintain but that is a price worth paying to avoid your country being taken over (or destroyed) by another.

Supporters of nuclear weapons argue that a nuclear option is necessary in the same way that any form of defence against aggression is. Avoiding war sometimes means that you have to appear able to hit back hard. In this way, the nuclear option brings peace through strength.

FIGURE 5.7 *Decommissioned nuclear weapons*

What do you think of Tommy Sheridan's argument?

FACTS AND FIGURES

◆ The global nuclear arsenal reached a peak in 1989 at 65,000 warheads. There are an estimated 41,000 warheads worldwide in 2000 (Worldwatch Institute).

◆ On 8 January 2000, Russian President Vladimir Putin made a new national security law that makes it easier for Russia to engage in the first-use of nuclear weapons.

◆ In 1931, Albert Einstein asked all scientists to refuse to take part in military work.

TAKING A STANCE

There are many anti-nuclear groups but few organised pro-nuclear organisations. Those who disagree with nuclear weapons may carry out protests or other acts of civil disobedience. Organisations such as Scottish CND carry out regular protests at the Faslane base on the Clyde.

However, the British government *could* argue that most people actually support nuclear weapons because the number of people who are members of anti-nuclear organisations is small in proportion to the population generally. Also, when elections take place, candidates who are against nuclear weapons don't always do very well. However, not all politicians feel this way though;

The mainstream parties tell us that we haven't got enough money to build publicly funded NHS hospitals – so they privatise our NHS. They say we can't afford demands for maximum school class sizes of 20; a living grant for students of at least 6000 pounds a year; free fuel for pensioners ... yet the government squanders 1.5 billion pounds a year on the administration of Trident. And they have turned Scotland into the nuclear dump of Europe.

Tommy Sheridan MSP

On the other hand, one politician, who wishes to remain unidentified, commented:

Of course nuclear weapons are evil and expensive – but so is a tank. What will our enemies say if we have no nuclear protection – 'Oh Scotland's a kind wee country, it has given up its nuclear weapons, isn't that nice ... let's leave it alone then and invade someone else'. Grow up.

TREATIES AND AGREEMENTS

The nuclear non-proliferation treaty was signed in 1968. It is reviewed every five years. Its aim is to:
◆ convince non-nuclear countries not to acquire nuclear weapons.
◆ encourage countries with nuclear weapons to gradually destroy their stockpiles.

The world stockpile of nuclear weapons has decreased recently as the major superpowers reduce their stocks. Some thought that the end of the Cold War and the break-up of the Soviet Union might mean that the nuclear issue was over. However, the concern now is that other countries may develop nuclear capability. It is clearly a moral issue that needs constant attention.

MORAL RESPONSES

Generally speaking, **Christians** oppose the use of nuclear weapons, as well as the threat to use them. The Church of Scotland's Church and Nation committee argues:

◆ The use of nuclear weapons goes against all Christian teaching including the 'rules' of the just war theory.
◆ Nuclear weapons may maintain some kind of world power balance but that this balance is unstable. Having these weapons does not contribute to the search for a lasting peace – instead it is an 'obstacle' to peace.
◆ The cost of maintaining stocks of nuclear weapons means that money is not being spent on issues such as homelessness, poverty and social problems.
◆ The arms trade generally means profiting from the misery of others. This can't be a Christian approach to trying to uphold what is right.

It states:

> The Church has, with increasing emphasis and urgency over the years, declared its abhorrence of nuclear weapons and its perception that not only the use of them but the possession of and threat to use them are incompatible with the word of God and with Christian revelation.

> *War & Peace,* Church of Scotland Education Department

However, many Christians support the nuclear option because they believe that for various reasons it is the surest way to peace. Christians also believe that it is the duty of the strong to protect the weak. Perhaps nuclear weapons are a good way to do that.

Muslim views of nuclear weapons can be quite different. Many Muslims believe they are wrong because they are indiscriminate. Muslims believe that justice should always go hand in hand with mercy and compassion. In conventional war, you can be compassionate to your enemy, by avoiding killing civilians, taking prisoners of members of the military and treating them humanely. In nuclear war, there's not much compassion because you have no control over who a weapon will kill – and nuclear bombs don't take prisoners. Also, the large costs of producing and maintaining weapons means that you are using the gifts of Allah for bad purposes and it may leave you unable to make people's lives better in other ways, like proper health and education services.

Some Muslims would say that nuclear war can be a part of Jihad, another way to protect the community of Islam. The Islamic country of Pakistan recently carried out nuclear weapons tests. Some Muslims stated that this was good because it meant that the Islamic world now had the means to defend and protect itself against its enemies. However, others say that these tests have to be understood in the light of tension between Pakistan and India. Claims that the Muslim world is aiming to have its own nuclear defence were responded to by Tariq Altaf, a Pakistani government spokesman:

> Nothing gives me more offence than the use of the term 'Islamic Bomb'. There is no such thing as an Islamic Bomb. This is a weapon for the self-defence of Pakistan – period.

An **Egoist** position in relation to nuclear weapons could take the following forms:

◆ *Using*: Egoists could support the use of the nuclear option provided that it won the war for their side and wasn't likely to lead to similar retaliation. They would have to take into account the possible wider effects of nuclear fallout from the use of nuclear weapons because this could have longer lasting effects on the environment and so ultimately their lifestyle – even if the use of the weapons had been a success. An Egoist would think that it was no better or worse to use nuclear weapons against an enemy than any other kind of weapon. The aim of conflict for the egoist is to win it and come out of it with as little harm to your way of life as possible. However, if the Egoist were convinced that the use of nuclear weapons would automatically trigger the same response by the other side, then he or she might be less keen to see them used.

◆ *Having*: If the Egoist believed that having nuclear weapons actually maintained peace – or at least deterred acts of aggression – then they might support their country's having them. However, the production and maintenance of a nuclear arsenal is costly and has potentially dangerous side-effects (for example the risk of accident when transporting weapons). If the egoist believed that this cost was at the expense of benefits which were more direct for them (for example a well-funded health service), then they might oppose having weapons. Also, if the Egoist believed that making and maintaining nuclear weapons could cause them harm (for example, in the release of radiation following accidents), they might reject them.

A **Utilitarian** response to nuclear war would probably be negative. The widespread and long-lasting effects of nuclear destruction – both as a result of the blast and the effects of radiation afterwards – surely couldn't contribute to the maximisation of happiness. Nuclear war could have consequences for everyone involved – winners and losers, as well as nature generally. In fact, a nuclear war could end all human life on earth. Obviously, this would go against any version of the happiness principle of Utilitarianism and so you would expect Utilitarians to be completely opposed to the use of nuclear weapons. However, a limited nuclear war might be acceptable, as long as it means more lives are saved in the long run. If the war in Japan hadn't been stopped so quickly by the use of nuclear weapons, then perhaps the war might have gone on for many more long years of pain, suffering and death. In this case, the use of the weapons produced short-term suffering in return for greater and longer-lasting pleasure.

The Utilitarian might question the process of making and storing nuclear weapons. The whole process involves great financial costs and a high level of risk. The Utilitarian might think that, weighed against the chances of actually using them, the disadvantages of producing them would be too great. For example, there's not much point in your government spending millions of pounds having nuclear weapons if that leaves it with no money to feed the hungry and heal the sick.

ACTIVITIES

Knowledge & Understanding

1 What did Oppenheimer say when he saw the effects of a nuclear explosion? What do you think he meant?

2 What have Scottish CND been protesting against?

3 What did Scottish CND's 1999 poll show?

4 State **one** argument against nuclear weapons.

5 State **one** argument for nuclear weapons.

6 In your own words, why does Tommy Sheridan oppose Trident nuclear missiles?

7 What view does the Church of Scotland have on nuclear weapons?

8 How might an Egoist explain their support for having nuclear weapons?

9 How might a Christian explain their opposition to nuclear weapons?

10 What reasons might a Muslim give for opposing the use of nuclear weapons?

Analysis

1 You are the President of a country which has nuclear weapons. You are engaged in a war. Your military generals have convinced you that you should use your nuclear weapons. You are about to go on live TV and announce your plans to your people. Write the script you would use. If possible, you should try to make a video of your presentation. After viewing a number of presentations from your class, you should discuss the reasons given.

2 You are a police officer at the Faslane nuclear base involved in policing anti-nuclear protests. Your family sees you on TV – your partner is a supporter of anti-nuclear protests. When you go home that night both of you discuss the day's events. Act out, in the form of a role play, the conversation that might take place.

3 Using newspaper/magazine cuttings and artwork, design your own poster on nuclear weapons. Try to balance out groups, making 'for' and 'against' posters in your class.

4 Have a balloon debate – class votes to throw all but one out of the basket! This should be based on the question: 'Should we ever use nuclear weapons?' Take on roles according to the four moral positions you have studied.

Evaluation

'Having nuclear weapons is not necessary.'
Do you agree? Give **two** reasons for your answer.

Assessment question

Outcome 2 You are the pilot of a bomber. You have been ordered to drop a nuclear bomb on an enemy's country. You are a Muslim. Explain what you would do and how this fits with your Muslim beliefs. Would an Egoist agree with your position?

Homework

Find out which countries currently have – or are believed to have – nuclear weapons. Prepare a table or graph to show your findings.

ACTIVITIES

Knowledge & Understanding

1 Do you agree with Albert Camus? Explain your answer.
2 How was the bombing of Japan justified?
3 Choose **one** argument against nuclear weapons. Explain how someone might argue against it.
4 Explain how someone could justify conventional war but not nuclear war.
5 Choose **one** argument for nuclear weapons. Explain how someone might argue against it.
6 Why might some think that the nuclear issue is out of date? Do you agree that it is? Explain your answer.
7 How might a member of the Church of Scotland justify supporting nuclear weapons?
8 Would the idea of Jihad give support to the use of nuclear weapons? Explain.

Analysis

1 You have just watched one of your Intermediate 1 classmates' 'Presidential TV presentations' . Write a letter to him/her explaining what you think about the decision which has been made.

2 Carry out your own 'Question Time' programme in your class. You may like to film it for later analysis. Around the table should be: a government spokesperson who supports having nuclear weapons; an anti-nuclear protester; a Christian (or Muslim); a scientist working on the development of nuclear weapons. Devise questions for the panel – it may help if you give them some warning.

3 Devise a piece of artwork expressing your own views on nuclear weapons.

4 Use you imagination. It is the year 2500. There was a global nuclear war in the year 2002. You have in your hand a holographic history book which explains how the nuclear war came about and what happened afterwards. What's in the book?

5 You are a Minister of the Church of Scotland. You must give a talk to your youth group – 'Why nuclear weapons are evil'. Write the speech you will give.

Evaluation

To what extent can you be a Christian and support having and using nuclear weapons?

Assessment question

Outcome 2 Your government wants to abolish its stocks of nuclear weapons. It has decided to carry out a referendum. Clare the Christian, Eddie the Egoist and Ursula the Utilitarian each receive their voting papers. Decide how they will vote and write a short explanation for the decision each one makes.

Homework

Design your own questionnaire about nuclear weapons. Ask your questions of as many people as possible and write up your findings.

6 GENDER ISSUES

DEPENDENCE AND INDEPENDENCE

CASE STUDY

A woman's education must therefore be planned in relation to man. To be pleasing in his sight, to win his respect and love, to train him in childhood, to tend him in manhood, to counsel and console, to make his life pleasant and happy, these are the duties of woman for all time, and this is what she should be taught when she is young.

Jean Jacques Rousseau (1712–78)

The 21st-century woman has certainly moved on from the little wife of the fifties. She now has a well-paid professional job which sees her work long hours and compete with men at the same level. However, her career break to have kids has meant that she's not been promoted just as far as her working husband. So when she goes home she does most of the housework – it's only fair. Her husband has to work late regularly, but she has managed to take work home. She may not cook the dinner, but she's organised the microwave ready meals. She'll do some ironing. Her husband was never taught how to. Anyway, people will assume she did it so she wants it to be done properly. She liaises with the childminder and acts as nursemaid when the kids are sick. When she spends time with the children she feels guilty because she's not working. When she works she feels guilty because the children are being neglected. She is the 21st century Superwoman – she even has time to make herself look good. A real improvement on the little lady at home of times past.

WHAT'S NEW?

Are women's lives better in the 21st century? Until World War One, most women stayed at home as housewives. Once they had shown they could do the same work as men (while the men were off fighting), many women began to ask for more in their working and social lives. In Britain, almost every job has now been done by a woman, including Prime Minister. Women professionals and businesswomen are common nowadays and it is not unusual for a woman to be 'the boss'. There are now househusbands (or genderless homemakers), and many jobs traditionally done by men are now done by women. However, some believe that women are still economically dependent upon men and that most men like to keep things that way. For many people, the 'new man' of the 21st Century isn't very different from the same old man he's always been.

PROVE IT

The UN's Universal Declaration of Human Rights states that in all respects, men and women should be considered equals. There should be no discrimination based on gender differences, in any society. However, such discrimination is often difficult to prove. This is especially true if it is very subtle. Is it discrimination if a woman is dependent upon a man? Also, does it count as discrimination if a husband 'persuades' his wife that she doesn't need to go out to work but should stay at home and raise a family? What about working practices, which make it very difficult for a woman to combine family life with working life? What about the use of women in advertising? What about the rebirth of events such as Miss World? Are these examples of the exploitation of women by a male society? Or are they examples of the new-found freedoms that the 21st Century woman now has?

WOMEN'S EQUALITY IS A HUMAN RIGHT

In September 1995, Hillary Rodham Clinton, now a US Senator, gave a speech to the UN's fourth World Conference on Women in Beijing. In addition to saying; 'Most women around the world work both inside and outside the home, usually by necessity', she also stated:

As long as discrimination and inequities remain so commonplace around the world – as long as girls and women are valued less, fed less, fed last, overworked, underpaid, not schooled and subjected to violence in and out of their home – the potential of the human family to create a peaceful, prosperous world will not be realised.

FIGURE 6.1 *Hillary Clinton*

Anita Roddick, founder of the Body Shop has said:

> *Women want to be free to choose from the same range of options that men take for granted. In our quest for equal pay, equal access to education and opportunities, we have made great strides. But until women can move freely and think freely in their homes, on the streets, in the workplace without the fear of violence, there can be no real freedom.*

DISCUSSION POINT

Is equality for women possible or desirable? Do we live in a man's world?

The Scottish Human Rights Centre campaigns for equal treatment for women. This is because anything else is an infringement of human rights. The Scotland Act (2000) and The Human Rights Act (2000) both aim to improve Scotland's treatment of human rights abuses. The Scottish Executive has put equal treatment of all sections in society as one of its first, and highest, priorities. The aim, eventually, is to set up a Scottish Human Rights Commission, which will oversee such issues, including the fair and equal treatment of women.

HAUD YER WESSHT WUMMIN'

Why do some people believe that women should be dependent upon men for their economic needs?

- Families are far more stable where there's a full-time mother at home looking after the children. Many social problems are related to lack of proper guidance at home. This is easier to do where a woman remains out of the workforce.
- It is more 'natural' for women to remain at home than go out and work. This is the way it has always been. Why should it change now? The 'instinct' of a woman is to look after children. Whereas a man's 'instincts' are more competitive and more suited to working life.
- Boys are not brought up to do domestic work, nor should they be, whereas girls are.
- A man is head of the household. He is in charge and makes the important decisions.

SISTERS ARE DOIN' IT FOR THEMSELVES

Many women find these arguments poor. They believe that a woman has the right to be independent from men and make her own way in the world:

- Being dependent on men is just another form of slavery. It is more likely to lead to the abuse and subjugation of women.

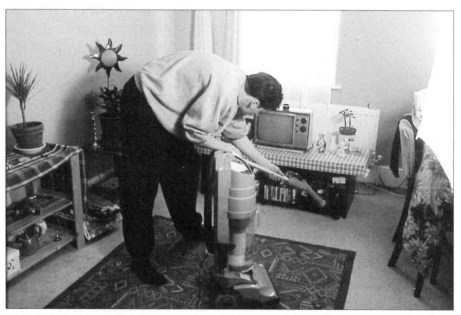

FIGURE 6.2 *A househusband*

◆ The ideas of gender roles are wrong. It's no more natural for a woman to stay at home than a man. Some men are better 'mothers' than women. Also what makes anyone think that a woman is better at housework than a man?

◆ Like men, women should have the right to make their own choices about their role in society. Society is based on what's best for men. Why should women have to fit in to that? Why should they change how they look to match men's ideas of 'attractive'?

◆ Even if women are different, why is this always seen as 'worse'. Even if women were more emotional, more caring, more 'irrational', why is this seen as bad? Just because women don't always do things in a 'man's way', does that make what they do any less valuable?

◆ Men and women must be educated – while boys and girls – to be able to do the same kinds of things. If a man hasn't been taught how to dust, vacuum and iron, he can easily learn.

◆ Why should a man be 'in charge'?

FEMINISM – REACTION OR REVOLUTION?

For some men, the word 'feminist' is often used as a term of abuse. However, feminism is a belief system or philosophy which is often backed up by very practical action. It sees itself as a very positive force.

Feminists believe that we live in a society dominated by men and a male way of looking at the world. They argue that in every respect, women should be treated as the independent equals of men. Early feminists, like the suffragettes, won the right for women to vote. Later, feminists contributed to improvements in how women are treated at work and also how they are treated at home. However, some feminists argue that feminism lost its way for a while. It achieved its limited goals and then let it end there, rather than pushing on and taking full advantage of them. In her famous book, *The Female Eunuch*, Germaine Greer claims that after the suffragettes, until quite recently, feminism became *'ever more respectable. Evangelism withered into eccentricity.'* She also argued that feminism needed to move on. It wasn't just about work but about the whole view of women by men and how women would try to conform to it. This meant, for example, that women would alter their body shape to please men. Or they might abandon their own 'feminine qualities' to be more like men. She finishes by saying that women's equality shouldn't just be tinkering with the details but a complete change in how women see their role in life:

Reaction is not revolution ... Revolution is the festival of the oppressed ... To be emancipated from helplessness and need and walk freely upon the earth, that is your birthright. The old process must be broken, not made new.

MORAL RESPONSES

The organisation, **Christians** for Biblical Equality argues that the Bible teaches that, in all respects, men and women are equal. Both are created in God's image (Genesis 1:26–8) as equal partners (Genesis 2:18). Both were jointly responsible for the Fall (Genesis 3:6). Jesus came to save all humanity, men and women alike (John 1:12–13). The gifts of the Holy Spirit are given to men and women equally (Acts 2:1–21). Women are to exercise all the religious duties of men (Acts 2:17–18 and 21:9; Philemon 4:23). Although men might be thought of as 'head' of the family (Ephesians 5:21–33), this just gives them responsibility not unlimited power. Children are the equal responsibility of men and women (Exodus 20:12; Deuteronomy 6:6–9; Colossians 3:20; Luke 2:51). It argues that, in the family: *Husband and wife are to defer to each other in seeking to fulfil each other's preferences... neither is to seek to dominate the other but each is to act as the servant of the other.*

Many Christians believe that the traditional family has been harmed by women going out to work but some argue that it is no more a Christian belief that the man should go out to work than the woman. Christians believe that men and women should complement each other but that they should be treated as equals, with equality of respect and opportunity. The treatment of a woman by a man should be just as caring and considerate as the treatment of humanity by God. To keep a woman dependent upon you as a way of keeping her 'beneath' you is therefore wrong.

Muslims believe that women should be allowed freedom in many respects. The Prophet Muhammed was once asked who you should obey. Three times he replied 'your mother'. Only after he was asked again did he reply 'your father'. Obviously women are thought of as very important in Islam. However, many people in the West still believe that Muslim women are kept in their place by their dependence upon men – at least compared to Western women. Many Muslim women reject this idea. They claim that their treatment is protective not smothering. Muslim men are 'head of the household' but, in practice, many Muslim men leave such responsibilities to the woman – if she is better able to oversee them than he is. Muslims also appreciate the different stresses and strains women may have to experience biologically – for example, menstruation and childbirth. Many rules have been designed to protect women especially during such times. Fatima Meruissi, a Muslim women's writer, argues in her book, *Beyond the Veil*, that Muslim women are not seen as submissive and passive, but 'powerful and dangerous ... All sexual institutions can be [seen as a way of] containing her power.' According to the Qur'an, women are to be treated as individuals in their own right. They have the right to own and dispose of property as they please, to buy and sell, and to spend their money as they please. Muhammed's own first wife, Khadijah, was a rich woman. Before he married her she was his employer. Islam doesn't accept discrimination based on race, wealth or gender. Men and women were created equal (Surah 49:13). Equal rights should therefore remain, they may just take a different form to what is common in the West.

Male or female **Egoists** might support the idea of the '21st century Superwoman'. For a man, the idea that a woman can work, look after the home, raise children will mean that the pressure is off him and he can pursue his own career – or just be very lazy. The female Egoist might like the idea of being competent at everything, although probably the thrill of being so 'super' might wear off before long. Egoists would think of equal treatment for women as a human right only if it brought them personal benefit. It would have to be shown that granting women full equality would do this. A male Egoist might like a woman being dependent on him because this might make him feel powerful and give him an excuse to 'lord it' over a woman. He might also dislike it because such dependence would be a drain on his resources, meaning that he has to work even harder to support himself and his woman too. A female Egoist might also like being dependent upon a man – this gives her freedom to do as she pleases. However, she might dislike it because it would mean that she has a lot less control over her own life. Both might reject feminism if it made their life more uncomfortable, by, for example, demanding better treatment for women. Also they might both support feminism because its actions might make their lives easier.

The **Utilitarian** John Stuart Mill argued that the fair treatment of women was necessary for society as a whole to flourish. He argued that men needed to listen to women in the first place to find out what their needs and wants were:

> We may safely assert that the knowledge that men can acquire of women ... is wretchedly imperfect and superficial and will always be so until women themselves have told all that they have to tell.

In his book, *The Subjugation of Women*, he wrote that society would only be truly happy when men and women were treated completely equally. In 1869, he wrote a letter to a friend, Alexander Bain, which is feminist in its tone: 'The most important thing women have to do is stir up the zeal of women themselves.' Here, he seems to be suggesting that women play an active part in securing their own rights. As far as women being dependent upon men is concerned he wrote:

> The principle which regulates the existing social relations between the two sexes – the legal subordination of one sex to the other – is wrong in itself, and now one of the chief hindrances to human improvement; and ... it ought to be replaced by a principle of perfect equality, admitting no power or privilege on the one side, nor disability on the other.

Utilitarians argue that the maximum social happiness is only likely where full equality of the sexes is in place. For one to be dependent upon the other makes little sense.

ACTIVITIES

Knowledge & Understanding

1 State **one** thing Rousseau said about a woman's education.
2 What things might the '21st-century Superwoman' do?
3 How did World War One make women ask for more in their lives?
4 What does the UN say about women's rights?
5 In your own words, state what Hillary Clinton and Anita Roddick said about women's rights.

6 Give **one** reason why someone might think a woman should be dependent on a man.
7 Give **one** reason why a woman might believe she has a right to her own independence.
8 What do feminists believe?
9 Give **one** reason why a Christian might think a woman is a man's equal.
10 Why might Muhammed's first wife be used as an example of the independence of women?
11 What might an Egoist think about feminism?

Analysis

1 Using newspaper and magazine cuttings, design a poster: 'The 21st-century Superwoman'.
2 Make your own class display of famous women. Include images as well as writing.
3 Draw up a code of practice for your school, which aims to ensure that life is made easier for mothers who are also teachers in your school. What things could be done?
4 The Miss World show comes to a town near you. Prepare a campaign in its support/rejecting it and carry out a class debate using the points you have covered.
5 Find out about the ways in which women are poorly treated around the world. Present your findings in a brief report.
6 What **three** things could feminist groups do to improve the place of women in society?
7 Have a class discussion: 'Women need men like a fish needs a bicycle'. Make sure that the two moral responses are represented in your discussions.

Evaluation

'It is more natural for a woman than for a man to bring up children'.
Do you agree? Give at least **two** reasons for your answer.

Assessment question

Outcome 2 'When a woman is dependent upon a man, it's just another kind of slavery.'
How might a religious person and an Egoist respond to this?

Homework

In what ways are girls treated equally/unequally with boys in your school? Write down some points for discussion in your next class.

ACTIVITIES

Knowledge & Understanding

1 In what way is the '21st-Century Superwoman' story being ironic?
2 Why is discrimination based on gender often difficult to prove?
3 Why did Hillary Clinton think that the fair treatment of women matters to everyone?
4 Do you agree that 'families are more stable where there's a full-time mother at home...'? Explain your answer.
5 Why might boys be brought up to think that some things are 'women's work'? Whose 'fault' is this? Should it change? How?
6 Why might some feminists oppose and others not mind the use of make-up?
7 What did Germaine Greer say feminism should be about?
8 Do all religious people believe that a woman's place is at home? Explain your answer.
9 How might an Egoist respond to the idea of the 21st-century Superwoman?
10 What does J S Mill's letter to Alexander Bain tell us about the Utilitarian attitude towards women's rights?
11 What did J S Mill think about women being dependent upon men?

Analysis

1 Debate the following: 'This house believes that society will never properly improve until women have full and equal rights'. Have representatives of each of the moral stances ask questions of the debaters.
2 Design **two** brief information leaflets: a) Why women should be independent; b) Why women need men.
3 You are a member of the Scottish Executive. You are setting up a Scottish Human Rights Commission to look at the rights of women in Scotland. a) Who might you have on this committee? b) What tasks would you give it to do? c) How might it go about finding out what the treatment of women in Scotland is like?
4 Prepare a short report based on a week's newspaper items on the rights of women (you may need to buy more than one newspaper). Use each article as the basis for a brief report on the issues involved.

Evaluation

'Society benefits where men and women stick to their traditional roles.'
How far do you agree?

Assessment Question

Outcome 2 'The role of a man is to protect a woman from the hardships of everyday life.'
How might a religious person, an Egoist and a Utilitarian respond to this statement?

Homework

What activities are modern feminists involved in? Find **one** example of feminist activity today and prepare a short talk for your class on what you have found.

OPPORTUNITY AT WORK

CASE STUDY

FIGURE 6.3 Equal Opportunities Commission poster

THE CLAIMS

Feminists and women's rights groups still claim that women are treated unfairly at work in relation to men. This unfairness can take a number of forms:

- Women doing the same job as men may be paid less for it. This is illegal under the Equal Pay Act, but employers might try to prove that the difference in pay is not based on gender.
- Women may feel that they have not progressed up the 'promotion ladder' as fast as male colleagues. Some also feel that there is a point of promotion beyond which women can't go. This is often called a 'glass ceiling' because you can see beyond it but can't get through it.
- Some jobs are still regarded by employers as 'men's work'. 'Men only' jobs are (almost always) illegal. However, it is often difficult to prove that women are being discriminated against based on gender.
- There is still great inequality between the types of jobs men and women have. For example, the 'lower' or more menial the job the more likely it is to be done by a woman, and 'higher status' jobs are more likely to be held by men.

MEN ONLY

Some women's groups argue that the reason for this inequality is simple. The world of work is still run by men. Men do not intend to give up their unfair advantage by promoting equal pay or treatment for women. This is just another example of men keeping women 'in their place'. Society is *patriarchal*; this means that it is run by men for their own benefit. This patriarchy, based on relationships in the home, spills over into working life. This is all based on the old-fashioned traditional idea that woman is the 'weaker sex' or that women take second place to men for other reasons. Some women's groups argue that these traditional views are held onto because they are beneficial for the men who hold them.

Women's groups point to the number of famous women throughout history – including those who have had positions of power in their working lives. These women show that women are just as capable of any job as a man. Some cultures in the world are matriarchal, although this is often only in relation to ceremonial or traditional matters.

I'M ALL FOR EQUALITY BUT ...

Some men believe that there are reasons for treating women differently at work. Judge them for yourself:

- Women are not suited to the same kinds of work as men – for a variety of reasons, from physical strength to emotional stability.

DISCUSSION POINT

Do you think that any of these claims are true? What evidence do you have?

DISCUSSION POINT

Do you think there are some jobs which are 'men's work' or 'women's work'?

◆ Women can get pregnant and may put work after family life. Besides, it is 'natural' for a woman to stay at home to look after children. It is the man's role to go out to work. This is not discrimination, it's a way of protecting women.

◆ Women don't have the same level of 'aggression' as men. This means they're not 'ruthless' or 'ambitious' enough at work. This is why they don't get promoted as far as men.

Feminists might respond:

◆ Women are suited to all kinds of work. There is no such thing as a typical woman – or man. You judge each *person* on their own merits for a job.

◆ Not all women want to raise a family. Why should a man not take on this role? Besides, perhaps working life should be built around family needs anyway.

◆ Some women are perfectly ambitious. It's just in a different form to men's. Why should 'aggression' be the only way to get on in working life?

Some men argue that the treatment of women at work is different because of the natural differences between men and women, which have always existed. Feminists respond that just because something has always 'been that way' doesn't make it right or unchangeable. Why should we still behave like cavemen and women in the 21st century?

FIGURE 6.4 *Not equal or just different?*

FORBIDDEN TO WOMEN

There is one category of work where even sex discrimination laws can't interfere. In the Christian Church, some denominations forbid women to become ordained clergy. The Church of Scotland, and other reformed denominations has had women Ministers for some years now and these seem to be widely accepted in the Church. The Episcopalian Church has more recently accepted the ordination of women. In England, this caused major disagreement within the Church of England – leading to people leaving the Church and congregations refusing to appoint women priests. The Roman Catholic Church remains opposed to women priests. At least, the Vatican and the Church authorities do. Whether ordinary Catholics feel this way is another issue.

The Roman Catholic Church argues that having women priests is wrong because:

- The tradition of the Church has been against the ordination of women. Traditions should be upheld.
- Abandoning this important tradition might mean that other traditions could be abandoned too, for example, the importance of marriage etc.
- Just because Equality is important in the modern world, it doesn't mean that the Church must blindly follow. The Church must be true to itself. It cannot change its views just to fit in with whatever is trendy at the time.
- Priests are meant to represent Jesus on earth. They are 'stand-ins' for the person of Jesus. As Jesus was male, so the priest must be male too.
- Jesus had no female disciples, so it is safe to assume that he did not mean women to act in priestly roles.
- There are many other roles for women in the Church. You do not need to be a priest to make your contribution or to live out your faith.

Supporters of the ordination of women (which include many men) argue:

- Jesus gave a high priority to women. He had no female disciples but many women followers. He made no distinction between men and women as followers.
- To say that a woman cannot represent Jesus is wrong. When a person represents Jesus, they represent what he taught and who he was in his nature – not his gender.
- The Church has changed its views to match changed situations throughout its history – why not on this?
- Tradition is valuable but it should be flexible to meet the needs of the day. God speaks to people now – not just in the past. God's message is to be understood in the circumstances in which we find ourselves. The Church must 'move with the times'.

DISCUSSION POINT

Do you think women should be able to become priests?

FIGURE 6.5 *A female Church of Scotland Minister*

Supporters of the ordination of women argue that it is not a matter of them choosing to be priests. God chooses them. They believe that the Holy Spirit gives them the necessary 'gifts' to be able to do the job. Why, then, do the human authorities of the Church deny women the opportunity to exercise their ministry? The Church replies that it has the responsibility of interpreting God's will. What people believe God is telling them to do has to be balanced up with the traditions of the Church and the thinking of those in power in the Church. There could be problems if the Church just accepted – from everyone – the argument that 'God told me to do it'.

How does your black waistcoat
Button me out of the Church?
Each button to be unfastened
Before I can creep in
through a button-hole
And hide in your handkerchief pocket
You fear me, and fasten yourself
neatly, tightly, up to the neck
So that I will not be your undoing.

Rev Flora Winfield: 'Dancing on Mountains'

In terms of doctrine there is no justification for women in the priesthood. This is not discrimination. It is a part of the plan of salvation that priests should be chosen from among men.

Vatican Declaration, 1977

FACTS AND FIGURES

◆ Since 1977, there have been 12,344 tribunals where women have claimed unfair discrimination at work in relation to equal pay with men. They won 632 of these (EOC).
◆ In 1998 in the UK, there were 18,700,000 men of working age, 15,700,000 had jobs. Of the 17,100,000 women of working age, 12,200,000 had jobs.
◆ In the same year, 26% of working women and 6% of working men had jobs classed as 'clerical and secretarial'.

Source: Office for National Statistics

MORAL RESPONSES

For **Christians**, the issue is whether equal treatment always produces the best society. Most Christians would oppose direct discrimination because 'all are one'. Man and woman were made equals at the creation. They would argue that freedom is important for each individual. For many people, work gives them a sense of identity and purpose. If you are a woman and choose to work, then that should be your affair. If you are a working woman, then there is no reason why you should be treated any differently to a man – either in what you are allowed to do or how much you're paid. However, many more traditional Christians believe that the problem with working women is the effect their work has on the traditional family. They believe that men and women are equal but different (complementarity). Women have different contributions to make to family life. Some Christians believe that it is a woman's 'nature' to nurture and look after children and so they should do this and not go out to work. However, there is no direct Biblical teaching on this, so it is mostly a matter of tradition.

The issue of women priests has caused great division in Christianity. Key Biblical texts are hotly debated:

◆ *Possible support for a strong role for women in Christianity*: John 20:10–18; Galatians 3:26–8; Romans 16; Philemon 4:11; 2 Corinthians 8:23; Acts 2:17–18.

◆ *Possible opposition to a strong role for women in Christianity*: 1 Corinthians, 14:34–35; 1 Timothy 2:8–14.

For Christians, the tension is between 'moving with the times' and 'sticking to their traditions'. However, many supporters of women priests argue that its not in human hands anyway:

People don't choose to be priests, God chooses you – if you're a woman, so be it.

In **Islam**, there is no restriction on working women. Also, women should be treated equally with men while at work – as everywhere else (Surah 2:228). In Muslim societies, women often have positions of power and responsibility. Many Muslims argue that Islamic society gave women full and equal rights long before the West (eg Surah 4:7–9). There have been women leaders in Islamic states (like Benazir Bhutto in Pakistan). However, there are traditionalists who believe that it is better for a woman to stay at home and have the responsibility of looking after the family. This is not seen as a way of keeping a woman 'in her place', but instead as a form of protection because working life is often hard and pressurised. If you can protect your wife from it then you are doing her a favour. Staying at home helps you avoid many unpleasant things 'outside'. Also, Muslims believe that the raising of a family is the most important thing. Work provides the money to support that important task (Surah 4:34), but the woman is given the most important role of all – ensuring that the children are brought up in a caring, believing environment.

Islam does not have a priesthood as such, however, there are Imams in each mosque, as well as other teachers and leaders. The role of women in these positions has not been the subject of debate in Islam in the same way. In Islamic society, there are women who are teachers of the faith. Again, however, there are traditionalists who argue that this should not be the case because it is giving women a 'pressure' that they should be protected from. The Islamic Propagation Centre says:

Islam makes one realise that ... the responsibilities of men and women are equally important in themselves but not exactly the same. The roles of men and women are complementary to each other.

Egoist views on women at work might depend upon whether you were a male or female Egoist. A male Egoist might support discrimination against women at work, because this means he'll have less competition for promotion and it might keep more competent female workers out of his way. The male Egoist might have no problem with unequal pay or conditions of work for women. However, if his female partner wanted to work and earn good money, he might support her right to do so because this would make his life better. A female Egoist might want to be treated equally in the workplace in all respects. On the other hand, she might quietly welcome discrimination because it could give her an 'excuse' to stay at home and be supported by her male partner. The same views might apply to the ordination of women. Male Egoists might reject it because it could have negative effects on them or support it if they thought it would bring benefits somehow. Female Egoists would uphold their right to do as they please – including becoming priests if they wanted to. They might also oppose it for many reasons. For example, they might quite like the role they have in their church and not want to feel pressure to take on more responsibility.

Utilitarians would need to take into account the wider social implications of working women. For example, if women working has harmful effects on social life generally, then they might oppose it. Some people argue that it is unfair that some families have 'two breadwinners' while others have none. Encouraging women to stay at home and raise a family might be a solution to this. Utilitarians might argue that family life is most stable where there is a full-time carer at home, rather than someone trying to juggle work and family responsibilities. If greater equality for women leads to fewer women at home then this could cause problems for society generally, leading to more 'latchkey kids' who are not as well supervised as they could be by a non-working mother. Of course, a Utilitarian might equally argue that a man could carry out this role. On the other hand, if work brings fulfilment, then why should a woman be denied this because of her gender. This would not produce pleasure for the individual, so perhaps also not for society as a whole. Furthermore, it would be an unhappy society where people were treated differently at work because of their gender. The maximum happiness is only likely where everyone is treated fairly in relation to their pay and conditions of work. Any form of discrimination brings unhappiness. If women choose to work, there can't be any reason to treat them differently, but the Utilitarian might think that society is best served by women choosing to take on family responsibilities.

ACTIVITIES

Knowledge & Understanding

1 Explain in your own words what the 'pocket money' quote means.

2 State **two** ways in which a woman might claim she's being treated unfairly at work.

3 Give **one** reason *why* a woman might be treated unfairly at work.

4 In what way might it benefit men to discriminate against women at work?

5 In your own words, state **one** response a feminist might make to discrimination at work.

6 Give **two** reasons why the Roman Catholic Church is against the ordination of women.

7 What point do you think Rev Flora Winfield's poem is trying to make?

8 Why do some traditional Christians oppose women going out to work?

9 What do Muslims believe is the 'most important task of all'?

10 State **one** way in which a male and female Egoist might disagree about equal pay for women.

Analysis

1 Design your own poster, like the one from the EOC, which encourages fair and equal treatment for women at work.

2 Carry out a survey of positions of authority in your school. What is the male/female balance? Now do the same for the parents of people in your class. Are men still in more important jobs than women?

3 Devise a role play as follows: *Susan recently had an interview at work for promotion. She didn't get it. However, someone she thinks is far less capable than she is and who hasn't nearly as much experience got it. He is a man. She goes to the boss who interviewed her to argue that she has been discriminated against because she is a woman.*

4 You are a member of a Roman Catholic Church. The Vatican has asked your Church to give its views on the possible ordination of women priests. Your Church meets to discuss the issues. Write two short speeches to be given. One in favour and one against.

5 To inform the people at this meeting, draw up a short information leaflet for and against the issue.

Evaluation

'Women should be treated equally with men in the workplace.'
Do you agree? Give at least **two** reasons for your answer.

Assessment question

Outcome 3 'A woman has as much right to become a priest as a man.'
Do you agree? Give **two** reasons for your answer.

Homework

Find one newspaper article about the rights of women at work. Make a short presentation to your class about it.

ACTIVITIES

Knowledge & Understanding

1 What might make it difficult for a woman to prove that being treated differently at work is gender discrimination?

2 Why might a 'patriarchal' society treat women unfairly?

3 State **one** 'reason' which might be given for treating women at work differently. Add your own criticism of this 'reason'.

4 How might a feminist respond to gender discrimination?

5 Why do you think the ordination of women priests in England has led to so much division?

6 Why does the Roman Catholic Church think tradition is important?

7 How might a potential female priest argue that she can still 'represent Jesus'?

8 Choose **one** Biblical reference for and **one** against the equal treatment of women. Explain its teaching in your own words.

9 What does a Muslim mean when he says that 'keeping' a woman at home is a form of 'protection'?

10 Why might a female Egoist support gender discrimination?

11 Would a Utilitarian support the idea of working mothers? Explain.

Analysis

1 Prepare a display board showing the two sides in the argument about equal treatment for women at work.

2 How might the Scottish Executive promote equal treatment of women at work? Draw up some suggestions for it to consider.

3 Debate the statement: 'A woman's place is in the kitchen.' Ensure that the moral stances you have studied are represented.

4 Using the Biblical references in Christianity, write a brief report either supporting or opposing the ordination of women.

5 In order to spread wealth around more evenly, the government takes the step of making it illegal for a husband and wife living together to both go out to work. How might a representative of the moral stances you have studied each respond to this idea. Write a letter from each one to their MSP outlining their views.

Evaluation

'A woman's place is in the home.'
How far do you agree?

Assessment question

Outcome 3 'Opposing the ordination of women is just another way for men to keep women "in their place".'
To what extent do you agree?

Homework

Using one of the moral stances you have studied, explain in your own words its views on the equal treatment of women at work.

VIOLENCE AGAINST WOMEN

CASE STUDY

Are you being abused?
These are some things that someone close to you could be doing:
Hitting you; threatening you; forcing you to have sex; threatening the children; abusing your children; breaking things in the house; keeping you short of money; playing mind games with you; accusing you of being unfaithful; ridiculing your beliefs; isolating you from friends and family; using contact with the children to abuse you or the children;
This could make you feel:
frightened; degraded; unable to make decisions; trapped.

If any of these apply to you, you are experiencing domestic abuse. You don't have to put up with it. No-one deserves to be abused, so it is not your fault in any way. Don't believe what he says to you – whatever you do won't change how he treats you.

North Ayrshire Women's Aid

DOMESTIC VIOLENCE

Most violence against women takes place in the home. One in 10 women experience domestic violence in the UK each year, one in four at some point in their lives. However, around 64% of women who have suffered domestic violence do not seek help. Violence at home is far more common than any other kind of violence. Domestic violence can take many forms, from subtle mental abuse – like putting someone down all the time – to serious physical and sexual abuse. Until relatively recently, sex in marriage was considered a right, and only within the recent past has it been accepted that marital rapes take place. Around half of all murders of women are committed by their partners or ex-partners.

VIEWS OF WOMEN

The charity *Zero Tolerance* found that a large number of Scottish teenagers said that it was sometimes acceptable for a husband to hit his wife. On Boxing Day 2000, a series of adverts about domestic abuse was launched – the campaign is called 'Domestic Bliss'.

Domestic violence depends in part on how people view women. For a long time, women were thought to be unequal to men and so did not deserve the same rights as men. Men saw themselves as 'head of the household', and so able to exert their 'authority' over women however they saw fit. Attitudes around the world vary, but it is only during recent times that the idea of equal treatment for women has become more accepted. Some women's rights campaigners and feminists say that we've still got a long way to go. They would argue that the fact that there is still so much violence against women shows that men still see women as second-class citizens.

DISCUSSION POINT

What do you think are the most common causes of domestic violence?

1 in 5 women
live with the
constant threat
of domestic abuse.

That's 1 in 5 too many.

A recent survey suggests that domestic abuse
is deeply entrenched in our society.
It affects women of all ages, across all
social classes. It can be physical, though it
doesn't have to be. But it's never acceptable.

FIGURE 6.6 *Domestic Bliss campaign*

A PERSONAL ISSUE OR A PROBLEM WITH SOCIETY?

The issue is not whether violence against women is right or wrong, but why it still seems to be tolerated in the 21st century. Women's rights groups argue that violence against women is an abuse of power by men – there are no excuses for it. It is a social problem. It's linked to social structures, values and attitudes which let inequality continue. The conditions for violence to occur are created by society favouring men's needs over women's.

What are the underlying features?

Personal issues

◆ Some violence against women may be caused by naturally violent men.

◆ Some men might see it as a way to exercise power. Using aggression to control another person may be thought of as a way of showing 'who wears the trousers'. This usually reflects an inadequacy in the man, because he feels the need to use such a tactic to make himself feel good. Oddly enough, many men who abuse their partners appear very respectable. No-one might ever guess that they are abusers.

- Much domestic violence occurs in situations where a woman is economically dependent upon a man. This will mean that she might feel that she has 'no choice' but to accept abuse – because she has nowhere else to go. However, domestic violence also occurs throughout the social classes.
- Many women might accept abuse as a way of protecting their children. Men who abuse women often abuse their own children too.
- Some women genuinely believe that their partner will change for the better. Some women think that they can 'cure' their men of the abuse. They might still love the person and make excuses for him. This kind of belief allows the violence to continue.

Social issues

- Society turns a blind eye to domestic abuse. Many people do not want to know about it. Some think that when it happens, a woman should just leave her partner.
- Society's view of men and women generally contributes to domestic violence. Women are treated as weak and submissive and men as strong and dominant. Women are still portrayed on TV and in the media generally as there for the benefit of men. The easy availability of pornography, including the subtle use of soft pornography (for example, 'page three girls') can lead men to think that women are there for their use.
- Such views of women are also probably major factors in acts of violence against women which do not take place in a relationship. Rapes, for example, are generally agreed not to be about sex but about the urge to control and exert power over a woman. Rapists are often people whose violent fantasies have been fed by attitudes towards women generally, including pornography.
- The traditional roles of men and women are difficult to unlearn. For so long, men have been thought of as the breadwinners and women the home-makers. This kind of view, where men are seen as 'head of the house' and therefore in charge, might lead some men to think that they can use whatever means they think they need to stay in charge. This might include the use of violence.
- Many women argue that society is biased in favour of men, and always has been. Therefore, violence against women is not tackled by society as seriously as it should be.

DISCUSSION POINT

Do you agree that society is biased in favour of men?

WHAT CAN BE DONE?

There are steps which many women's groups suggest might help end violence against women:

- less use of women in submissive and weak roles in the media.
- tighter controls on pornography, including soft porn.

- more serious treatment of violence against women by the legal system. For example, tougher sentences for rapists and abusers.
- better funding of agencies which help abused women – for example, rape crisis centres and 'women's refuges'.
- better education about the relationship between men and women.
- zero tolerance of any kind of ill treatment of women and girls from primary school onwards.
- a move away from a male-dominated society.

CASE STUDY

Karen (not her real name) speaks of her years of abuse:
'I married my husband in Glasgow in 1983. We're both professional people. He was as charming as you could be before we were married. Soon after our wedding though, he began to change. It started with simple things like criticising how I looked, or that there was no bread left – stupid things like that. This was often after he'd had a drink or two. We had a little girl and this seemed to stop him being nasty to me ... for a while. When she was about three it started again. He was working very hard, and would come home and drink and then get quite aggressive with me and our daughter. Soon, he got more abusive. One night, he was shouting at our daughter for spilling something. I 'got in his way', and he hit me. I was shocked, but I just put it down to him being tired, stressed and having had too much to drink. However, this became common. He'd get worked up and thump me for no reason. To all his friends and relatives he was the perfect gentleman – you'd never have known the temper on him. One night I told him he should get some help and he really let me have it. I told friends I'd fallen down the stairs, but I think by then they knew what was going on. I kept hoping that he'd 'snap out of it'. Maybe his work would get easier or something. Then one day he hit our daughter. Then I knew he was beyond our help. One night, when he was away on business, we left. My daughter's now 12, she hasn't seen her father since she was eight. I'm still terrified that one day he'll find us. I don't know what he'd do.'

FACTS AND FIGURES

- Women aged 20–34 are most likely to experience domestic abuse.
- Between February and November 1998, police in Scotland attended almost 7000 domestic incidents. This is around one every hour (Strathclyde Police, 1998).
- Around 1,155,600 adult American women have been forcibly raped by their husbands (University of South Carolina, 1992).

FIGURE 6.7 *A womens' rights activist in Islamabad burns bed sheets taken from hospital beds on which two female victims died. Their injuries were burns-related, and they were caused by domestic abuse*

MORAL RESPONSES

The overall message of **Christianity** is anti-violence. Christians are taught to respond to violence with understanding, not with further violence. The principle is one of 'turning the other cheek' (Matthew 5:39). However, this doesn't mean that a wife should accept violence from her husband. Christians believe that the marriage relationship is special (often sacramental). In this relationship, both partners have responsibilities towards each other and should care for each other. Being violent towards each other would not meet this requirement. Some Christians believe that the Genesis creation story suggests that men are 'in charge' of women but Christians do not believe this means a man can treat his wife any way he wants. Jesus responded to women with respect – even those who had committed sin or were outcasts. He treated a prostitute with respect and kindness (Luke 8:1–3). He also forgave the woman who had been caught in adultery, protecting her from the violent reaction of others. Violence against women, whether it is physical, emotional or of any other kind, goes against the whole principle of Christian teachings. Paul's ideas about women are mixed. On the one hand, he says that 'the husband is the head of the wife' (Ephesians 5:23) and that women should 'obey their husbands' (Colossians 3:18), but he also suggests that 'male and female are equal' (Galatians 3:28). Paul's writings about the relationship between men and women may be related to specific situations. However many have used his teachings to justify treating women as 'inferior' to men. Nevertheless, Paul unmistakably opposes domestic violence:

Husbands, love your wives and do not be harsh with them.

Colossians 3:19

Muslims think that the treatment of women in Islam is an example for all to follow. In Muhammed's final sermon, he made a point of reminding his followers to treat women with respect. Men and women are to have responsibility towards each other (Surah 30:21). This obviously suggests that violence against women should be avoided. The Qur'an teaches that men are 'the protectors and maintainers of women'. This means that men have the responsibility of looking after women. However, this Surah goes on to say:

> As to those women on whose part you see ill conduct, admonish them (first), (next) refuse to share their beds (and last) beat them (lightly, if it is useful).
>
> Surah 4:34

Modern Muslims argue that this is not to be an excuse for violence against women because:
- It is far less than the much harsher treatment that a woman might have received from her husband in Arabia before Islam – and so, at the time, it was an 'improvement'.
- It is to be 'used lightly' and as a way of turning someone away from evil and back to good – and so is 'helpful'.

Muslims argue that the treatment of women in the Qur'an stresses care and kindness far more than this Surah. Women are to be equal partners in any relationship. To use this Surah as a justification for violence against women is wrong. It is certainly wrong to use it as a way to suggest that a man should exercise his 'authority' (Surah 2:228) over a woman by the use of violence.

For the male **Egoist**, violence against women for any reason is obviously a possibility. If being violent against a woman can result in your own self-interest, then you may see it as an acceptable option. What you do in the privacy of your own home is your affair and no-one else's. On the other hand, the female Egoist would want violence against women for any reason subject to severe punishment so that she was protected. Being a female Egoist in a relationship with a man should not give that man complete rights over you as if you belonged to him. This is probably a very crude view of Egoism, however. It would be hard to show just how violence against women could be in an Egoist's self-interest whether the Egoist was male or female. For the male, violence against anyone – including your partner, carries with it serious risks. She might hit back or 'repay' you in some other way. You might be prosecuted and go to prison. She might leave you; or she might, as has sometimes been the case with people who are domestically abused, respond by killing you. Such acts have often been treated 'kindly' by the courts who realise that the woman has been provoked to the point where her actions were 'unavoidable'. Knowing all this, the male Egoist will want to avoid being violent towards his partner. Also, other people may treat you badly if they know (or even suspect) that you are an abuser. This is not in your self-interest. So, although the Egoist will decide based on his own wishes whether or not to be violent towards women, its probably true that on balance it's more likely *not* to be in his interests.

Utilitarians would oppose violence against women in all forms. The only 'happiness' such violence might produce might be the abuser's (and that's doubtful). For the majority, it is not likely to produce a happy and well-balanced society. In his book *The Subjugation of Women*, J S Mill says that not treating women equally with men is bad for both men and women. Equality of treatment is most likely to produce the greatest happiness for all. Obviously, this could be extended to include the issue of the violent treatment of women by men. A society which accepted or tolerated this would not be a very pleasant society in which to live. A lot of domestic violence is conveniently 'ignored' by society. Even here, this does not mean that the Utilitarian will accept it. Even if actions which produce pain are hidden, the pain is still real. Besides, a society which ignored this kind of violence might be more likely to ignore other kinds of violence too. The problems of domestic violence can also 'spill over' into other areas of life too – affecting people's work or social relationships. Domestic violence can also lead to children in such families being more likely to repeat this kind of behaviour when they are adults. This means that the violence has consequences far beyond any one relationship. All of this could have negative consequences for everyone. It is therefore in everyone's interests to be aware of domestic violence and to put an end to it wherever possible.

ACTIVITIES

Knowledge & Understanding

1 State **two** things which North Ayrshire Women's Aid calls abuse, and **two** things this might make you feel.

2 What proportion of women are likely to experience domestic abuse in their lifetime?

3 State **one** way in which how men see women and domestic abuse might be linked.

4 What is meant by the phrase 'a male abuse of power'?

5 Why might some women 'put up with' domestic violence?

6 How might pornography lead to violence against women?

7 State **one** thing which could be done to help end domestic violence.

8 Which age group is most likely to suffer domestic abuse?

9 State **one** way in which Jesus showed respect for women.

10 How might a Muslim explain Surah 4:34?

11 What different attitudes towards violence against women might a male/female Egoist have?

Analysis

1 Design and make a short information leaflet: 'What is domestic violence?'

2 Prepare a short TV advert, which raises awareness of violence against women.

3 Without using examples of soft pornography, make a collage of images from newspapers which might encourage men to have a negative view of women.

4 Draw up a list of conditions which you think might lead to domestic violence. Put them into two groups: *Personal* and *Social*.

5 Write a letter to your MSP. Outline your suggestions for helping to end violence against women in Scotland.

6 Write two letters to 'Karen', one from a religious person, one from an Egoist. What might each say?

7 Design your own poster opposing violence against women.

Evaluation

'Violence against women is everyone's problem.'
Do you agree? Give at least **two** reasons for your answer.

Assessment question

Outcome 2 How might a religious person and an Egoist argue that violence against women is wrong?

Homework

Find out about the work of **one** women's aid organisation. Prepare a short presentation for your class.

ACTIVITIES

Knowledge & Understanding

1 Why do you think so many women do not seek help when being abused?

2 Using the definitions of abuse from North Ayrshire Women's Aid: Do you think there are some forms of abuse which are 'worse' than others? Explain.

3 What does it mean to say that domestic abuse is a form of 'control'?

4 Why might society 'turn a blind eye to abuse'?

5 What 'excuses' might a woman make for her husband's violence?

6 In your opinion, which of the suggested responses to violence against women is likely to be the most effective? Explain.

7 What views did Paul have about women in general and violence against women?

8 In your opinion, does Surah 4:34 support violence against women? How might a Muslim explain this?

9 How might an Egoist (male or female) support opposition to violence against women?

10 State **two** arguments a Utilitarian might use in opposing violence against women.

Analysis

1 Discuss what you think the 'social structures, values and attitudes' might be that allow violence against women to continue. Write a summary of your ideas.

2 You are about to set up a 'refuge' for 'abused women'. Draw up a list of things you would need to consider in your preparations. How might you best support the victims of domestic abuse?

3 You are to tackle the subject of violence against women with a class of S3 boys. The aim is to raise their awareness of the issues and direct them away from violence towards women. How might you go about this? You should devise a short programme that you would run with them. You may like to make up information sheets, a presentation of some kind, activities etc. It might be possible to try this out with a class in your school (perhaps in SE or RE).

4 Have a class debate: *Education is the way to end violence against women.* Include representatives of each of the moral stances in your debate.

Evaluation

'In a male-dominated society, violence against women is inevitable.'
How far do you agree?

Assessment question

Outcome 3 'The most effective response to violence against women is tougher prison sentences for offenders.' To what extent do you agree?

Homework

Find out more about the extent of violence against women in Scotland. Prepare a short presentation for your class.

ECOLOGY AND ENVIRONMENT

TREATMENT OF ANIMALS

CASE STUDY

FIGURE 7.1 *Sue Savage communicating with Panbanisha*

Sitting on the forest floor opposite a haughty female ape I was completely taken aback when she tipped her head on one side and as she pressed the buttons on an electric keyboard, a synthesised voice said, 'Has the visitor brought a surprise?' Thankfully Bill, a researcher at the Georgia State University Language Research Centre, came to my aid saying, 'Yes, yes she has – she brought you some jello.' 'Good' came the satisfied response.

Julie Cohen talks with Panbanisha, a 14-year-old pygmy chimpanzee,

Geographical Magazine, May 2000, p58

WHAT RIGHTS?

Julie Cohen believes that we have to look again at the issue of animal rights. Harvard Law School has recently introduced an animal rights law course. New Zealand has made it illegal to use great apes in experiments. On the other hand, there are at least 200 laws relating to the treatment of animals in Britain today and many of these are routinely ignored.

Animals can't tell us how they would like to be treated, so we have to decide for ourselves. Humans have the 'power' to treat animals however we want. How should we use that power?

There are different views about how far animals should have rights.

- *Animals should have no rights*. Rights can only be given to creatures who can understand them and accept the responsibilities these rights involve. Animals can't understand the idea of rights so they shouldn't have any. Besides, if they had rights, then you would have to arrest animals who hurt each other.
- *Animals should have some rights*: Although not human, animals have their own value and should be respected. Just because something can't communicate with us shouldn't mean we can do what we want with it. We give rights to humans who can't understand what rights are, so why not animals?
- *Animals should have the same rights as humans*: Humans are just another form of animal. What makes us more special than any other species? If we don't give animals rights, then we are guilty of discrimination.
- *Different kinds of animals should have different rights*: It might be good to give animals some rights, but you couldn't give a fly the same rights as a horse.

There are also different reasons given for *why* animals should or should not have rights:

- Animals have their own worth (intrinsic value). They should be treated fairly because that's right.
- Animals should be treated fairly because they are of value to us (instrumental value). If we do not protect them, then we will lose the benefits they can bring to human life.
- Humans have a duty to protect the weak. Animals are 'weak' because they don't have our abilities. If an animal could communicate with us it would not want to be eaten. Besides the question should not be 'can animals communicate?' but 'can they suffer?'.
- If we respect animal life, we'll be more likely to respect human life too.
- The relationship between humans and animals has nothing to do with rights, it's just a part of nature. We have always used animals for our own benefit and should still do so. There's no good reason to give up our natural advantage.
- Human life comes first. If the use of an animal helps a human, then it should be done, whatever the 'cost' to the animal.

ANIMAL RIGHTS ISSUES

Animals as food

Arguments for:
- It is natural for humans to eat meat.

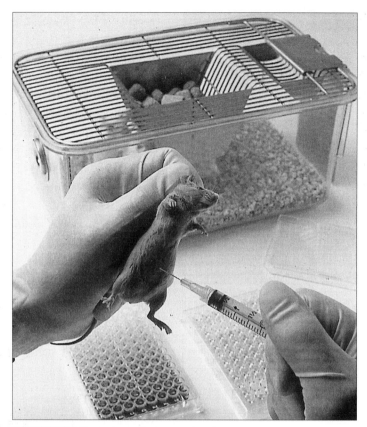

FIGURE 7.2 *Experimenting on animals*

- ◆ Humans need certain vitamins, which can only come from meat.
- ◆ The production of meat and slaughtering is controlled and not cruel – even 'factory farming' has improved recently.
- ◆ Animals eat each other too.

Arguments against:
- ◆ Meat is not necessary: all nutritional requirements can come from non-meat sources.
- ◆ Killing is always cruel and the treatment of animals in 'factory farms' is still unacceptable.
- ◆ It is an abuse of the weak by the strong.
- ◆ It is a waste of resources.

Hunting

Arguments for:
- ◆ It is traditional and maintains a way of life.
- ◆ It keeps the countryside in balance, protecting farm animals.
- ◆ Sometimes it is the only means of survival.
- ◆ It is a natural activity.

Arguments against:
- ◆ It is unnecessarily cruel.
- ◆ It harms the countryside more than it helps it.
- ◆ There is no need to hunt, agriculture and modern farming provide all our food needs.
- ◆ Just because something is 'traditional' doesn't make it right.

Cosmetic experiments

Arguments for:
- We need to ensure that products are safe for human use.
- There is no other reliable way to test cosmetics.
- Other methods would make the cosmetics too costly.

Arguments against:
- There are alternative ways to test cosmetics.
- The results of tests on animals are not always reliable anyway.
- Many tests are unnecessary – 'new' products are not needed, these are just ways to keep us buying the same 'old' things.

Medical experiments

Arguments for:
- We need to ensure that the products work and are safe for humans.
- You could not test a medicine, which might kill someone on a human.
- There is often no other way.
- The death of some animals could benefit many people – and other animals.

FIGURE 7.3 *Youngest member of a pro-hunting lobby protesting outside the Scottish Parliament*

◆ Human life comes first.

Arguments against:

◆ Drugs may not work the same way on humans as they do on animals.

◆ What makes it any more right to kill an animal during medical experiments – why should human life come first?

◆ There are alternative ways to test drugs.

◆ A lot of testing is not on life-saving drugs but things like headache pills and contraceptives.

Zoos

Arguments for:

◆ They help preserve endangered species.

◆ We can learn about animals and so be more likely to care for them in the wild.

◆ Animals in zoos are well looked after.

Arguments against:

◆ Repopulation of wild stocks from zoo-bred animals is very small – so they don't help endangered species.

◆ People don't learn much when they go to a zoo (other than that humans are in charge).

◆ No matter how good it is, a zoo is still an unnatural place for an animal to live.

Pets

Arguments for:

◆ They help us to learn about animals and so care for them.

◆ They are comforting for many people, particularly the elderly.

◆ They are well looked after.

◆ They often carry out important tasks for us, like guide dogs for example.

Arguments against:

◆ No-one really learns much from a pet, it just convinces children that animals are 'below' humans.

◆ Keeping an animal as a pet is unnatural, no matter how well they are treated.

◆ Pets are often expected to 'perform' for us – this is unnatural and degrading.

THE BIG PICTURE

For many people, the issue is this: If we change how we treat animals, what will be the effects on human life and the 'balance of nature'? Is our relationship with animals something that we should examine, or should we just accept 'how it's always been'? Should we go the whole way and give all animals rights or just some? Who should make these decisions and based on what? Could we work out a way to ask the animals themselves? What might they say? On the other hand, we could just leave things as they are.

DISCUSSION POINT

Does it matter how humans treat animals?

FIGURE 7.4 *A sleeping brown bear in Edinburgh Zoo*

MORAL RESPONSES

The first **Christians** followed the Jewish food laws about eating meat (see Leviticus). Soon they decided that it was acceptable to eat any kind of animal (I Corinthians 10:25).

Jesus gave no direct teachings on how to treat animals. Christians have to try to work out what he might have thought about modern animal issues.

One of the miracles of Jesus involved five loaves and two fish (Luke 9:13), so Jesus was probably not vegetarian. However, the message of Jesus was one of love and respect for others. So Jesus would not support cruelty to animals. His most important teaching was that we should 'love one another'. Jesus said that God expects us to treat others as we would like to be treated ourselves (Matthew 19:19). Maybe this also includes our treatment of animals.

Many Christians believe that animals have rights because they belong to God. As humans, we have been given responsibility for God's creation (Genesis 1:28). Part of that responsibility involves looking after animals.

Other Christians believe that it is right to be concerned about animals but feel that humans come first. This means that the use of animals in many ways is acceptable if it is for human benefit. The Church of Scotland says that animals can be used in medical experiments as long as there isn't unnecessary suffering for the animal. Most Christians believe that God cares for all his creation.

Aren't five sparrows sold for two pennies? Yet not one sparrow is forgotten by God.

Luke 12:6

In **Islam**, there is also a set of food rules where some food is clean (*halal*) and other food unclean (*haram*).

Although Muslims may eat meat, they should look after the animals well before slaughter. Muhammed told someone sharpening his knife in the sight of an animal to be slaughtered not to do so because this would frighten the animal and 'inflict death on it twice'.

Muhammed showed concern for animal life. He is reported to have said, 'Whoever is kind to the creatures of God is kind to himself.' Muhammed also forbade the use of animals for sport and said that animals should be 'killed without torture'. Some Muslims take this to mean that experiments on animals are wrong. Others say that our actions towards animals will be judged by what our *intentions* are. For example, using animals in experiments may be acceptable provided that the intention is to produce benefits for humans or animals. Muhammed did say, 'Kill even a sparrow without its deserving it, and God will question you about it.'

The point for the Muslim is that animals should not experience unnecessary pain or cruelty. Animals have their own value which should be respected as far as possible.

There is not a living creature on earth, nor a bird that flies, but they are communities like you.

Surah 6:38

An **Egoist** would want to make sure that the treatment of animals produced real benefits. It would depend on how you measured those benefits and what you took into account.

For example, if you thought that experiments on an animal could produce drugs to save your life (or even make your life easier), you might not worry much about any suffering for the animal. But if you thought that cruelty to animals might somehow harm you (eventually), you might not be so happy. For example, cows are often injected with chemicals to make them grow faster and avoid illness. This can help produce cheaper meat, but some people worry that these chemicals might get into the person eating the meat and do them harm.

The Egoist would have to weigh up the benefits they could get from cheap meat against the possible dangers it might have for them.

The Egoist would want to make sure that the balance of benefits over drawbacks was in their favour – no matter what that means for the animals or even for other people. Egoists don't worry a great deal about cruelty as long as it doesn't affect them. If an Egoist believed that cruelty might eventually affect them then they might want to avoid it. For example, some people think that treating animals badly makes it easier for humans to treat each other badly. If this is true, it could eventually cause problems for the Egoist.

Utilitarians would want to make sure that most people benefited from the ways in which we use animals. They would accept a small amount of suffering if it produced a greater good.

The Utilitarian might say that the treatment of animals is carefully watched over by the law and so cruelty can be avoided. However, some things can only be done on animals but not humans – for example, you couldn't give a person cancer on purpose to test a new anti-cancer drug. The Utilitarian would weigh up the possible benefits of the use of animals for the greatest number. If the use of animals brought benefits for humans, then we should think of it as a 'necessary evil'. Some Utilitarians don't see any difference between humans and animals and think that the way to minimise pain is to minimise suffering generally whether it is human or animal. Peter Singer says that if we treated animals as equals (not 'abusing' them as we do now), then we would have to end all experiments, close zoos, ban circuses etc.

As a result, the total quantity of suffering caused would be greatly reduced: it is hard to imagine any other change of moral attitude that would cause so great a reduction in the total sum of suffering in the Universe.

Practical Ethics, p61

Knowledge & Understanding

1 Why was Julie Cohen surprised by Panabisha?
2 What has Harvard Law School recently introduced?
3 Give **one** reason someone might have for believing that animals should have no rights.
4 What does it mean to say that an animal has 'instrumental value'?
5 In your own words, give **one** argument for and **one** argument against eating meat.
6 In your own words, give **one** argument for and **one** argument against keeping animals in zoos.
7 What were two youths charged with in 1997? Why was this special for the SSPCA?
8 Give **one** reason why a Christian might be concerned about animals.
9 What did Muhammed do when he found someone sharpening their knife in front of an animal?
10 Give **one** reason why an Egoist might agree with the use of animals in experiments.

Analysis

1 Imagine you could speak to Panabisha. What would you ask her?
2 Make your own list of rights for animals. Should some animals have more rights than others?
3 Write a short talk that you can give to your class. This should either support or oppose rights for animals.

4 Design a poster, 'Should we eat meat?'.
5 Design an information leaflet: 'The Christian View of Animals'.
6 You are a Muslim.
   You need a drug to keep you alive but it has been tested on animals. Explain how you would feel about taking this drug.
7 Take each of the issues on animal rights and explain how an Egoist might feel about each one.

Evaluation

The hunting of foxes in Britain today is wrong.
Do you agree? State your opinion clearly and give **one** reason why you have this view.

Assessment question

Outcome 2 Eddie the Egoist is trying to persuade Malcolm the Muslim to become a vegetarian. Write a short dialogue where each sets out his beliefs and reasons for them.

Homework

Imagine you are a chimpanzee. You live in a zoo. However, you have been trained to communicate like Panabisha. Describe your life and how you feel about captivity.

 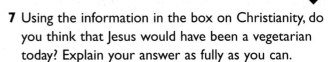

Knowledge & Understanding

1 Why do you think Harvard Law School has recently introduced the new course in animal rights law?
2 In your opinion, who should make decisions about what rights animals should have?
3 What does it mean to say that an animal has 'intrinsic value'. Do you agree that this is true?
4 Explain and justify your own views on meat-eating.
5 Some people think there's a major difference between the use of animals in cosmetics experiments and medical experiments. What do you think? Give reasons for your answer.
6 Do you agree that the keeping of pets is really an 'issue'? Explain your answer.

7 Using the information in the box on Christianity, do you think that Jesus would have been a vegetarian today? Explain your answer as fully as you can.
8 How might an Egoist be persuaded to support banning the use of animals in medical experiments ?
9 Explain your views on the quote from Peter Singer.

Analysis

1 Carry out a class debate: 'Fox-hunting is a traditional feature of British country life, which should be maintained.' Ensure that all the moral responses are represented in your audience.

2 Act out a short role play which involves a discussion between an animal rights supporter and a scientist involved in the use of animals in medical experiments. Imagine both are Christians.

3 Imagine a circus came to your town. The circus included animal acts. Your school plans to visit the circus. Explain your reasons for either supporting or opposing the circus in the form of a letter to your headteacher. Imagine that you are a Muslim and refer to your Muslim beliefs in your letter.

4 You are the parent of a child who wants a pet. As a Utilitarian you are unsure about the rights and wrongs of keeping pets but want your child to think it through. Write the discussion you might have.

Evaluation

'Christians believe that humans have responsibility for God's creation, so they should not eat meat.'
How far do you agree?

Assessment question

Outcome 3 Answer the following question using this format: The argument for; the argument against; your own personal conclusion. 'The use of animals for cosmetic experiments should be banned by all governments.'

Homework

Imagine that the government plans to ban the keeping of pets. Write a letter explaining your views on this.

DEPLETION OF RESOURCES

CASE STUDY

In 1838, John Muir was born in Dunbar in East Lothian.

At the age of 11, he and his family moved to the USA. Here, as he grew up, he took an interest in the preservation of wilderness lands. These lands were then thought of as 'wastelands' or as dangerous places which needed to be 'tamed'.

He believed that areas such as the Sierra Nevada and Yosemite were places where humans could find true spiritual contentment. He argued that these places should be protected, not only because of their own worth but because their existence would remind humans of their 'place' in the universe. He founded the Sierra Club, the world's first environmental organisation. His work led the US government to create National Parks, like Yosemite, where nature and wilderness would be preserved for future generations.

John Muir is now known by many as the 'Father of American Conservation'. The John Muir Trust, based in Musselburgh, successfully bought Ben Nevis in order to preserve it for future generations. The Trust shares John Muir's belief that nature has the right to be preserved, both for itself and for the benefit of all living things who share Earth.

Everybody needs beauty as well as bread, places to play and pray in, where nature may heal and give strength to body and soul alike.

John Muir, *The Yosemite* (1912), p256

FIGURE 7.5 *Statue of John Muir, Dunbar*

GIVE AND TAKE

Humans have needs. We need resources to make things, energy to fuel our activities, food to eat. We depend upon nature in everything we do. Do we use natural resources wisely? Do we take and give back or just take? Are earth's resources for us anyway or are they to be shared? Do we take just what we need or more?

Should our use of resources be regulated or should we use now and worry later? Anyway, what is nature – aren't we a part of it?

SHOULD NATURE HAVE RIGHTS?

'Deep ecologists' believe that because nature is 'living' it deserves to be treated fairly. Many religious or spiritual people believe that nature has a spiritual dimension, which should be protected. Many also believe that nature belongs to God. We should therefore care for it because it is his.

Some claim that the way we treat nature has consequences for our own identity. For example, if you find it easy to chop down a tree, then you are one step closer to finding it easy to kill a person.

DISCUSSION POINT

What do you think of as 'nature'?

Others argue that if we abuse nature we might suffer the consequences – or our descendants might. Pollution has direct effects but running out of natural resources would also be a problem. Nature should have rights because of its value for humans. We only have one earth so should look after it.

Of course there are many who argue that nature can't have rights, because giving something rights has to involve a contract that both parties agree to uphold. Obviously nature can't do this. However, we do give rights to babies even though they can't agree to a contract, so this suggestion has flaws.

COMPARING THE PRINCIPLES

1 The environment is very complex and not completely understood. Once we have decided that something is an environmental problem (and that's not easy), we then have to decide what to do (which also isn't easy). Once we've done that, the result might be an even bigger problem than the one we were originally trying to solve.

2 Why should we do anything? Nature will sort itself out without our help, as it has always done. Besides, the problems are too big for us to cope with. Even if we could do anything, why do it now, why not wait until we begin to suffer the effects of some environmental problem? Then human intelligence will work out the solution.

3 What we think of as 'environmental problems' are just natural cycles that the earth has always gone through – and will carry on going through. Once we run out of one resource, we'll simply learn to use another.

4 Humans are part of the environment. *Everything* we do has environmental impact – it's unavoidable. We need to use the earth's resources to survive.

1 We can't just do nothing because we don't know what the outcome might be. Environmental issues are very complicated but we have to study them and try to work out the best course of action to take – and then take it. This means living in a sustainable way. This means living now in a way which protects nature for the use of future generations. Perhaps nature will solve the problems 'itself' – by destroying humans.

2 We have a responsibility to use the earth's resources wisely so that future generations can enjoy the same quality of life we do now. We can't just stick our head in the sand and hope it all goes away.

3 Nature does go through cycles but the impact of humans on the earth has been very great, very quickly. We can't wait, environmental problems are already here – resources are running out.

4 Humans are a part of nature – but the most powerful species. Our impact on nature is great but we have the ability to understand our actions. A lot of the harm we cause nature is avoidable.

USE OR EXPLOITATION?

To survive as a species humans must use natural resources, but the use of these resources almost always involves conflict between using nature and abusing it. This may lead to disagreements as human rights conflict with the rights of nature.

◆ For example, in China, the building of the Three Gorges dam (by 2009) will mean that 1.9 million people will lose their homes. The reservoir will be 370 miles long and flood vast areas of natural beauty. However, it will bring economic benefits to millions of Chinese, allowing them to enjoy things that we take for granted here.

◆ Scottish fishermen must regularly tie up their boats because of European Union rules about the amount of fishing that a member country may allow. The EU – and so the Scottish Executive – argue that this is a way to preserve fish stocks for future genera-tions and so is a sustainable practice. Many fishermen, however, argue that they need to continue fishing in order to survive and be able to support their families.

◆ On the Isle of Harris, in the Outer Hebrides, there are plans to construct a large superquarry. This quarry will provide aggregates for use in building and road construction. Environmentalists are strongly opposed to it because of the harm it will do to the local environment. However, many locals support the idea because the existence of such a quarry would provide a boost to the local economy, which has suffered from the movement of people out of the area in search of work.

◆ There are also concerns that Scotland's native forests are being destroyed to be replaced by commercial forestry which uses a much smaller range of trees. Again, however, locals often support this because it brings jobs and benefits the local community. The Forestry Commission also argues that its commercial forests are open to the public – whereas privately owned woodlands might not be.

◆ There are regular appeals to 'save the rainforest'. However, who has the right to deny the governments of countries with rainforest the right to exploit their natural resources for the benefit of their people? Developing world countries often point back at us in the developed world and argue that our current wealth is the result of our exploitation of nature in the past.

◆ The petrol price protests of September 2000 almost brought Britain to a standstill. The government argued that part of the reason petrol is so high is to reduce consumption of it and so pro-tect the environment. But is it fair to expect those who depend on the use of fossil fuels to do their job to bear the burden of such environmental protection?

DISCUSSION POINT

Should human needs come before protecting the environment?

FIGURE 7.6 *Open-cast mining*

SPECIFIC ISSUES

Resource: Fossil fuels

Problems:
- Over-extraction means that stocks might run out in the near future; however, the world economy depends heavily on fossil fuels.
- Extraction, processing and use can all be environmentally damaging, for example, fossil fuels produce 'greenhouse gases' which could cause serious climate change.
- Limited supplies.

Difficulties:
- Many jobs depend on fossil fuels.
- Change to other sources could produce world instability.
- Alternatives, like renewable energy, need heavy initial investment and may also be environmentally damaging.

Resource: Raw materials – ores, minerals etc

Problems:
- Extraction, processing and use can be environmentally harmful.
- By-products may also cause pollution and contamination of natural systems.
- Limited Supplies.

Difficulties:
◆ Sometimes no economically viable alternative.
◆ Jobs tied up with such resources.
◆ Once stocks are used up, could be impossible to replace.

Resource: Organic materials – wood, plant resources

Problems:
◆ Use and production can be directly harmful.
◆ May have side-effect of destroying habitats for other species.
◆ Could alter climate locally and/or globally. Would take a long time to replace once lost.

Difficulties:
◆ May need to be used to support local economy.
◆ May not be an alternative.

Resource: Food stocks

Problems:
◆ Extraction may result in the extinction of other species.
◆ Can have poor side-effects for the rest of the ecosystem; for example, changes to one form of life (eg fish) can badly affect other forms of life which depend upon them for food too.

Difficulties:
◆ Humans need to eat.
◆ Population increases need to be matched with increasing production.
◆ Jobs and whole ways of life might be involved.
◆ May be no real alternative for some human communities.

Earth's resources, with the possible exception of energy, are finite – they can't last forever. Also, the use of certain resources might have unpredictable side-effects which might eventually cause harm for humans far into the future. Perhaps John Muir's ideas about conservation were right – or perhaps we clever humans will work out a different solution to the problem of balancing the need to survive with the need to ensure the survival of future generations.

FACTS AND FIGURES

◆ In Europe, the demand for drinking water has increased by 500% since 1950.
◆ A global increase in fossil fuel consumption of 5% could mean that there will be no fossil fuels left by 2047 (David Bellamy).
◆ The River Clyde may have increased its flow by 50% due to the effects of Global Warming (Dundee University).

MORAL RESPONSES

Christians believe that the Old Testament story of the creation puts them in charge of nature. This idea of dominion (Genesis 1:28) means that, although we need to use nature to survive, we must look after it too because it belongs to God. This means it's only 'on loan' to humans. Most Christians followed the rules about treating the environment which were handed down to them from Judaism. Judaism has always had very strong ties to the land. Part of the Covenant Promise, which God made to the Israelites, was that he would give them their own land. As this was a gift from God it was to be cared for and used wisely. Treating the land badly would be a rejection of God. The earth belongs to God (Psalm 24:1), the human job is to look after it as stewards. This belief led to many Jewish laws which controlled the use of land, including giving it a 'rest' every seven years, known as Jubilee years.

However, some people believe that Jesus had a mixed view of nature. He accepted laws about how we treat nature, but ignored them when they came into conflict with human need:

◆ Matthew 21:19. Jesus cursed a fig-tree for not bearing fruit. Does this mean that he saw its only value in producing food for humans?

◆ Luke 6:1. Jesus allows his disciples to pluck and eat corn on the Sabbath. Jewish law forbids this – part of the reason being to let the land rest on the Sabbath too. Jesus says that the Sabbath laws were for man's benefit. Does this mean we can treat nature however we want for our own good?

◆ Luke 5:1–11. Jesus performs a miracle, which some might take to mean that he supports overfishing and so the exploitation of nature.

Many Christians also argue that caring too much about nature means that we might end up worshipping the created and not the creator. However, many Christians are involved in environmental organisations as their way of looking after God's creation.

Muslims also believe that the earth belongs to Allah. How the Muslim treats Allah's creation will be a question asked during his final Judgement. In particular, actions which have been unnecessary will result in punishment – if these actions have caused harm for no good reason. This means that the Muslim will have to live on earth as if he will have to answer for everything he does.

In many Arab countries, the issue of water supply is important. There is an awareness that water is scarce in the desert and so to be used wisely. Complicated rules have grown up around water use. However, in Arab countries, one principle about water is important; it is there for all to share equally because all are equal in the eyes of Allah. This should include all of nature, not just humans.

Like many other faiths, Muslims believe that nature can be used for human benefit, provided that it is not abused. The earth's resources are for the benefit of mankind. The problem is in deciding when use becomes abuse. This decision is important considering who nature belongs to:

He created man, and gave him the ability to speak. The sun and the moon rotate in their orbits ... The plants and trees bow down in adoration. He raised heaven on high and set the balance of all things so that mankind may not upset the balance. Keep the balance fairly and do not fall short in it.

Surah 55:3–13

Even an **Egoist** might support responsible use of the earth's resources. This wouldn't be for the benefit of the earth, but in your own self-interest. You would want your needs met, no matter what the cost to nature generally, but if meeting your needs now meant that things would be worse for you in the near future, then you might think again. For example, if over-consumption of food sources – like overfishing – meant that in five years the Egoist would go hungry, then perhaps he or she could accept the need for cutting back now. Egoists want to make sure that their needs can be comfortably met throughout their life. If resources are finite, they want to make sure they last – at least until they've died!

If you could convince the Egoist that sustainable use of resources was actually less expensive (in total) than unsustainable practices, then he or she might give them his support. For example, if the total costs (to him) of solar energy production were far less than using fossil fuels he might be interested.

Also, if an Egoist thought that the use of resources now might lead to harmful side effects, you'd want to avoid that. Extraction and production of raw materials can often have harmful side-effects, like water pollution. Such pollution wouldn't be in an Egoist's best interests, so you might either want to stop the production (if you thought it was 'unnecessary') or to find an alternative.

For Egoists, nature can only have rights as long as that doesn't 'cost' them anything.

The **Utilitarian** would argue that the use of natural resources should benefit the many. It should provide for people's needs more than it costs them in other ways. Nature can only have rights as long as those rights don't negatively affect the happiness of the majority. If a particular use of resources could be shown to have serious environmental side-effects, then there would be more 'pain' than 'pleasure' involved. A Utilitarian would want to make sure that use of resources didn't have such bad side-effects now that it cancelled out the benefits such use would bring.

The Utilitarian would also be more likely to support sustainable practices. This is because that would take into account the needs of future generations. This might mean that people today would have to make small sacrifices – like cutting back their use of fossil fuels – in order to benefit future populations. If our use of resources now left generations to come with none, then that means that the minority now benefit at the expense of the majority in the future – the opposite of Utilitarianism.

> [An environmental] ethic would regard every action that is harmful to the environment as ethically dubious, and those that are unnecessarily harmful as plainly wrong.

Peter Singer, *Practical Ethics*, p285

ACTIVITIES

Knowledge & Understanding

1 Why did John Muir think that nature should be protected?

2 What did the John Muir Trust recently buy?

3 What do 'deep ecologists' believe about the rights of nature?

4 Why might a Christian look after nature?

5 Why do some people think that there's no such thing as an environmental problem?

6 Why might someone support the building of the Three Gorges dam?

7 What **two** points of view are there about the Harris superquarry?

8 What does the word 'dominion' mean?

9 How might a Christian argue that Jesus supported overfishing?

10 Why might a Muslim worry about how he treats the earth?

11 Give **one** reason why an Egoist might support cutting back on our use of natural resources.

Analysis

1 Find out more about John Muir. Prepare your own display board on his life, work and beliefs.

2 Design an information leaflet, 'Should Nature have rights?' Include arguments for and against.

3 Imagine you live on Harris. A public meeting has been called about the superquarry. Prepare a role play in your class where you discuss the issues. Who would be there? What might they say?

4 Choose one example of the use of natural resources. Prepare a short report on the issue. This could be in the form of a written report, a short class talk or a TV news item.

5 Imagine you are a Muslim. You are standing before God answering his questions about how you have treated nature during your life. Write an imaginary discussion that might take place.

6 Draw your own strip cartoon illustrating the story of Luke 5:1–11. Explain underneath what this teaches about how we should treat nature.

7 An open-cast mine is to be worked in an area of natural beauty near your town. Letters have been flooding in to the local newspaper. You are an Egoist. Write your own letter explaining your views about the mine.

Evaluation

Some people believe that the resources of the earth are just for human benefit.
Do you agree? Give at least **two** reasons for your answer.

Assessment question

Outcome 1 To save energy, the government has decided that cars should be banned one day every week.
What might an Egoist and a Christian or Muslim say in response to this?

Homework

List **four** things *you* do to help the environment and **four** things you do that harm it.

ACTIVITIES

i2

Knowledge & Understanding

1 In what ways do you think nature might help people to find 'spiritual contentment'?

2 In your own words, explain why some people believe that nature should have rights

3 How could someone justify not giving rights to nature?

4 How might 'human intelligence' overcome resource depletion?

5 In your opinion, should Scottish fishermen 'regularly tie up their boats'?

6 How might someone support commercial forestry?

7 Explain, in your own words, how someone might say that Jesus had a 'mixed' view of nature.

8 Do you think an Egoist would be likely to be a member of Greenpeace? Explain your answer.

9 Why might a Utilitarian support sustainable resource use?

Analysis

1 An area close to you is being considered as a national park. You believe it should be. Devise a campaign to convince the government. You may want to include speeches, letter, leaflets etc.

2 Carry out a class debate: 'This house believes that Scottish fishermen should accept fishing quotas.' Ensure that the moral responses you have studied are represented.

3 Create your own display on the petrol crisis of September 2000. Focus on the arguments for and against.

4 If John Muir were alive today, what might he make of our treatment of nature? Write a short speech which he might give to your school assembly.

5 You are the Minister/Priest of a local Church. You have to give a talk on the use of God's Earth. Plan out what you will say in the form of a set of headings which you will use as the basis of your talk.

6 Two people in your congregation respond to this sermon as they leave your church that morning. One is an Egoist and one a Utilitarian. What might they say?

Evaluation

'Nature exists for human use.'
How far do you agree?

Assessment question

Outcome 3 'Humans have a responsibility to use natural resources wisely now for the benefit of future generations.'
Set out the arguments for and against this view and include your own personal conclusion.

Homework

Draw up and carry out your own questionnaire which tries to find out about a range of views people have on the use of natural resources. You should be prepared to discuss your findings in class.

POLLUTION

CASE STUDY

Serious water pollution incidents have increased by almost 50% in Scotland to a three-year high, according to SEPA's annual report. A board meeting this month heard details of 50,000 fish being killed in a 'major pollution incident' at North Queich, near Loch Leven, Kinross. It was suspected chemicals from a swimming pool had been poured down a drain. In another incident, 400 trout died at Finglen Burn, Campsie Glen, allegedly because of pollution from a sheep dip product.

The Herald, 22 October 1999

EVERYBODY'S DOING IT

Breathe in. Breathe out. You have just polluted the atmosphere. No need to call Greenpeace. CO_2, the by-product of breathing, has been labelled a harmful 'greenhouse gas'.

Whatever we do, we cause some kind of pollution. The earth works as a 'closed system'. This means that it can only cope with change which is gradual enough to allow its regulation mechanisms to take effect. Sudden or dramatic change throws the system out of balance. Every activity of life produces by-products. Normally, the earth can cope with these but for a number of reasons it's sometimes more difficult:

- If a pollutant exists in large quantities or is concentrated in a small area its effects can be greater than normal.
- *Where* a pollutant is can cause harm – some places are more environmentally sensitive than others.
- Some pollutants are worse than others – because they last longer or have more serious direct effects.

So, should we hold our breath?

DISCUSSION POINT

In what ways do you think you contribute to pollution?

A GRADUAL PROBLEM

Many environmentalists argue that, since humans began using fossil fuels, living in cities and carrying out large-scale industrial and agricultural practices, global pollution has increased.

◆ Agriculture uses far more chemical fertilisers nowadays. These chemicals, like nitrates, easily find their way into rivers, seas and the air. The most recent issue is whether growing genetically modified (GM) crops might cause pollution, as pollen from GM crops 'accidentally' fertilises non-GM crops. This could lead to changes in non-GM crops, which could be unpredictable.

◆ Industrial processes can lead to pollution. The burning of fossil fuels leads to air pollution – particulate and gaseous. This can lead to problems like acid rain. Many other processes have effects too. For example, many substances, like mercury, which are part of the process of making some batteries, can find their way into water supplies or into the food chain. Mining for raw materials can not only alter natural landscapes but lead to pollution, as leftover materials (spoil) get into water sources.

◆ Many human activities produce waste products. This ranges from nuclear waste all the way to our own personal waste products. What's to be done with it? Depending on what kind of waste it is, some of it is recycled, buried, burned and some is dumped at sea.

FIGURE 7.7 *Pollution: this oil spill is a disaster for the local wildlife*

All of these can lead to pollution. For example, the practice of landfill – burying household waste in large pits – produces methane (CH_4). This is a 'greenhouse gas' and also very explosive. A lot of sewage is dumped at sea – some treated, some not. This can kill marine life by producing toxic blooms, which reduce the oxygen-carrying capacity of the water. It can also lead to viral infection of species that use the seas – including us.

CASE STUDY

Throughout the year 2000, Friends of the Earth Scotland has been monitoring 117 Scottish beaches. 25 of these had faecal coliforms (harmful bacteria from sewage) above 10,000 per 100ml of water. The report stated that beaches where the water was of acceptable quality were: Arbroath, Carnoustie, St Andrews, North Berwick and Yellow Craigs. Many others were 'unacceptable'.

Friends of the Earth Scotland

CASE STUDY

Winds from the Baltic States and Poland are posing an air quality problem in Edinburgh.

The finding emerged yesterday as the City of Edinburgh Council reported it was seven years ahead of schedule in meeting government standards on air quality. Mike Drewry, Environmental Services Director, said that the difference in air quality now and in the days before smoke control zones in the 1970s was 'quite stark'. He also added that 'Emission of certain pollutants from motor vehicles are now the main sources of concern in relation to air quality.'

The Herald, 2 December 1998

WHOOPS!

Accidental pollution is often the most harmful because it can be rapid, widespread and 'alien' to a natural environment. Oil spills cause problems very quickly. Accidental dumping of waste products can also lead to pollution of water sources. Also, there are some cases where pollution is deliberate. This might be when you last dropped litter or when some large company decided to dump dodgy chemicals somewhere no-one might notice for a while.

SO WHAT?

Pollution can harm or destroy whole ecosystems. Acid rain destroys forests and everything that depends upon them. Pollution can find its way into the food chain. It might even alter the balance of the planet's atmosphere.

Why do some believe this matters?

DISCUSSION POINT

Why do you think some people/organisations choose to cause pollution on purpose?

◆ Pollution directly harms nature. If we value nature for its own sake we'll want to avoid this.

◆ Even if we don't value nature, pollution incidents might eventually lead to harm for our own species.

CASE STUDY

Dramatic new evidence blames pollution from fish farms for causing the poisonous algae that is devastating Scotland's 50 million pound shellfish industry.

A report to be published tomorrow by the World Wide Fund for Nature (WWF) ... will conclude that the vast amount of waste excreted by the millions of salmon penned in 350 cages along the west coast is linked to toxic algal blooms. Scottish Ministers have always denied such a link, and the results will come as a blow to the Executive.

Sunday Herald, 17 September 2000

FIGURE 7.8 *Anti-pollution protest*

SURELY SOME MISTAKE?

On the other hand, many argue that pollution is something we can't avoid.

◆ Agriculture must be carried out intensively and chemical fertilisers widely used to keep up with demand. This is the only realistic way to feed the rapidly increasing human population. It is also a way to deal effectively with the food needs of the developing world. This will involve increased pollution – but that's better than starving.

◆ Industry produces pollution. However, the benefits outweigh the drawbacks. Industrialisation brings a much better quality of life, like improved healthcare, greater physical comforts. People who live in industrialised nations generally live longer than those in non-industrial countries. A small increase in pollution might be a price worth paying. Besides, industry has been very successful in improving its treatment of nature. Air and water quality in many places is much better now than it was in the past. Many people put this down to improvements in pollution control made possible by industrial development. Some argue also that industrial nations cause less pollution than non-industrial ones. Smoke from cooking fires is one of the major causes of cancer in the developing world.

◆ When accidents – like oil-tanker spills – happen, the answer is not to turn back to some primitive pre-industrial society but to improve the way we respond to pollution.

◆ Some people will always pollute on purpose. You can't use this as an excuse to return the world to the stone age.

DISCUSSION POINT

What benefits has modern industry brought life on earth?

FIGURE 7.9 *An example of sustainable energy*

FACTS AND FIGURES

◆ Of 173 large waters classified by SEPA 30 lochs are 'fair, poor or seriously polluted'.

◆ 4% of Scottish estuaries and coastal waters are 'sub-standard'.

◆ Almost 10% of rivers and 65% of canals are 'polluted'.

Improving Scotland's Water Environment, Scottish Environmental Protection Agency (SEPA), 2000

A BALANCING ACT

Pollution might always be a feature of human existence. Some argue that the key is to avoid unnecessary pollution and to keep necessary pollution levels as low as possible. This might mean:

◆ making industry and agriculture more efficient so that there's less pollution (like waste) in the first place

◆ carrying on as we are and find better ways to deal with pollution; with waste, for example, some have suggested sending it into space

◆ changing our lifestyles so that we use less of the materials which cause pollution as they are produced – or alternatives, like biodegradable materials

◆ doing nothing at all because there's no real problem. Nature will find its own way to deal with pollution – besides, pollution is part of the cycles of life, which nature has coped with perfectly well so far.

MORAL RESPONSES

Christians believe that caring for God's creation is important. For this reason alone they might want to avoid pollution. Christians also value highly an attitude of mind which puts others first and tries to do as little harm to those around us. The Golden Rule of Christianity is that you 'do to others that which you would have them do to you'. For Christians the command to 'Love one another' means that you have to put the needs of others before your own. Because of this a Christian could be confused about his response to pollution:

◆ If pollution caused direct harm to other people, then obviously it should be avoided. If you don't like walking in air polluted by car exhaust fumes, you must remember that the next time you use your car. Your pollution affects others, so you should live your life in a caring way so as not to cause pollution.

◆ However, if pollution is an unavoidable product of something which brings benefits to others, then you may have to accept or even support it. For example, if burning fossil fuels is the best option to provide energy for a developing country, who are you to deny that country the benefits that this might bring? If you objected to pollution in this case, then you might harm others.

Christians have had a long tradition of trying to treat others with care and consideration. The message of Jesus was one of love and justice. If pollution goes against this principle then it should be a matter of concern for the Christian. Christians have also had a long tradition of concern for nature. Such concern isn't best shown by polluting nature.

Praised be my Lord for our sister water,
who is very serviceable to us, and humble and precious and clean
Praised be my Lord for our mother the Earth, which sustains and keeps us ... .

St Francis of Assisi

The **Muslim** believes that all of the gifts of Allah should be used wisely. Extravagance is seen as something which is wrong. In the Hadith, it is stated:

> *Do not be extravagant wasters. Those who are extravagant are kinsmen of Satan.*

This means that the Muslim must guard against unnecessary pollution because, if what causes it is not necessary, it must be extravagance. The Muslim is to live in harmony with Allah's creation, not spoil it for his own use. He must take what he needs and no more. In taking what he needs, he should still avoid harming nature without good reason. There is also a saying from the Hadith, which says:

> *If any of you sees something which is objectionable, he should change it with his hand, but if he cannot he should change it with his tongue.*

So Muslims are permitted to fight against what they think is wrong and, if they can't take action, they can at least speak out. So, for example, a Muslim could be part of an anti-pollution protest. All life is to be respected and unnecessary harm is to be avoided. So the Muslim should oppose pointless pollution.

For the **Egoist**, there could be various responses to pollution.

- One response would be where the Egoist would want to ensure that pollution didn't happen at all. They might even sacrifice some of the benefits which potentially polluting activities might bring. They would do this if they believed that pollution was going to be harmful for them. This could be either directly – as they suffered the effects of a pollution incident – or less directly, as pollution led to other changes, like climate change – which would harm the Egoist in the long run.
- An Egoist might support processes which resulted in pollution, as long as the pollution didn't end up near them. For example, if dumping raw sewage at sea was cheaper than treating it and not dumping it at sea, they might support the dumping (as long as they lived far inland perhaps!).
- An Egoist might just ignore pollution – especially if it was a by-product of something they wanted. For example, they might want to travel only by car, even when they didn't need to, because their own self-interests outweigh their desire to cut pollution. They might especially ignore pollution which would only cause harm in the future – because an Egoist is only interested in their own life after all.

Utilitarians would want to think about the possible effects of pollution and how these effects were balanced against possible benefits. If we accept that all actions cause some kind of pollution, then we have to decide which pollution is acceptable and which is not. Utilitarians would want to make sure that the effects of pollution were small and certainly not harmful. If pollution could be 'handled' by nature's systems without harm to most people, then we could agree that some amount of pollution would be permitted – provided the benefits were great enough to make the pollution 'worthwhile'. The Utilitarian wants to make sure that people's lives are made better – leading to happiness. But, if making people happier now can only be done at the expense of people's future happiness, then that has to be questioned.

For example, society today is very dependent upon the use of oil for energy. This brings us many benefits but, if environmentalists are right, using oil might harm the global environment in the long run. The choice is whether we should accept the benefits now even if they will cause suffering for future generations. The Utilitarian would want to be sure that future generations didn't suffer for our pleasures. If we accept that the use of oil now will cause serious long-term problems for countless generations, then that means that the minority (everyone today) benefits at the expense of the majority (everyone who will live after us). This is the opposite of Utilitarianism. On the other hand, some Utilitarians could argue that human technology might solve the problems of the effects of pollution in the future. If so, we'll have been wrong to deny people the benefits of activities which cause pollution today.

ACTIVITIES

Knowledge & Understanding

1 State **one** source of pollution.
2 When can the effects of pollution be 'greater than normal'?
3 What reasons do some environmentalists give for increased pollution?
4 In what ways can waste cause pollution?
5 In what ways is pollution of the sea a problem?
6 Why might humans want to avoid pollution.
7 Why do some people support intensive agriculture?
8 How might we reduce pollution?
9 How does the 'Golden Rule' in Christianity help us understand what a Christian might think about pollution?
10 State one opinion an Egoist might have about pollution.

Analysis

1 Find out more about specific kinds of pollution and complete a table with the headings: type of pollution; possible causes; possible effects; possible solutions. You should include as many types of pollution as you can.
2 Design an illustrated poster showing how we all contribute to pollution. Use some humour! Think about many different possible types of pollution that we cause and how, individually, we do it.
3 Create a piece of sculptured artwork, using waste materials, which highlights the possible problems of pollution.

4 Find out about **one** of the specific examples of pollution mentioned in the text. Write a short report outlining **both** sides of the argument.
5 You discover that a landfill site is to be set up in your area. List the concerns you would have and the questions you would ask the operators.
6 Some argue that the polluter should pay. Devise a way to make producers of non-biodegradable packaging pay for its disposal or recycling. How could you enforce this?
7 You're an Egoist. You work in a chemicals company. Your boss has just asked you to 'accidentally' dump some chemicals in a river that flows past your own home. Explain what you do and why.

Evaluation

'Pollution shows that humans don't care about nature.' Do you agree? Give at least **two** reasons for your answer.

Assessment question

Outcome 3 The government has increased petrol prices to help cut air pollution. State what you think about this and give at least **two** reasons for your opinion.

Homework

Find out about a major accidental pollution incident. Describe how it happened and what the effects were. How was it dealt with? Be prepared to present your findings to the class.

ACTIVITIES

Knowledge & Understanding

1 What does it mean to say that the earth works as a 'closed system'? How does this affect its ability to handle pollution?
2 In what ways might modern agriculture contribute to pollution? Why are some prepared to accept this possibility?
3 Why is accidental pollution so potentially damaging?
4 How might a fish-farmer justify the practice of fish-farming?

5 How might someone argue that pollution caused on purpose shouldn't be used as a reason for criticism of all possible polluting activities?
6 Which of the ways of keeping pollution levels low do you think is likely to be the most effective?
7 In what circumstances might a Christian support polluting activities?
8 In what ways does the Utilitarian take into account future generations when making his decisions about the issue of pollution? How helpful do you think this is?

Analysis

1 Carry out some research into specific pollution issues. Choose the one which you think is most important. Prepare your own short report about it, which you should present to your class, using a variety of visual aids.

2 Compile your own resource pack on an issue of pollution in your local area. You could interview people involved and display your materials.

3 Devise and carry out a survey of people's attitudes towards pollution. Try to find out how much people know about local/global pollution; how 'big' an issue they think it is and what they might be prepared to do to help solve the problem.

4 Protesters have destroyed a field of GM crops. The case goes to court. Write the speeches which the lawyers might make, summing up the argument in favour of the protesters and then in favour of the farmer who has had them charged.

5 You are a Christian. Your minister/priest has asked you to sell your car and buy a bicycle because this will cause less pollution. Explain how you would respond and why, basing your argument on your Christian belief as well as practical issues.

Evaluation

'Pollution is an unavoidable feature of human activity on earth, so there's nothing we can do about it.'
To what extent do you agree?

Assessment question

Outcome 2 How might a religious person, an Egoist and a Utilitarian justify the acceptance of pollution caused by the use of fossil fuels?

Homework

Find out about the ways in which pollution has been reduced globally during recent times.

8 REVISION AND STUDY GUIDE

The course 'Making moral decisions' is about how we reach decisions about what is right and wrong. Life is full of complicated issues. These issues have to be thought about and decisions made about them. Even though you might never actually have to face some of the issues in this book, thinking about them and working through the process of making moral decisions should help you with moral decisions you will have to make in your life. Why is this important?

◆ You already have to make moral decisions. These range from the very simple, all the way to much more serious. Teenage life is full of choices:
Should I behave well and work hard – or be nasty to the teacher?
Should I admit to being given too much change in a shop?
Should I lie to cover up my friend's actions?
Should I try drugs?
Should I take part in beating someone up?

◆ In just a few years' time, you'll be an adult – you might even be a parent. The responsibility for creating and maintaining a fair society will be yours. Younger people will look to you for guidance about what's right and wrong – and follow your example. Remember too that you'll have to live in the world your generation creates.

◆ You'll also have to elect governments. These will shape the future and play a part in making the world the way it is. You'll want to understand what the big issues in life are and have your say about them, in a reasonable and informed way.

◆ You may actually have to face some of the issues explored here. This might be while doing your job, for example, you may do a job that is environmentally damaging. It might be in your personal life, for example, you may have to decide when to switch off a relative's life support system.

The point of studying a course like this is to give you a mental toolkit. This toolkit means that when you approach an issue you've never dealt with before, you've got the right 'tools' to deal with it.

LEARNING OUTCOMES

A Learning Outcome (LO) is what you are supposed to be able to do after studying a topic. To achieve the LO you'll have to go through a series of steps. For example:

Learning Outcome: The student should be able to saw a piece of wood.

Step 1 – Know what a saw is.

Step 2 – Be able to match a particular type of saw to a particular kind of wood.

Step 3 – Watch and learn sawing action.

Step 4 – Be able to position wood so that it is stable for sawing.

Step 5 – Carry out the task to completion.

Once you have achieved all the steps, you'll have achieved the LO.

INTERMEDIATE I LEARNING OUTCOMES

Outcome 1

You should be able to describe each of the moral stances, showing that you understand each one. For example, explaining that the moral stance based on Religious Authority means following the teachings of your faith.

You should also show that you know how each moral stance affects someone who follows it when they are making moral decisions. You are expected to do this for **two** of the moral stances – Egoism & Religious Authority (= Knowledge & Understanding).

Outcome 2

You should be able to outline **two** viewpoints on a particular topic – each related to a different moral stance. For example, what different attitudes might there be on capital punishment from people who base their moral decisions on Religious Authority and those who base it on Egoism (= Analysis).

Outcome 3

You should be able to express your own opinion on a moral issue. You should be able to give two reasons for your opinion. For example, I think that capital punishment is ... . My reasons for this belief are ... (= Evaluation).

INTERMEDIATE 2 LEARNING OUTCOMES

Outcome 1

You should be able to describe each of the moral stances, showing that you understand each one. For example, explaining that Egoism is based on the idea of self-interest.

You should also show that you know how each moral stance

affects someone who follows it when they are making moral decisions. You are expected to do this for **three** of the moral stances (= Knowledge & Understanding).

Outcome 2

You should be able to apply the three moral stances to a particular issue. For example, why might an Egoist, Utilitarian and Christian refuse to fight in a war? In what ways do their moral stances affect their actions? (= Analysis).

Outcome 3

You should be able to show that you understand **at least two** sides for any given issue. For example, arguments for and against euthanasia. You should also be able to offer your own personal conclusion on a moral issue. This should be supported by **at least two** relevant reasons (Evaluation).

ALL TOGETHER NOW

You will see that there is a lot of overlap in what you're expected to do. You might be in a class where there are students aiming for Intermediate 1 and others for Intermediate 2. You'll cover the same coursework. The kind of assessments you'll do will be slightly different. Also, Intermediate 2 students will be expected to go into some more detail than Intermediate 1 students.

Your teacher will discuss with you whether you should go for Intermediate 1 or 2, but remember:

AIM HIGH!

THE SKILLS

The skills involved in the course 'Making Moral Decisions' are the same for Intermediate 1 and 2. This shouldn't be surprising because **they are the same skills which apply to RMPS generally.**

KNOWLEDGE:

This means being able to grasp the facts and opinions in a topic. It means being able to work out what matters in a particular topic and what doesn't. You should keep this store of knowledge as up to date as possible. Many of the topics you'll study change very quickly. New ideas and discoveries change how we see things. You should keep a file of newspaper cuttings on the topics you study. You should also use the internet, which often has the most up-to-date information on a topic. But watch out, sometimes *opinions* are presented as *facts*! Learn to spot the difference.

UNDERSTANDING:

This means being able to make the *link* between different pieces of knowledge. It also means being able to *fit new knowledge into your old knowledge* and fit it in the right place! Understanding is also about *applying* what you know. This means taking individual bits of knowledge and fitting them together to make the big picture. Think of a piece of knowledge as a bit of a jigsaw puzzle. Looking at it on its own, it might not mean much or make much sense. Understanding is when you can look at the bigger jigsaw picture and work out where your single piece goes. The piece of knowledge is now slotted in and you have improved your understanding.

ANALYSIS:

This means being able to pick out all the bits that go together to make up something complete. By being able to take apart and put together, you increase your understanding. To do this you need to be able to see all the smaller bits which form the big picture. You can work on each of the smaller bits so that they improve the overall understanding. For example, imagine you are a swimmer who wants to win Olympic gold. You can analyse your performance by looking at all the parts which go to make up your complete swimming technique: breathing, entering the water, timing of stroke, body position and so on. You can then do specific exercises to improve one aspect of your performance. This will then improve your performance overall.

EVALUATION:

This is like a set of scales where you 'weigh up' all the elements of the topic you are studying to come to a conclusion. You might, for example, put all the arguments for having nuclear weapons on one side and all the arguments against on the other. You can then give each bit of the issue some kind of 'value', which makes it heavier or lighter. You can then see whether the balance is heavier on the for or against side. Of course, to do this you have to: *know* the information, *understand* how it fits together and analyse the relationship between all the different bits. Then you can achieve the final stage.

CONCLUSION:

This means being able to express your own opinion on something, which is based on study of the issue. You have your facts and opinions to hand, you understand them and you've been able to analyse how they fit together. You can then weigh them up and 'announce' your result. Following through this process means that your conclusion is not just an opinion plucked from the air, but is the end result of a lot of thought and reflection. Of course, somebody else's opinion might be different to yours but now that you've carefully worked it through, you'll be able to take them on!

HOW DO WE LEARN?

Have you ever watched a baby learning to walk? It clambers up, it wobbles and then it falls over. Then it tries again and again until it gets it right.

What about the same child learning to talk? Its parents point to things and say the name over and over again. The child tries it. Sometimes its words sound funny but eventually they make sense. The child fits the new word into its new vocabulary. It eventually learns how to fit many words together to make sense. Imagine the baby wants a drink of water – here's a few stages it might go through as it gets older.

1 Cries, and only stops when it gets water (parents have to work it out!).
2 Learns where water is and points to water and grunts/screams/cries.
3 Asks for 'waaaaaaa'. Parents associate this word with water and they then say 'water'.
4 Asks for 'wawa' – parents recognise closeness of word to water.
5 Asks for water.
6 Works out where water comes from and how tap works etc.

In all of this, the child is continually processing the information, fitting old knowledge into new situations and working out how all the bits fit together to achieve the desired outcome.

This is what you have to do with your topic materials. You must process the information. There's no point in just reading it once and hoping it'll stick in your head (unless you're very lucky). You have to approach it from different angles, develop different ways of seeing it and using it and work on specific bits of it.

Imagine you're a professional footballer. Naturally you'll practise your game but you'll also work out in the gym, perhaps do weight-training, running, swimming, study of the game. In other words, build up your overall fitness so that you're better at the one thing you want to do best. Studying's the same. If you want to learn and learn well – you have to work at it. So what kind of 'training' is best?

Gathering the information:

There are many sources for this. This book. Your library. The internet. Newspapers. Your teacher. Gather together as much as you can on your topic, including different opinions. Use as wide a variety of sources as possible – books, videos, TV, radio, computers, newspapers and magazines. You'll find that these days there's no shortage of information. Remember, simple things can often be very effective. For example, go through your TV guide once a week and highlight programmes that are related to your course. There are a great many programmes on about moral issues topics. Even some films and TV series often have strong moral issues storylines. It doesn't have to be an RMPS textbook for you to learn about RMPS topics. It also doesn't have to be obviously 'religious'.

Sorting the information:

Organise this information. Put it in a folder with dividers/polypockets. If you have a workbook, keep it organised. Put the date on pieces of work, keep a record of your course, your attendance. If you don't understand something, ask. For each moral issue sort the information into categories, such as facts; opinions; for; against; history of topic; recent developments. Create your own index so you know where to find materials quickly. Make your own vocabulary dictionary of terms.

Processing the information:

Reduce 1000-word articles from newspapers to bullet-point headings. Re-read your notes and make them into diagrams or bullet points. Take the sections in this book and, using the subheadings, write summaries of what each section is trying to explain. Mix this in with information you've taken from other sources. Cover your subheadings and read what you've written – work out what the subheading might be. Write all the subheadings for a topic out on a page and add your own text to explain each one from memory. Make your own list of questions for each topic. Put them aside for a week and then try to answer your own questions as fully as you can. Work together with friends. Quiz each other – introduce an element of competition. Devise a TV-type game show on a topic, for example, *Who wants to be a Millionaire?* (top prize 50p!), where all the questions are on human rights issues. Turn your notes into board games, – for example, a *Trivial Pursuit*, where all the questions are on environmental issues. Put yourself into different people's shoes. Imagine you are a Christian, Muslim, Egoist or Utilitarian. How would you respond to the topics and the issues if you were one of these. Act out role plays or dramas. Write imaginary letters or reports. Turn the material into artwork, poetry or stories. Make up mnemonics to help you remember things, for example Fossil Fuels Fuel All Greenhouse Gases (FFFAGG). Turn ideas into artwork. The list is endless!

Reviewing the information:

Test yourself regularly. See if you can remember key ideas, work out links to other parts of the course. Re-read your work – see if it still makes sense. Set yourself assessment tasks. Do tasks in the book you've done already. Compare your new answers with your original answers. Ask your teacher for more work! Mark your friend's work and get them to mark yours. Explain what you have given them marks for and what they've missed out. Be prepared to explain how they should have done it if you think it could have been better!

ASSESSMENT

Your teacher will have what are called 'Instruments of Assessment', which he or she will use to check your progress and work out your marks. These instruments are just questions designed to let you show that you have achieved the Learning Outcomes. Your teacher will also have sample answers, which they will use to help them mark your answer. These come from a collection of items known as the National Assessment Bank. This isn't a place, just a way of making sure that the same standard of question is given and the that same standard of answer is expected, whether you live in Clydebank or Kirkwall. At Intermediate 1, you'll answer set questions with restricted response answers. These will usually be about 100 words long. At Intermediate 2, you'll do what are known as extended responses of around 200 words.

A response of 200 words might seem a little scary at first, until you realise that you're trying to gather together what by then should be a fair amount of information. You will be trying to show in only 200 words that you understand the main parts of some detailed study you have done – as well as express your own opinion and give supporting reasons for what you think.

(By the way, between the first and last words of the section on assessment you have just read, there were 203 words!)

Finally, if for some reason, you don't quite achieve the Learning Outcomes the first time, you'll get another shot at it.

All through this book, there have been examples of Assessment Questions, which you will have attempted. Now let's look at and analyse some typical responses to these kind of questions.

ASSESSMENT QUESTIONS AND SAMPLE ANSWERS

Note: In a real assessment exercise, all three questions at each level would all be on the same topic (for example, human rights).

The answers here are just examples to show you how different types of question should be answered using different topic material.

Intermediate 1

Outcome 1

Question 1

Describe the two moral stances you have been studying and show how each one relates to the issue of caring for the environment.

Religious Authority: People here base their moral decisions on the teachings of their religious leaders, as well as holy books and answers to prayers. For example, Muslims follow the teachings of the Qur'an first. In the Qur'an it says you should care for nature because it belongs to Allah. Also, you will be judged at the end of your life. If you have been careless about the environment you'll be punished.

Egoism: Egoists base their moral decisions on what's best for them personally. An Egoist wouldn't really care how he treated the environment as long as what he did didn't cause him any problems. If he thought his actions would harm him (like if he made Global Warming worse by driving his car), he might change his ways.

(128 words)

good — varied explanation of what 'Religious Authority' means

use of actual sources is good

relates idea of judgement to caring for the environment

good, two possible ways an Egoist could respond to environmental issues are identified

Outcome 2

Question 2

What viewpoints might Egoists and religious people have on the issue of embryo research? Explain how each viewpoint is related to its own moral stance.

An Egoist would support embryo research because using embryos could help scientists cure diseases. This would be good for the Egoist because <u>he looks after his own interests</u> first. If it meant he could be cured from some disease, he'd support the use of embryos. But if he thought that such research was dangerous (for example, actually causing genetic problems), he might not be so happy – especially if these problems could somehow harm him.

Christians believe that life is sacred. Some think it should never be taken because life begins at conception – so embryo research is always wrong. Others think that we sometimes have to take lives if that benefits people – so embryo research is a 'necessary evil'. All Christians think we should treat life carefully because it is God's gift to us.

(136 words)

good, clearly sets out what egoism means

again, good variety shown of different possible Egoist responses

good, links sacredness of life idea to this specific issue

Variety of Christian viewpoints examined

good — reference to what Christians have in common with reference to this issue

Outcome 3

Question 3

'Capital punishment should be brought back in Britain. It's the best way of making sure people do not commit serious crimes.'
Do you agree or disagree? Give reasons for your answer.

(I disagree.) (In countries with capital punishment there are just as many murders as in countries where there's no capital punishment.) (It's also a very strange way to say that murder is wrong by murdering murderers.) (People should be punished, but no-one has the right to take away someone else's life) – even governments.

(54 words)

good clear statement of opinion

solid evidence used back up opinion (Reason ①)

good clear & reasonable argument (Reason ②)

Additional reason given – pupil obviously understands the issue and has evaluated it well

Intermediate 2

Outcome 1
Question 1
a) Give a brief outline of the three moral stances you have studied.
b) Choose *two* of these stances and state how they might affect someone's attitude to voluntary euthanasia.

a) *People who are Egoists make their moral decisions based on their own self-interest. They put themselves first, in other words. As far as they're concerned their moral choices in life are based on what's best for them.*

Utilitarians try to make decisions which produce the most benefit for the most people. They try to produce as much happiness for as many people as possible, and also as little pain for as many people as possible.

People who make their moral decisions based on religious authority follow the teachings of their holy books or listen to their holy leaders. They may also pray and hope to be told what's right and wrong 'directly' by their God.

(116 words)

Clear explanation of what the stances are

good variety of ideas about how religious people arrive at moral decisions

b) *An Egoist would think that it's entirely up to him if he wants to opt for euthanasia or not. He might decide that his life no longer has much quality and so he'd be better off dead. Also, if he was in pain, he'd want that to go away – pain isn't in his self-interest. If the only way to make it go away was to end his life he'd want that. Finally, an Egoist might avoid suicide because it could be painful and go wrong, so he'd want to know that he could choose to die but be helped by a qualified doctor.*

good varied ideas about what 'self-interest' actually means

A religious person would most likely not choose voluntary euthanasia – although there are differences of opinion about this. This is because he'll probably believe that life is a gift from God and so should be cherished. If he chooses to end his own life he 'rushes into God's presence uninvited', meaning he makes a decision that only God should.

(164 words)

good use of relevant quotation

Has identified conflict within a moral stance

Outcome 2
Question 2
Following recent scares about BSE, Clare the Christian, Eddie the Egoist and Ursula the Utilitarian meet in the pub to discuss whether or not they should become vegetarians. How might each explain their own viewpoint?

Eddie the Egoist would want to know how likely it was that he would get ill from eating meat. If he found out there was a high chance, then he might give it up. Eddie's only concern would be his own well-being, the animal's wouldn't matter. If you could convince Eddie that vegetarianism was safer, healthier or cheaper for him then he might think about it – as long as he benefited.

relates self-interest to vegetarianism/ meat-eating

clear statement about Egoism

Clare the Christian might say that eating meat wasn't what God intended. _Only after the Fall were humans allowed to eat meat – but some Christians think this was just a temporary measure that people should 'grow out of'_. Clare would also say that humans have a responsibility to care for all God's creatures because humans have _dominion_ over them. Eating an animal is not a good way of caring for it, so Clare would probably become a vegetarian happily.

good use of actual material but should have quoted book of Genesis

good use 'technical vocabulary'

Ursula would want to make sure that not eating meat would benefit the majority. For example, if you could show her that vegetarianism was better for the environment – and so everyone – then she might give up eating meat. Also, if meat-eating was linked to serious illness (like BSE-CJD), then she would give up, because such illness would not produce the greatest happiness for people, but misery.

(221 words)

clear exposition of utilitarian reasons for action

Outcome 3
Question 3
'Keeping nuclear weapons is morally wrong.'
How far do you agree?

good link to other ideas of study of war

Nuclear weapons kill indiscriminately and so break the rules of a just war, which say that civilians should be protected. They also harm the environment, and their effects can last long after the bomb itself has been dropped, like after the bombing of Hiroshima. Also, spending money on nuclear weapons is money that should be spent feeding the poor and helping the sick. Nuclear weapons' production and storage is also dangerous – nuclear weapons have been transported on motorways across Scotland. If there was a road accident, the effects could be very serious.

good, a number of arguments briefly put

clear explanation of some reasons behind an anti-nuclear stance

On the other hand, some say that maybe having nuclear weapons is why we have had no major wars since World War Two. Having them has been enough to make countries think again about acting aggressively. In fact, having them makes it more likely that they'll never be used, whereas not having them could actually cause a war as a country could use them knowing that it can't be hit back.

good explanation with supporting evidence

On balance, I think that having nuclear weapons is morally wrong (but that we don't really have a choice. You can't un-invent them, so getting rid of them now would just cause more problems than it solved.) (Also, an enemy country wouldn't use them against us if it knew that we could strike back in the same way – so they are a good _deterrent_.) (Finally, nuclear weapons are evil, but all weapons are in one way or another.) Giving them up would just be pointless.

(249 words)

Reason ①

Reason ②

Reason ③

good use of technical vocabulary

THE EXAM

By the time you reach the exam, you will have:

◆ completed a large amount of coursework, which your teacher will have supervised; this will include homework items, questions, and more extended tasks like short essays

◆ completed a range of Unit Assessments, which you will have had marked, indicating your achievement of the Learning Outcomes

◆ probably completed a Prelim exam, which will give you some idea of what the real exam will be like

◆ tried out practice exam papers and exam questions designed by your teacher.

All of this means that by the time the final exam comes you will be well practised in the core skills that you have been developing as the course progresses. Provided that you 'know your stuff' you should be able to achieve a pass in the exam without too much difficulty. But how do you move this pass from a C up to an A band 1?

The most important skill at this stage is **exam technique**. You must take all that you have learned over the course of a school year and squeeze it into a few short hours in such a way that the examiner is convinced your knowledge, understanding, analysis and evaluation is worthy of the mark you get.

The author of this book has marked examinations for the SQA for many years. Here are some vital tips for exams in RMPS:

◆ **The marker is on your side.** The aim is to support the candidate by giving him/her the benefit of the doubt. Markers are teachers just like your own. They like teaching and they like pupils. They want pupils to do well (even if we've never met you!). Markers will try to award you marks wherever they can. At Intermediate 1 and 2 levels, we know you aren't meant to be final year University students and will do our best to spot the fact that you know what you are writing about. But you can help yourself!

◆ **Answer the question as fully as you can.** When a question asks you to explain, this means that you should answer fully – not just give a vague idea about what you mean. Don't waffle pointlessly or write pages and pages for a question that is worth two marks, but if you think it's a relevant point put it in. Remember, you're trying to convince someone who doesn't yet know that you know the answer.

◆ **When you state something, also explain it if necessary.** Many answers are let down because candidates leave the answer 'in the air'. Round off your question as best you can. There's nothing worse for the marker than the candidate who obviously knows what they're on about but just doesn't go far enough in the answer. We're supposed to help you but not write the answer for you or give you marks for what we think you know.

◆ **Learn how to respond to specific exam phrases** (see below). There are definite unspoken rules about exam performance, which everyone the world over (almost) agrees upon. The trick is to write the right response for the right question.

◆ **Give your answers a structure where you can.** Your marker has a 'marking scheme'. This gives suggestions about what really should be in the answer and what might be there. He or she has some flexibility too. However, if your answer rambles all over the place it will be more difficult to pick out the important parts from the padding. Think about what the question is 'looking for' and answer accordingly.

◆ **Remember, it's an exam in RMPS.** You will, of course, have to express your opinion. However, this course is designed to make sure that your opinion is based on reason, evidence and beliefs. You probably had opinions at the start of the course. They might not have changed. However, the aim of this subject is to help you develop your opinions by taking into account the views of others, and putting your own views through a process of critical examination. In the exam, you should try to show that you have thought your opinions through and that you are aware of the opinions of others (in particular, those who follow the moral stances you have studied), even if you still don't agree with them. RMPS tries to help you to see things from other people's point of view. So, for example, you should be able to argue as if you were a Christian even if you are a committed atheist.

◆ **Back up your answers with course material and ideas, where you think it's relevant.** The marker would like to know that you have actually studied the *Making Moral Decisions* unit. It's your job to show it.

◆ **Watch carefully how you present your work.** Present your answer as neatly as you can and as clearly as you can. Try to express things simply but accurately. Don't try to write big fancy words if you don't know how to use them. The smartest people are those who can make very complex issues quite simple, clear and straightforward. Be formal in your answers but not 'stuffy', but watch out that you don't become too flippant! Watch your spelling, grammar, punctuation etc. The easier something is to read, the easier it is to spot when it's going in the right direction. If you have to 'translate' a scruffy, rambling scrawl, it makes it more difficult to find where you deserve to get the marks.

◆ **Give yourself time to re-read your answers.** It's amazing how many times I've marked things where the candidate obviously hasn't gone back through it all to check that it makes sense. Sometimes an idea gets lost in the middle of a long sentence and never re-appears. If the candidate had re-read the answer he or she would have spotted this and could have put it right.

SOME TYPICAL *EXAMSPEAK* IN RMPS

Like all subjects, Religious, Moral and Philosophical Studies has its own way of doing things, which may be a little different to other subjects. Here's a list of common instructions in RMPS Intermediate 1 & 2 exams and what they mean.

◆ **Describe:** This just means that you state the important features of an issue. For example: *Describe two viewpoints which people might hold in connection with capital punishment.* This means that you simply state two typical ideas which people have about capital punishment and what these ideas are based upon. For example, *Christians believe that no-one has the right to take another person's life because ...* **and** *Christians think that capital punishment is a just reward for crime because ...* .

◆ **Outline:** means the same as above.

◆ **Explain:** You go one stage further than describe here, because you are giving a fuller account of the reasons behind a particular belief. At this level, you'll often be expected to *Explain how viewpoint X is related to Moral Stance Y.* In your answer, you would be expected to give an explanation of what the moral stance is (briefly) and how it links with a particular view expressed. For example, *Egoism is based on the idea of self-interest, this means ... . Because of this, an Egoist might believe ... about [moral issue].*

◆ **Do you agree or disagree?** At some point in your answer you should explain whether you do or don't. You can even say that you're not sure – it's not compulsory to have an opinion one way or the other. For example: *In my opinion ... ;* or; *I agree/ disagree/ don't know whether I agree or disagree with X because ...* .

◆ **Express a personal opinion about/on:** means the same as above.

◆ **Give (or support your answer with) reasons:** Sometimes the number of reasons is stated. Stick to it. You won't get any extra marks for giving more reasons than required. Make sure your reasons are related to the issue you're talking about and that they make sense. Express your reason(s) as fully and as clearly as you can. Watch out that they are reasonable and not vague or too way out. If you have particularly strong viewpoints, watch out that you don't get carried away with your own argument. Also, if you have viewpoints that most people would think unacceptable, you might like to be careful about how you express them. For example: *I think X because [reason(s)].*

◆ **Justify your opinion with:** means the same as above.

◆ **How far do you agree?** At Intermediate 2 level this is the extended version of *Do you agree or disagree? Give reasons for your answer.* This goes one stage further, however, because it asks you to **evaluate**. The question is often in the form of a quote, and you're then asked just 'how far' you agree with it. This means that you should show awareness of more than one point of view, as well as reach your own personal conclusion (supported by reasons of course) about a moral issue. The generally expected response to this kind of question is that you outline and explain opposing viewpoints on the issue under consideration, then explain which of them (if any), you are most likely to agree with and why. The examiner expects you to give at least two – usually opposing – points of view as well as your own conclusion. This is the only way you'll get full marks for this kind of question. So for example: *'Marriage is out of date.' How far do you agree?* Your answer should take the following format: *Some people argue that marriage is out of date because [explain their viewpoint as fully as you can]. Others think it is not out of date because [explain their viewpoint as fully as you can]. My conclusion is [explain, with reasons, which of the preceding viewpoints you agree with most and why].*

◆ **To what extent?** Another way of saying *How Far?* Same procedure as above.

◆ **'Double-barrelled' questions:** Some questions have **two** parts, make sure you answer both or you won't be able to get full marks. Perhaps you could highlight them on the exam paper in different colours to remind yourself that there are two parts to the question. For example: *Describe the two moral stances you have been studying in relation to Human Rights.['part 1'] Explain briefly why they are important in making moral decisions. ['part 2']*

There are plenty of books on exam technique, structure, tips and tactics and it's up to you how much attention you pay to these. However, it is safe to say that there are two important principles about this exam that should ensure you pass:

1 **Work hard all through your course.** Some people are good at 'cramming'. But for most of us, learning takes time to sink in. If you have worked hard throughout the year's courses you should do well.

2 **Practice.** Take every opportunity your teacher gives you to test yourself. Submit work when asked and pay attention to comments made. Practice exam questions repeatedly in class or on your own. If you follow these two important principles, by the time you get to the exam hall it should be a doddle! Good luck.

INDEX